Management Issues in China: Volume II

As the 1990s progress, China is emerging as an economic giant. The World Bank expects that it will become the world's largest economy early in the next century, if it maintains its recent rate of growth. This is largely due to the fact that China presently enjoys the largest amount of foreign direct investment among developing countries and is generally perceived as the next 'big thing' in international business circles.

The ten chapters in this book illustrate many aspects of China's path to internationalization. They also raise important questions that still require further clarification and study. What becomes clear is that to succeed in China's sometimes harsh business environment, foreign business strategists need to become better informed of the type of challenges China presents. The contributors – from the UK, US, Europe, Hong Kong and China – address the strategic issues facing international firms in China, the challenge of managing international enterprise in China and the international activities of Chinese firms.

The editors have extensive first-hand experience of Chinese management practice over many years. With the increasing interest in China, there is a need for an authoritative discussion of the situation which will be of value to the corporate sector, as well as researchers and MBA students following specialist options.

John Child is Guinness Professor of Management Studies at the Judge Institute of Management Studies, University of Cambridge. **Yuan Lu** is Rothmans Research Fellow at the Judge Institute.

Management Issues in China: Volume II

International Enterprises

Edited by John Child and Yuan Lu

London and New York

First published 1996
by Routledge
11 New Fetter Lane, London EC4P 4EE

Simultaneously published in the USA and Canada
by Routledge
29 West 35th Street, New York, NY 10001

Typeset in Times Ten by Florencetype, Stoodleigh, Devon
Printed and bound in Great Britain by
Clays Ltd, St Ives plc

British Library Cataloguing in Publication Data
A catalogue record for this book is available from the
British Library.

Library of Congress Cataloguing in Publication Data
A catalogue record for this book has been requested

ISBN 0–415–13003–4 (hbk)
ISBN 0–415–13004–2 (pbk)

Contents

Part III International activities of Chinese enterprises

Illustrations

Notes on contributors

Anne Carver was educated at Cambridge and since 1984 has been a lecturer in the Faculty of Law, University of Hong Kong. She specializes in teaching Commercial Law to fourth year law students in the Faculty of Law, and Business Law to BBA and MBA students in the Department of Management Studies at the University of Hong Kong.

She is the author of numerous articles on the creation of an industrial jurisprudence for Hong Kong, and is interested in the convergence of the international business community's legal norms. She is currently researching the invention of a new legal tradition in China's commercial developments, and her latest book is *Hong Kong Business Law*.

Aimin Guo joined the He-nan Institute of Finance and Economics in 1988. He was appointed Associate Professor in 1993, and in 1994 he was made head of Department of Industrial Economics. He was also a visiting scholar at Aston Business School, 1992–94. Aimin Guo is the author of numerous articles on technology imports into China, as well as *Engineering Profit Theory and Application*, *Superior Business Administration*; and *Industrial Enterprise Production Management*. His current research interest is in the theory and practice of machine translation of Chinese legal texts into English.

Robert Akroyd was called to the Bar of the Middle Temple in 1972 and was awarded a PhD on 'The Coalescence of Foreign and Indigenous Elements in Japanese Commercial Law' in 1978 at City University, London. He joined Aston Business School in 1976 and became the Head of Legal Studies in 1988. He was also Japan Foundation Professional Fellow at Tokyo University, 1978–1982. During 1987 and 1991 he was a visiting scholar at the People's University of China in Beijing. Dr Akroyd is the author of articles dealing with the role of law in a business context, particularly with reference to Japanese law and culture; and of *A Guide to Contracting for the Sale of Goods* and *A Guide to Contracting, Negotiation and the Law*. He was the joint ESCOM Award winner with the decision support system Sales Contractor, 1990–1991.

Jiatao Li was on-leave Associate Professor of International Business and Strategy at the College of Business Administration at the University of Hawaii. His research interests focus on international business strategy, global competition in service industries, and joint venture success in China. He has published widely in leading academic journals such as the *Strategic Management Journal, Journal of International Business Studies*, and *Management International Review*. He has also served as a consultant to the United Nations and private organizations on issues related to international strategies. He is with McKinsey & Company, a leading management consulting firm, in Hong Kong.

Oded Shenkar has degrees in East-Asian Studies and Sociology from the Hebrew University of Jerusalem, and a PhD from Columbia University, New York. He is with the Leon Recanati Graduate School of Business Administration at Tel-Aviv University, Israel, and the College of Business Administration and the Centre for Chinese Studies at the University of Hawaii, Manoa. Oded Shenkar has edited *Organization and Management in China: 1979–1990* and *International Business in China* (with Lane Kelley), and published numerous articles in such journals as *The Academy of Management Review*, *The Academy of Management Journal*, *Organization Studies, Management Science*, *The Journal of International Business Studies*, *The Journal of Applied Behavioural Science* and *Human Resource Management*.

Ingmar Björkman is an Associate Professor in the Department of Organization and Management at the Swedish School of Economics in Helsinki, Finland. He has done research on various issues in the area of international management. During the last few years, his research has focused on the operations of Western companies in China. He has studied the internal management of Chinese-Western joint ventures, human resource management issues in Sino-foreign joint ventures, and industrial sales by Western companies in China.

Elizabeth Weldon is Associate Professor of Management at Indiana University. Her current research focuses on innovation in empowered work teams and conflict management in bicultural work teams.

Karen A. Jehn is Assistant Professor of Management at the Wharton School of the University of Pennsylvania. Her current research is in the areas of intragroup and intergroup conflict, strategic decision making and cross-industry and cross-national comparisons of values, goals and conflict styles.

Aimin Yan is an Assistant Professor in the Department of Organizational Behavior, School of Management, Boston University. He received his PhD from the Pennsylvania State University. His current research focuses on negotiations, structuring, and effective management of international strategic alliances. His work has appeared in *Academy of Management Journal, The Journal of Applied Behavioral Science, Advances in International Comparative Management*, and *Advances in High Technology Management*. Professor Yan teaches in the areas of international management, organizational behaviour, and organization theory at the undergraduate, MBA, and doctoral levels. He is also a consultant to many Chinese and Western organizations on international joint ventures in China.

Barbara Gray is a Professor of Organizational Behavior and Director of the Center for Research in Conflict and Negotiation at the Pennsylvania State University. She has been studying organizational and international conflict and the negotiation processes for 20 years. Dr Gray's interest in negotiations is reflected in her books *Collaborating: Finding common ground for multiparty problems* and *International joint ventures: Economic and Organizational Perspectives* as well as in numerous academic publications on collaboration, dispute resolution and joint ventures. She is a trained mediator and a trainer for the NTL Institution. She has also worked in industry, in education and in academia as a consultant to numerous public and private sector organizations.

Roy Rimington, BA (Hons), PhD, MIQA, has spent 20 years in quality management in several major electrical/electronics companies in the United Kingdom and Taiwan, and has been employed in design/development and production management. He is currently with GPT Business Systems Group in Nottingham. He received his BA in Business Studies from the University of Staffordshire and his doctorate in Management Science from the University of Keele. He is also a Registered Lead Assessor. Dr Rimington has developed ISO 9001 Quality Management Systems into the joint venture in Shanghai described in his contribution to this book. He has presented papers and workshops in companies, universities and at conferences in the United Kingdom, China, Taiwan, Malaysia, Singapore, Indonesia and the United States.

Hai yan Zhang graduated from the University of International Studies of Shanghai, China, in 1980. He gained a Master's degree in Public Administration and Management from the Institute of Administrative Sciences, University of Antwerp in 1990, and became a PhD student and research assistant at the University of Antwerp-RUCA. His PhD thesis deals with the business activities of Chinese and overseas Chinese, in particular their international investment operations. His research interests include management issues of international joint ventures in South-East Asian countries, on which he has published several papers.

Daniel Van Den Bulcke is Professor of International Management and Development at the University of Antwerp and Director of the Centre of International Management and Development-Antwerp (CIMDA). He received his PhD from the University of Ghent, 1974. He has taught at the University of Limburg, the College of Europe in Bruges, and ICHEC, Brussels, and also became Professor of International Management at UFSIA and the University of Ghent in 1990. He is a former president of the International Trade Invest Institute (ITI) and the European International Business Association (EIBA); and has been scientific co-ordinator of the European Institute of Advanced Studies in Management (EIASM) since 1988 and the Intercollegiate Centre of Doctoral Studies in Management from 1988 to 1994. He has also been visiting professor at the University of Brabant, the Netherlands, University of Padjadjaran, Indonesia, China-EC Management Institute, Beijing, the National Institute of Development Administration in Thailand and Ateneo de Manila University, the Philippines. He is a Fellow of the Academy of International Business, and author of several books and articles on foreign direct investment issues and the activities of multinational enterprises.

Danming Lin is a lecturer in the Department of Economics, Shantou University, People's Republic of China and a PhD candidate in the Department of Management Studies, University of Hong Kong. His research interests focus on foreign direct investment in China with special reference to the operations of Sino-foreign joint ventures.

Alasdair MacBean is an Emeritus Professor of Lancaster University, and was a Professor of Economics in the Management School from 1967. He has been a research associate at Harvard University, and visiting professor at the universities of Michigan, Fudan (Shanghai), and the People's University (Beijing). His main publications are *Export Instability and Economic Development* and *Institutions in International Trade and Finance*. He is a consultant on international trade and economic development, and has been a consultant to the World Bank, the Asian Development Bank, OECD, and the UN.

Introduction
China and international enterprise

John Child and Yuan Lu

As the 1990s progress, China is emerging as an economic giant. By 1993, it already accounted for the world's third largest Gross Domestic Product measured at purchasing power parity, after the United States and Japan. If China maintains its recent rate of growth, the World Bank expects that it will become the world's largest economy early in the next century. This rapid economic expansion has been accompanied by China's increasing engagement in world trade. Its rank in world trade rose from thirty-second in 1978, accounting for $20.64bn, to eleventh by 1993, accounting for $195.71bn (*People's Daily*, 6 October 1994).

This impressive economic development has resulted from the two major components of China's economic reform policy: the transformation from a centrally planned towards a market system and the opening of the economy through the so-called Open Door Policy. The companion volume to this book, edited by David Brown and Robin Porter, examines various aspects of the internal reform and its impact upon domestic enterprises. The present volume focuses upon the internationalization of business in China, which is evident in three developments.

First, there has been an internationalization of China's domestic market. China has become the largest recipient of foreign direct investment among developing countries. By the end of March 1994, there were more than 186,000 foreign-invested firms accounting for $241.5bn of contracted capital and $67.2bn of utilized capital. The proportion of domestic industrial output value accounted for by foreign-invested firms rose from almost zero when the Open Door Policy was initiated in late-1978 to 11 per cent in 1993. Such firms contributed as much as 37 percent of China's foreign trade in 1993 (*People's Daily*, 18 May 1994). The great majority of foreign-invested firms in China are equity joint ventures, though the number of wholly-owned subsidiaries is increasing more rapidly (*Statistical Yearbook of China 1994*: Table 16–2).

Second, Chinese firms are seeking opportunities through investment abroad. By 1993, China's overseas investment had reached $5.16bn, accounting for a total of 4,497 projects (*Beijing Review*, 16–22 August 1993: 29). This relatively new trend has not as yet been well studied, and there is a need to understand how Chinese firms cope with their overseas investment and the ways in which Chinese expatriate managers administer the companies into which Chinese investment has been placed.

Third, China has established intermediary organizations which link domestic firms to international markets. This calls attention to the reform in China's foreign trade companies, which have been transformed from bureaucratic governmental agencies into business units with an interest in the pursuit of their own profit.

The Open Door Policy and China's economic internationalization strategy raise many questions. One concerns the dynamic resulting from contact between Chinese and foreign approaches to management, particularly in cases such as joint ventures where ways have to be found of reconciling the two. The key differences between the Chinese approach and that fairly typical of the Western international corporation are set out in Table I1. Although it reflects certain cultural influences, the Chinese approach was largely shaped under the pre-reform centrally planned economy. Most Chinese enterprises until the mid-1980s operated within a command system under which planning quotas for inputs and outputs were imposed on them. As a consequence, managers had to involve themselves closely with the higher governmental officials upon whom they were dependent, giving rise to a system of personal rather than formalized relations and roles. Chinese managers were generally political appointees. They had to reach physical performance targets and their decisions had to take account of multiple criteria which derived from social and political considerations as well as economic requirements. By contrast, the approach to management which has developed in the market economy emphasizes competence for the job, devolved strategy-formulation, formalized organizational procedures, and financial performance criteria. During the early period of internationalization, there were many accounts of conflict between these two approaches at a time when most Chinese joint venture partners were still subject to strong direct governmental influence. As Table I1 indicates, the authority system under which many Chinese managers spent their formative years was characterized by a considerable level of vertical dependency, and there was only a small amount of formalization in terms of procedures, definitions of responsibility, performance criteria and the like. If it had the appearance of bureaucracy, this was somewhat of a 'mock' character (Gouldner 1954) since it actually functioned to a great extent through informal sponsorship, personal obligation and a good deal of political control. The implicit and personalized nature of this management system has been thrown into sharp relief within many Sino-foreign joint ventures where it contrasts markedly with the conventions now followed by many foreign companies, especially multinationals (Child 1994: 294–5).

Moreover, governmental agencies and the regulations they administer continue to contribute to the unique characteristics of China as an

Table II: A comparison of Chinese and Western approaches to management

Concepts and practices	Chinese management under a centrally planned economy	Western management under a market economy
Corporate governance structure	Planning authorities acting on behalf of state ownership	Boards of directors acting on behalf of shareholders
Decision-making authority	Industrial bureaux or ministries	Boards of directors and CEOs
Managerial autonomy	Little before the reform, much improved now	CEO enjoys autonomy under the board
Organizational performance criteria	Multiple rationality – economic, political and social obligations	Economic rationality, tempered by social responsibility
Degree of procedural formalization	Low formalization, but highly personalized processes	Highly formalized and relatively impersonal
Information communication	Mainly vertical; little horizontal flow	Multi-directional
Management training and development	Not emphasized before mid-1980s	Highly emphasized
Reward policies and incentive systems	Rewards dependent on age and long service; incentives not closely related to performance	Performance-related

environment for foreign investment. These include the persistence of state monopoly over certain strategic sectors such as telecommunications and the importance that firms, including joint ventures, have to attach to their relationships with government agencies. While for most foreign firms local government agencies now play the most significant role and are rather more approachable than are the central bodies, they can still generate some inflexibility in both the negotiation and operation of foreign-invested firms (Beamish and Speiss 1992; Howell 1992). As Beamish and Speiss put it:

> The joint venture process in China is different from that in developed countries and different than with joint ventures in developing countries which have market economies. These differences stem as much from politics as they do from the short time period in which the regulatory infrastructure has been enacted.
>
> (Beamish and Speiss 1992: 160)

Joint ventures can offer a number of economic and managerial advantages. Partners investing in a joint venture can share risks, seek complementary contributions of technology and know-how, overcome barriers to entering a host-country market, and establish a strategic position which reduces opportunities for competitors (Root 1987; Contractor and Lorange 1988; Young *et al.* 1989). Joint ventures can also be an effective vehicle for improving management by transferring tacit knowledge from one partner to another (Hennart 1988).

On the other hand, there are certain tensions built into the relationship between the partners investing in a joint venture, as well as into those between the partners and the venture itself. What distinguishes a joint venture from other forms of international business organization is that it has two or more parent firms from different countries. These parent firms share in the ownership of the joint venture according to the investment they commit to it. Each parent firm has a claim on revenues derived from the venture, and the right to exercise control over it, according to its commitment (Buckley and Casson 1988; Kogut 1988). However, each partner may have incongruent objectives and they may apply different criteria to the evaluation of its conduct and performance (Geringer and Hebert 1991). The relationship between parent firms is therefore liable to have a critical bearing on the venture's performance. Moreover, the stability of a joint venture is heavily dependent upon the partners' intentions; they can terminate the venture, or one partner may acquire it even if it is successful (Bleeke and Ernst 1993). In addition to these complexities which are embedded in joint venture relationships, contextual factors can also play a role. Datta (1988) has, for instance, pointed to differences in the partners' management styles, cultures and experiences as influences which can create difficult managerial dynamics within a joint venture.

Joint ventures, which are extremely important channels for technology transfer and the injection of managerial expertise which so importantly assist China's economic development, present a particularly difficult managerial challenge. However, the management of joint ventures in China presents challenges that are additional to the normal tensions built into the complex web of relationships within which such ventures are embedded. The first such feature is the political and economic institutional setting already mentioned, in which governmental agencies exercise a more significant role than is normally the case even in many other developing countries. It is necessary for senior joint venture managers to spend time and effort on securing the sympathetic understanding of key officials in these agencies.

A second additional feature concerns the impact of traditional Chinese culture. Five prominent elements of this culture are commonly identified: respect for age and authority, group orientation, the importance attached to family relationships, close personal connections (*guanxi*), and 'face' (*mianzi*). These factors, together with the intervention of the governmental bureaucracy, often contribute to lengthy processes of negotiation both in the formation and the operation of foreign ventures in China. Patience and the explicit cultivation of good personal relations are essential to navigating a way through the Chinese cultural and institutional context.

A third challenge arises from the underdeveloped state of the Chinese market. The attraction of this potentially huge market is for many foreign companies the single most important motive for engaging in joint ventures. Glaister and Wang (1993) conducted a survey of 21 British companies which have established joint ventures in China and found that 'faster entry to market' and 'to facilitate international expansion' were ranked as the two most important strategic reasons. The potential of the Chinese market, however, is not automatically transformed into a profitable reality. National distribution can be very difficult, while supply can also be a problem especially regarding the availability of raw materials, the quality of components and the ability to secure modern packaging. Moreover, in some sectors the high rate of foreign entry in the past few years has depressed rates of return from the attractive levels previously available. Foreign companies in China have to take an active role in exploring ways of generating and servicing market opportunities as well as exercising careful control over all aspects of quality.

The chapters in this book illuminate many of the features of international enterprises in China on which this introduction has touched. The ten chapters are grouped into three parts. Part I is concerned with strategic issues facing international companies in China. Anne Carver, in Chapter 1, examines the Chinese legal framework and the constraints it can impose on foreign firms. As she notes, the Chinese system of economic governance is largely run on the basis of internal documentation, due to the government's practice of maintaining secrecy. Chinese society is in this respect run quite differently from the civil societies of Western countries in which the processes of law and regulation are much more open. Her example of the Chinese government's control over the telecommunication industry vividly illustrates how hidden internal procedures affect policy and practice.

Chapter 2 is concerned with the barriers to technology transfer into China. Guo and Akroyd identify five such barriers to do with information, communication, decision criteria, infrastructure and perception. They present three case studies which indicate how such barriers can be overcome.

In Chapter 3, Li and Shenkar examine the relationship between the structure of joint ventures and the transfer of skills. They find that 'soft technology' – tacit knowledge and skills such as marketing and managerial expertise – are more likely to be transferred through equity joint ventures than through co-operative ventures. They argue that an effective transfer of technology must combine its hard and soft components.

Chapter 4 reports on the approach adopted by Western companies to entering the Chinese market and to selling their products within it. Björkman argues, through his investigation of 24 Finnish companies which exported to China, that doing business in China is not only a matter of market competitiveness deriving from technology, quality and price. More importantly, judging from the experience of these companies, it is the access to networks and the capability of managing them, which was a particular challenge for these companies. Such networks are largely built upon unique Chinese cultural and institutional characteristics. For instance, personal relations (*guanxi*) played a crucial role in business transactions and a company with good *guanxi* would enjoy competitive advantage.

Part II contains three chapters which examine how foreign management challenges the traditional Chinese approach and therefore acts as an agent of change and transformation. Weldon and Jehn in Chapter 5 develop a programme for research which suggests that conflicts in joint ventures arise from both inter- and intracultural factors. While the former arises largely from national differences, the latter derives from differences in people's tasks and personal interests. Weldon and Jehn's research is intended to distinguish between the approaches employed respectively by American and Chinese managers to solve such conflicts, including the ways they attempt to relate with each other. In Chapter 6, Yan and Gray present the findings of their research on the relative influence of foreign and Chinese partners in the formation and operation of joint ventures and the impact this has on venture performance.

Chapter 7 presents a case study of a telecommunications equipment joint venture in Shanghai. Rimington reports on the key factors which have contributed to the company's successful development, which he formalises into a set of guidelines for practitioners. He discusses both the process of technology transfer and complementary managerial initiatives such as the training of Chinese staff and the localization of supplies.

Part III changes focus and is concerned with Chinese companies that are engaged in international operations or transactions. Zhang and Van den Bulke note in Chapter 8 some specific features of Chinese multi-national companies. These companies are usually state-owned and are thus encumbered by many of the bureaucratic features associated with state enterprises in China. State ownership tends to inhibit good management, and the companies studied by Zhang and Van den Bulke were also weakened by poor integration with their parent companies. Their findings suggest that, so far at least, Chinese overseas companies have extended the domestic style of management to their foreign operations.

The subject of Chapter 9, by Lin, is the reverse investment in mainland China undertaken by Chinese Investment Companies (CICs) in Hong Kong. Lin notes that CICs have some advantages which stem from their strong links to domestic organization, such as local firms and governmental authorities. Moreover, as they are located in Hong Kong, CICs can use this prestigious position to secure competitive advantages in the domestic economy. For example, they benefit from incentives offered to foreign investors by the Chinese authorities. What makes Lin's chapter particularly interesting is his argument that CICs are actually socialist firms operating in a capitalist society. This double identity creates some operational difficulties for them. On the one hand, they are constrained by their Chinese headquarters as to the practices they can adopt and, as a result, their management bears some similarity to that of state enterprises. On the other hand, CICs have to accept the business values, norms and practices of a market economy. Lin argues that CICs, as an experiment in the transplantation of business practices, should have some influence on mainland Chinese management.

Chapter 10 examines the position of China's foreign trade companies under the economic reform. Foreign trade companies serve as intermediaries between domestic enterprises and the international market. MacBean observes the development of foreign trade companies and provides an insight into their structure and management. He notes that such companies continue to exercise considerable monopsony powers, despite the fact that the past decade of decentralization has given many domestic enterprises the right to engage directly in foreign trade. Foreign trade companies share the typical characteristics of state-owned enterprises, including the presence of a soft budgetary constraint and multiple performance rationales.

The ten chapters of this book illustrate many aspects of China's path to internationalization. They also point to questions which still require further clarification and study. The connections between norms inherent to Chinese society and Chinese management style provide one example, bearing directly, as they do, on the ease with which soft technologies can be transferred and on the real meaning of the stated Chinese aim to endow foreign approaches with 'Chinese characteristics'. Foreign business strategies towards China need to be better informed of the type of environment China presents, and the chapters in Part I show that researchers are addressing that issue. Second, there is a need to bring analysis of joint venture management more into the mainstream of thinking on management, especially as joint ventures and other types of strategic alliance are fast becoming a major form of business organization. Investigations, such as that by Weldon and Jehn, are attempting to do this with respect to conflict management, and the other chapters in Part II also throw new light on managing joint ventures in China. Third, China is expanding its overseas investment quite rapidly, and the management of Chinese overseas companies deserves examination following the important beginnings provided by the chapters in Part III of this book.

The contributions to this book were presented in an earlier form to the Conference on Management Issues for China in the 1990s, which was held at St John's College Cambridge in March 1994. Our thanks are due to

Alisa Colley who was the registrar for the conference, to the other conference organizers, David Brown and Robin Porter, and to the two conference rapporteurs, Patricia Wilson and Dr Yuan Yijun. Without their help and encouragement, and without the very lively participation of all the conference members, this book and its companion volume would not have been possible.

REFERENCES

Beamish, P. and Speiss, L. 1992 Foreign direct investment in China, in L. Kelley and O. Shenkar (eds). *International Business in China* 152–171, London: Routledge.

Beijing Review 1993 'China invests more in overseas business', 16–22 August: 29.

Bleeke, J. and Ernst, D. 1993 'The way to win in cross-border alliances', in J. Bleeke and D. Ernst (eds) *Collaborating to compete*: 17–34, New York: Wiley.

Buckley, P. and Casson, M. 1988 'A theory of co-operation in international business', in F. Contractor and P. Lorange (eds) *Co-operative strategies in international business*: 31–51, New York: Lexington.

Child, J. 1994 *Management in China during the age of reform*, Cambridge: Cambridge University Press.

Contractor, F. and Lorange, P. 1988 'Why should firms cooperate?' in F. Contractor and P. Lorange (eds) *Co-operative strategies in international business*: 3–30, New York: Lexington.

Datta, D. 1988 'International joint ventures', *Journal of General Management* 14(2): 78–91.

Geringer, J.M. and Hebert, L. 1991 'Measuring performance of international joint ventures', *Journal of International Business Studies* 22: 249–263.

Glaister, K. and Wang, Yu 1993 'UK joint ventures in China', *Marketing Intelligence & Planning* 11/2: 9–15.

Gouldner, A. 1954 *Patterns of industrial bureaucracy*, New York: Free Press.

Hennart, J.-F. 1988 'A transaction cost theory of equity joint ventures', *Strategic Management Journal* 9: 361–374.

Howell, J. 1992 'The myth of autonomy: the foreign enterprise in China' in C. Smith and P. Thompson (eds): *Labour in transition*: 205–226, London: Routledge.

Kogut, B. 1988 'Joint ventures: theoretical and empirical perspectives', *Strategic Management Journal* 3: 319–332.

People's Daily 1994 (overseas edition) 'Prosperity of the future' (*qianjing guangkuo, dayou kewei*) 18 May: 1 and 3.

People's Daily 1994 (overseas edition) 'China's reputable foreign economic collaboration in the world' (*xiangyu shijie de zhongguo duiwai jingji hezou*) 6 October: 1.

Root, F. 1987 *Entry strategies for international markets*, Lexington, Mass.: Lexington Books.

Statistical Yearbook of China 1994 Beijing: China Statistical Press.

Young, S., Hamill, J., Wheeler, C. and Davies, J.R. 1989 *International market entry and development*, Hemel Hempstead: Harvest Wheatsheaf.

Part I

Strategic issues facing international enterprises in China

1 Open and secret regulations and their implication for foreign investment

Anne Carver

ABSTRACT

China has placed a high priority on telecommunications in the 1990s and seeks to create an 'information society'. There is however a legal and practical dysfunctionalism between the long-term investment strategies of the foreign investors in the telecommunications industry and the interests of the Chinese government.

Western insistence on transparency contrasts with the Chinese government's use of secret or *neibu* regulations as part of China's legal system inaccessible to both the foreign investor and non-government Chinese. Can there be a convergence of the two different styles of legal systems and business cultures? This chapter further contrasts the private law regimes of Western business dependent on their belief in a civil society, and the lack of recognition of a private law regime in the China of the 1990s.

The expectations of the foreign investor who comes from the traditions of a civil society cannot be met by the Chinese partner whose 'mother-in-law' in government plays a disproportionate role in business philosophy in terms of access to information and changing the rules.

INTRODUCTION

In a report (Chen 1994) prepared in February 1994 on direct foreign investment in the People's Republic of China (PRC) by large multinationals, McKinsey & Company were quoted as describing the 1990s' investor as passing through three distinct phases: first, the opportunistic experimenter; second, the strategic investor; and third the dominant local player. The key features of a business involved as a dominant local player appear to be the acceptance by Chinese consumers of the business as truly local and the recognition by the Chinese government that this business is a long-term partner in the PRC's economic development.

There are already several examples of the would-be dominant local player in place. AT&T and Northern Telecom have already signed agreements with the State Planning Commission to develop a 'nationwide multi-venture presence that encompasses all their product lines' (Chen 1994). Since the telecommunications industry is primarily under the control of the central government (the Ministry of Posts and Telecommunications) and is felt to be of strategic importance, entering into direct agreements with the State Planning Commission is the way for foreign multinationals involved in telecommunications to become accepted in China as dominant local players.

The telecommunications industry in China is a 1990s' issue. According to the French telecommunications multinational Alcatel: 'Although China opened up to foreign investment in 1979, it was not until a year ago that telecommunications acquired such a high priority' (*South China Morning Post* 28 November 1993). The reason for the lack of priority accorded to telecommunication investment was the presence of 'soft loans' which China obtained in the course of the last decade from countries such as Japan, Canada, Germany, Sweden and France.

> China's telephone links were very poor as recently as 1989 but they have managed to link up all 24 provinces and expand to ten cities in each province in the last couple of years. By now, they have progressed to join the submarine network along the east multinational coast.
> (*South China Morning Post* 28 November 1993)

The list of telecommunication firms interested in becoming dominant local players includes Eriksson, NEC, Motorola, Siemens, Fujitsu and Nokia (based in Finland). Siemens, for example, has a long-term strategy towards the acquisition of infrastructure projects in China (*South China Morning Post* 1993).

The PRC, like the rest of the world, places a high priority on telecommunications in the 1990s, since it appears to be a universal truth of the 1990s that telecommunications based upon global public networks are an essential element of growth, competition and productivity – hence China's focus on the latest technology and the development of the industry to create an 'information society'. There is also an emerging decentralization of the government infrastructure together with the prominence of the service industries. China needs 'fast, cheap communication resources, especially in the areas of voice, text, data and image transmission' (*South China Morning Post* 28 November 1993).

The paradox for foreign investors is that the government bureaux, commissions and industry associations who sit like powerful 'mothers-in-law' (Stewart 1994), watchfully protecting and guarding their interests, represent the best route to permissions, tax concessions, locked-in customers and central funding. Therefore the foreign investor will often be keen to bring government agencies into the business, sometimes according these agencies too much authority in management decisions. It is government which has the power to make most of the decisions, as for example 'rulings on the use of foreign exchange or state funds and sometimes even fiscal concessions' (*South China Morning Post* 16 February 1994). In addition the foreign investor may be looking for a special relationship with those in power as a way of making things happen (Stewart 1992: 166).

These mothers-in-law of government in China can be seen as one of the inevitable symptoms, if not the cause, of what has been described as China's 'arbitrary authoritarianism fostering the wrong values, even economically. Its crony capitalism with Chinese characteristics places a premium on connections, not skill' (*Asian Wall Street Journal* 16 December 1993). The issue is particularly relevant at a time when, for example, foreign businesses protest against what they regard as 'illegal surcharges imposed on foreigners on some prices and services' following the uni-fication of the yuan in January 1994, which caused a devaluation of the yuan and in some cases led Chinese organizations to increase prices including salaries, aeroplane tickets and airport tax (*Asian Wall Street Journal* 7 February 1994).

The President of the American Chamber of Commerce in Beijing main-tained that surcharges imposed on foreigners because of the devaluation of the yuan were illegal. 'This issue is at the heart of many problems in China. It's a question of whether China is willing and able to live by rule of law in this part of its development' (*Asian Wall Street Journal* 16 December 1993).

The implications are clear for management of a foreign business in China. There is a disjunction between the continuing expectations of the foreign investors and the business environment in which they operate whether as opportunistic experimenter, strategic investor or dominant local player. The problem is further illustrated by comments made by the President of the Shanghai Academy of Social Sciences at a symposium in February 1994 in which he referred to Shanghai's 'poor and under-developed legal system' (*South China Morning Post* 15 February 1994). Mr Zhang went on to say that Shanghai must now 'integrate with the world market before the city could truly claim it had recovered its past glory'. Perhaps more pessimistically, one American commentator at the symposium claimed that foreign investors had become sceptical about their investment plans in the face of 'the strong role of the government in economic development' (*South China Morning Post* 15 February 1994) and that the strong link between business development and senior Chinese leaders had been counter-productive.

This strong link between the Chinese bureaucracy and the 'mothers-in-law' of government and foreign business development is discussed in the context of the cancellation of the Goldman Sachs China Venturetech deal. The Goldman Sachs deal was cancelled in December 1993 as a result of 'secret' or *neibu* regulations concerning the appropriate rate of return for foreign investment and thereby emphasizes the disjunction between Western business's reliance on the terms of reference of a civil society and the Chinese partners' acceptance of the importance of the role of government in business.

Is there, however, a possibility of a theoretical and/or practical convergence of the Chinese mother-in-law and the Western rule of law styles? As an example of the problem of convergence this chapter focuses, in particular, on developments in the telecommunications industry and highlights the basis for the disjunction of views. It examines the question from two different perspectives – is it possible to arrive at a definition of the rule of law that is universally accepted and if so how do developments in the telecommunications industry fit within that definition? First, however, who makes the rules and are there any examples of convergence in international business practice in China that will serve as a model for management?

One possible model emerging is the United Nations Development Programme (UNDP), which launched a US$ 6 million project in 1994 to assist 20 Chinese industrial companies to upgrade their management standards for potential listing on international equity markets. The international consultants provided by the UNDP will apparently advise on

> the reform of internal management, and the main areas of focus will be the adoption of modern accounting methods, the establishment of clear lines of organization, the use of accepted quality standards, and the introduction of new technology and modern cost effective manufacturing controls.
>
> (*South China Morning Post* 4 January 1994)

In the meantime, the World Bank has also funded a project for the management consultant firm of McKinsey & Company to 'reform' leading Shanghai enterprises and to recommend long-term strategies and organizational priorities to enable them to remain competitive in the rapidly developing market economy (*South China Morning Post* 4 January 1994).

It is relevant that, in the eyes of the UNDP and of the World Bank at least, a concept of international management standards for business exists that can not only be quantified but also be taught transnationally. One example of the international standardization of business practices willingly received in China is the National People's Congress's Standing Committee's revision to the 1985 Accountancy Law which came into force on 1 January 1994, and has 'all the necessary features of a well-structured regulatory framework' (*South China Morning Post* 18 January 1994). Article 1 reads

> The purpose of this law is to establish the standards of professional conduct of certified accountants. This law also delimits the role and purpose of Certified Accountants in the economy and society. This law is necessary to protect the public interest, to protect the lawful rights and interests of investors and to promote the healthy development of the socialist market economy.
>
> (*People's Daily* 31 December 1993)

Is there, by analogy, an internationally accepted body of legal rules which international business can expect transnationally from those involved in business? In other words, can the international business community agree upon a universal set of criteria that make up an acceptable bottom line of legal rules, procedures and remedies for international business?

UNIVERSAL DEFINITIONS OF LAW?

Universal definitions of law are notoriously difficult to agree upon, and the problem of cultural and – by extension – legal relativism was once again heard as the voice of pragmatism in the Bangkok Declaration of April 1993 (Agence France Report 1993). The ministers and representatives of Asian States met in Bangkok from 29 March to 2 April 1993 (pursuant to the United Nations' General Assembly Resolution 46/116 of 17 December 1991) in the context of preparing for the World Conference on Human Rights. Australia and New Zealand were only allowed to observe rather than participate in the conference since these countries were considered too Western. The conference adopted the Bangkok Declaration to put forward an Asian voice to be heard together with the African, European and Latin American positions at the World Conference in Vienna in June 1993. This was the first United Nations Conference on Human rights for 25 years, and the participants set out to re-affirm and strengthen the Universal Declaration of Human Rights proclaimed on 10 December 1948 in the General Assembly of the United Nations. As a matter of historical interest, in 1948 the communist bloc, South Africa and Saudi Arabia abstained from voting while pre-PRC China was one of the members of the Drafting Committee headed by Eleanor Roosevelt (Jayawickrama 1990: 348).

At the Vienna Conference in 1993, the Singaporean Foreign Minister emphasized the pragmatism of the Asian voice and spoke of the impossibility of establishing absolutes: 'We are not the prophets of a secular god whose verities are valid for all time. We should act more pragmatically and I hope modestly as diplomats dealing with a difficult international issue' (Wong Kan Seng 1993).

The difficult international issue in question was whether human rights can be universal or whether culture, which includes religion, nationality, history and language must, by definition, preclude absolutes. The Vienna Conference delegates compromised on the final text by incorporating a general reference to the different historical, cultural and religious backgrounds of different communities. This outcome would seem to suggest that law, like language, is bound 'within particular historical, social contexts' (Haley 1991: 4) and that it is not possible to give a universally accepted definition of the word 'law' itself. Nevertheless it may still be possible to provide a universally accepted definition of some of the characteristics of a legal system within different prevailing belief systems, despite the different historical, cultural and religious backgrounds of different communities.

CIVIL SOCIETY: GOVERNMENT AND LAW

One of the essential purposes of the law that can perhaps be universally agreed upon is that law provides conformity, and that consequently the ultimate aim of law is order. In contrast to China's so-called 'arbitrary authoritarianism' (*Asian Wall Street Journal* 1993), in liberal states 'the most important rules are rules against rules, above all constitutional rules that restrict the power of government or political organs in order to conserve and protect the liberal order itself' (Hayley 1991: 12). On this cornerstone of Western political thought rests the concept of the civil society existing independently of the state, but regulated by law. Civil society in the Western use of the term is the realm in which individuals seek the attainment of their selfish aims, and is that 'arena where the "burgher" as private person seeks to fulfil his or her own interests. Civil society is thus that arena where – in Hegelian terms – free, self determining individuality sets forth its claims for satisfaction of its wants and personal autonomy' (Seligman 1992: 5).

At the heart of the Western concept of the civil society is the recognition of privateness, addressing the question of how the social bonds of the individual to society can be strengthened and what ethical virtues can be assumed or hoped for. Just as the Bangkok Declaration proved the impossibility of universal notions of human rights, so – as this paper will show – the Western concept of civil society is still unrealized in the context of the PRC's attitudes to the marketplace. However, the focus of Western law on the rights of the individual has important implications for the philosophy of management styles in China if we accept Fukuda's definition of the philosophy of management as being 'implied and express attitudes of *organization* towards employee, consumers, suppliers, owners, government and society' (Fukuda 1989: 45). It must be the case that the very act of holding implied and expressed attitudes of organization towards third parties involves management in attitudes towards the creation of and reliance upon rules, and profoundly held beliefs about rules as constraints upon behaviour or upon the values inherent in the rules themselves. It also has implications for making decisions, and agreement upon who makes the rules and how they are to be made and enforced.

In any discussion about the regulation of civil society by a legal system and who makes the rules that regulate the values inherent in that society, it is necessary to examine the preconditions of the legal system thus in force. It has been argued that a legal system can only exist if it is effectively 'in force', and there are two minimum preconditions that must exist before a legal system can be said to be effectively in force (Lloyd 1985: 404).

These two minimum conditions concern, first, the rules that private citizens should generally obey the law and, second, the 'common standards of official behaviour' by officials of the system who must accept the rules, and 'observe them from, what Hart calls the internal point of view' (Lloyd 1985: 405): that is to say, unlike officials, citizens do *not* need an 'internal point of view' of the law or indeed to understand the cohesiveness of the legal system. It is, however, necessary that the officials of the legal system have an internal point of view and understand the cohesiveness within the legal system which they operate, and this requires from officials a demand for conformity and criticism together with an acknowledgement that criticism and the demand for conformity are justified. While the existence of a civil society in which the 'burghers' pursue their selfish aims is seen as creating a self fulfilling wish for obedience to the law it is, even in Western societies, sometimes difficult to assess the attitudes of officials towards coherence, restraint and common standards of behaviour. How much more difficult is it, therefore, for the foreign investor to assess the attitudes of the officials (the mothers-in-law of government in a Sinicized legal system) to rules, to management styles and towards the legal system itself? These are serious problems which confront the foreign investor in China. Thus this whole argument seems relevant to the question whether the international business community can expect a convergence of management styles and the rule of law in China in the 1990s.

PRIESTS AND WORSHIPPERS

If we accept the difficulty in identifying the internal view of Chinese government officials in the 1990s (and further recognize that the interests of Western business, the 'burgher' and the 'mothers-in-law' of government in China may well diverge at profound levels of cultural and group interests) can we nevertheless identify any common attributes of law, legal processes and attitudes towards rules, underlying the profound levels of cultural and group interests which may have converged in China as a result of the international business community's participation to date? It might be assumed that searching for the common attributes of law and rules in international business should prove easier than searching for universal absolutes about human rights or the views of officials. Here – at least – we can set out one of the basic external rules introduced by the West to the China of the 1990s – the search for 'transparency' in the development and enforcement of the law relating to the telecommunications industry in China. 'Transparency' implies that government officials are not only accountable for their decisions but that the policies and rules for those decisions are a matter of public scrutiny and comprehension. It may be helpful here to recall T.S. Eliot's observation about the function of the priest within a community of believers: 'A religion requires not only a body of priests who know what they are doing, but a body of worshippers who know what is being done' (Eliot 1948: 24).

In the context of Chinese legal culture in the 1990s, substitute the word 'law' for 'religion', 'government officials' for 'priests' and 'private citizens' for 'believers' and the ironic significance of Eliot's observation is all too clear. As this chapter will show, taking Eliot's observation further, it would seem that in the Chinese legal system of the 1990s it is deemed by the priests/government officials to be in everyone's interests that the worshippers/citizens are unaware of 'what is being done'.

In China it may well be that there is a serious disjunction between the two – priests and worshippers – and that the legal memory, in other words the legal tradition of transparency, is relevant only to the very few, perhaps only to the foreigner steeped in the civil society's traditions of thought.

However, before examining the introduction of the concept of transparency into Chinese law the question must be asked as to whether there is a key distinguishing characteristic separating Western and a Sinicized society's legal ideologies. If there is a key distinction, can the concept of transparency be introduced from one to the other and what effect does such a transplant have on the legal culture as it is understood by the business community?

CHINESE AND WESTERN LEGAL TRADITIONS

The key distinction between Western societies and Sinicized societies in terms of legal ideologies rests on the latter's lack of a 'broadly shared belief in transcendent universally applicable moral values or standards' (Haley 1991: 15). This belief in transcendent universally held moral values, has produced 'a remarkably expansive legal domain' in Western societies (Haley 1991: 15). In this context perhaps the most significant historical distinction between the Western and the Sinicized legal systems, however, is the victory of Roman justice with the conversion of Constantine and the substitution of ecclesiastic for secular rule. The fundamental contrast in the legal traditions between Western and Sinicized societies was not simply the concept of natural law rooted in religious beliefs, but also the establishment of Christianity as the state religion. Thus the bonding of law and Christian morality constituted an essential element of the Western legal tradition. In Sinicized societies, on the other hand, law did not originate in a religious order; legal rules were nothing more than the commands of those who exercised political authority. Hence it may be that the internal rules of the legal system are not understood in China in terms of criticism and transparency.

In addition to the problem of the official's view of the rules, there is the lack of recognition of a 'private' law system in a Sinicized society. Sinicized legal regimes can be classified as public law regimes that preclude the development of the concept of legal rights, knowing only duties: duties towards the state and towards one's elders and betters, in contrast to the Roman system of rights defined by specific procedures and remedies for the claims of the individual.

Only within the Western model of an adjudicatory private law system was a mechanism for allocating control over enforcement necessary: to determine who may bring what actions against whom for what remedy or sanction. The crux of Western law is therefore the concept of a legal right as a legitimate demand for state enforcement of a legal rule. By contrast, however, legal rights have little place in public law regimes, which recognize no such entitlement or right to the formal procedures for law enforcement beyond the discretionary control of political authorities. Furthermore, one of the most significant contributions of the Roman private law regime was the transference of the private law process to the public law domain in the recognition of citizens' rights against the state, a situation not hitherto recognized in Sinicized societies as a necessary or even appropriate tradition.

In examining Western and Sinicized legal traditions it may be the case then, that there is no universal definition of law except in the sense of its conservative function to support the norms and values, with the aim of protecting social order. Thus in the China of the 1990s it may be that there is a serious disjunction between what is being done in the name of the law (the priests, to use Eliot's analogy) and what is understood by the laymen or indeed business community (the worshippers). The legal tradition of the international business community may therefore be salient only to the very few in China and considered to be relevant by even fewer of those whom it affects.

The next step in this argument, therefore, is to understand that in the Western legal tradition the concept of the individual includes business corporations and that these occupy the same place in Western private law as the private individual. For individual, read AT&T or Motorola in the private law system of the Western concept of the rule of law, and the disjunction at the basis of the two management philosophies becomes clear.

THE CHINA–US MEMORANDUM OF UNDERSTANDING

The international community expects a universal set of rules in its cross-cultural business transactions, and remains free for the purpose of trade to accept the claims of cultural relativism such as those articulated in the Bangkok Declaration. On the other hand, politicians may, for complex reasons, insist upon publicly asserting the universality of the Western rule of law as a genuine universal. This brings us to the question of bilateral treaties; the rule of law imposed as a model for development; and of the international business communities' quasi-religious belief in the values inherent in the Western concept of the civil society.

On 10 October 1992 the governments of the People's Republic of China and the United States of America signed the Memorandum of Understanding also called the China Market Access Agreement. (The full title is The Memorandum of Understanding Between the Government of the United States of America and the Government of the People's Republic of China Concerning the Market Access.) The memorandum demonstrates the West's insistence upon transparency, and China's apparent willingness to accept transparency as an important international objective and the basis for international trade.

The importance of the agreement lies in its focus on the transparency of trade related rules and regulations in China, and in the Chinese commitment to eliminate secret or *neibu* regulations as a part of China's trade law (Massey 1993: 11). The three other basic areas covered by the Memorandum of Understanding (MOU) were import bars and quotas; the import licensing system and technical barriers to trade. Article 1 of the MOU requires the PRC to publish all laws, regulations and administrative guidelines affecting or governing foreign trade, and to publish a list of all authorities that must be consulted before a particular activity can be approved. It commits the Chinese to issue regulations by 10 October 1993 stating that only laws and regulations published and readily available to foreign governments and traders are enforceable. It also commits China to the creation of an administrative and judicial process to ensure the enforcement of the MOU's provisions, and the good faith of the Chinese government in establishing recognized administrative and judicial processes under constant scrutiny by GATT members and the US government. In exchange the United States promised, *inter alia*, to liberalize controls on telecommunications equipment to China and the procedures of the Co-ordinating Committee for Export Controls (COCOM) which restrict exports to China.

Has the MOU had an impact on the transparency of China's trade laws and regulations? The telecommunications industry, while in itself 'one of the sovereignties of state' according to a spokesman for the Ministry of Posts and Telecommunications (*Xinhua News Agency* 1993) – and thus necessarily a state monopoly – is an example of the obvious lack of any developments on transparency. Compounded with the difficulties of imposing transparency on Chinese bureaucrats are complex ideological and diplomatic developments in the liberalization of basic telecommunication services and the multilateral trade rules in the General Agreement on Trade in Services (GATS) Telecommunications Annex negotiations, of the Uruguay Round of Trade Talks, agreed in December 1993 (The Bureau of National Affairs Inc. 1993). The 117 members of the General Agreement on Tariffs and Trade (of which China is not yet a member) approved the Uruguay Round of trade talks, intended specifically to reduce tariffs and open markets. The GATS annex dealt with general principles for access to a basic voice telecommunications network for users.

The United States proposed three points of particular significance to China's developing telecommunications industry concerning:

1 permission for *foreign investment* to provide long distance services
2 permission for *foreign entities* to provide long distance services
3 the establishment of fair and transparent regulatory procedures.

The points were taken and the result of the Uruguay Round on the telecommunications services industry has been to extend the liberalization of basic telecommunications services to all GATS members. It represents the development of multilateral trade rules for telecommunications services to meet the needs of the international business community, and specifically includes transparency requirements to publish all relevant laws and regulations, and encourages recognition requirements through internationally agreed criteria (Bureau of National Affairs Inc. 1993).

THE EXPERIENCE OF FOREIGN COMPANIES WITH CHINESE LAW

Turning to the developments in China's telecommunications industry since the signing of the MOU in 1992, what impact has the requirement for transparency had on Chinese regulations and legislation? Despite the MOU in 1992 and the expectations of international business the situation as regards transparency does not appear to have changed.

The practice of producing internal secret or *neibu* regulations continues. There is for example the *neibu* State Council document dated June 1993 prepared by the Ministry of Posts and Telecommunications (MPT) concerning ideas for strengthening and developing the market management of the Telecom Business, supplied to the author by a private source and added as an appendix to this chapter.

Three obvious points emerge from the document. First, that the contents of the regulations are internal, and thus unavailable to foreigners. Second, that the regulations require everyone to obey the law, and specifically to obtain licences to operate and to use frequencies. And third, that foreign investment in the operation of telecommunications in China is prohibited by any method. These are examples of regulations created and promulgated in confidence with 'punishment' to be imposed if the exploitation of private benefits occurs. The lack of transparency has serious implications on two levels. First, there are no definitions of liaising procedures or, in particular under paragraph 3, of what constitutes intervention in the 'normal operation and construction of the national public telecommunication network and other professional communication networks'. Second, the wording is so vague as to be opaque and the question of who decides upon its 'suitability' has been left unanswered. The document cannot be read or interpreted in terms of statutory definitions or legal authority and retains the hallmarks of a central edict that may or may not be amended as circumstances change, without notice.

As a result of this *neibu* publication of the Ministry of Posts and Telecommunications, the 'Radio administration regulation of the People's Republic of China, from the State Council and Central Military Commission of the People's Republic of China', was published in the *People's Daily* to implement publicly the opinions stated in the internal document for 'Strengthening the Management of Telecommunications Business Market' (*People's Daily* 11 September 1993).

Examining the regulation from a Western legal perspective, that is to say, searching for the definitions and guides to interpretation of the rules, and examining how the rules are enforced and the exceptions permitted, there are no definitions nor are the exceptions (if any) to the rules stated. Articles 8 and 9 give the local non-military radio administration and the related departments of state the power to draft delegated legislation at the provincial level. However Article 12 causes problems of interpretation since at the time of writing there are no national technical standards for radio equipment and those that exist are introduced on a piecemeal basis without the force of legislation. Article 30 causes similar problems of interpretation; it states that the production and sale by enterprises must meet national technical standards and the quality control laws and regulations of the product, although such technical standards appear not to be in place.

Chapter 7 of the *Radio Administrative Regulation* deals with the united national policy relating to foreign Radio Administration, and requires the co-ordination of foreign-related radio frequency affairs to be submitted to the national radio administrative section. It requires foreign investors to report to the national or local radio administration for approval under the terms of Article 13 of the regulation. Article 13 further causes problems of interpretation since, despite a detailed explanation of what 'the relevant radio administration sections' are, to which an application should be made, Article 13 (3) requires 'agreement from the higher administration sections' in advance, without stating to which higher administrative sections the application should be made. We can only presume such authority should come from the highest level of government authority, but the drafting and implementation of the regulations is an example of the lack of transparency in the current regime as it relates to the telecommunications industry.

We have seen from the *neibu* document discussed earlier that *internally*, as a matter of confidential policy making, the PRC government will not allow foreign entities to operate as a business in the telecommunications industry. Instead foreigners should only produce and sell the equipment. Finding a public regulation or rule for this generalized statement requires a search through the various statements made by the Ministry of Posts and Telecommunications. On 10 May 1993 the following statement was issued:

To stop further attempts by companies outside of China to continue to raise the issue of joint management of the telecommunications market, it is necessary to stress that China will not allow any *individuals, organizations* or *companies* [emphasis added] outside of the Chinese mainland to manage its public and special networks' wire and wireless communications services. To become shareholders is not allowed either.

(*Xinhua News Agency* 1993)

MPT statements issued through the newspapers are not generally the West's idea of legal transparency.

There are many cases where foreign firms have been confronted with *neibu* regulations in the telecommunications industry but for obvious reasons the foreign companies concerned do not wish to have their names mentioned. The cases supplied to the author (from a private source) cover the north east, the eastern coastal belt and the west of China. In each case the pattern was the same: the foreign investor concerned was led by a Chinese agent into a situation where a potential Chinese customer began negotiations with memorandums of understanding and letters of intent. In each case the Chinese agent and the potential customer claimed that the authority of the customer was such that permission would be forthcoming to use a private radio frequency network already in existence (such as a railway network or a defence network) for their own purposes. Both agents and the potential customers claimed that their connections and influence with the mothers-in-law of government were such that permission was forthcoming. After perhaps a year of negotiation it became clear to the foreign investor that the customer not only did not have permission to use the radio frequency under discussion but also had no likelihood of receiving such permission. This was particularly true of potential customers who were members of important government departments involving defence, railways and oil. When pressed by the foreign investors' legal advisors who had exhausted the public records on radio frequency regulations, the agent and potential customers would claim that *neibu* regulations, unavailable to foreigners, existed for public purposes in the telecommunications industry and that it would be impossible, if not illegal, to show the foreign investor such *neibu* regulations.

It may be that in the future there will be more transparency for the foreign investor in the telecommunications industry particularly since the Ministry of Posts and Telecommunications has now lost its monopoly over the industry. Two new companies, Jitong Communications Company and Liantong Communications Company were established in early 1994 under the control of the Ministry of Electronics Industry. Liantong, however, is now said to be under the management of MPT according to MPT's Chief of Information who would not confirm that Liantong had received State Council approval. Rather, he stated that 'Regulations to split the Ministry's regulatory and business functions would be published this year as soon as they gained State Council approval' (*South China Morning Post* 3 February 1994).

It may also be the case that the new developments create a new ambiguity for foreign investors. There is as yet no discussion of the legal authority of Liantong, nor is there any clear explanation of the relationship between Liantong and the MPT. Not only will the foreign investor have to choose whether to work with the MPT or the Ministry of Electronics Industry, but it may also be that the authorized activities of the new companies themselves will be limited.

AT&T, however, takes a more robust view of the rule of law, and on questions of transparency stated:

> In the context of our partnership with China AT&T will respond to all reasonable requests for technology, products and services. Currently we are actively working with MPT. If Liantong and Jitong invite us, we will be ready to address their needs.
>
> (*South China Morning Post* 7 February 1994)

The evident lack of transparency in China's telecommunications industry is also reflected in the developing power industry: according to the minister responsible for the power industry 'Enterprises in the power industry are subsidiaries of administrative organs. They tend to be controlled by arbitrary orders which can mean poor investment' (*Far Eastern Economic Review* 1994: 74).

The minister was probably referring to the Goldman Sachs Joint Venture with China Venturetech to build a power plant in Shandong Province, which was terminated by Beijing in December 1993. The proposal had been 18 months in the making and offered a group of foreign investors a 30 per cent stake in existing power plants in Shanghai in exchange for capital for new projects. It is alleged that a 30 per cent stake was thought to be too generous, and that the rate of return to the foreigners was considered to be too high and therefore unacceptable to some elements in the State Council who vetoed the project. One investment banker is quoted as follows:

> Nobody understands the approval process, and China won't explain it. Deals are cut within the family (the Party); things happen where the light of day does not shine. It is difficult to work out which approvals you need and what the sequence is.
>
> (*Far Eastern Economic Review* 1994: 75)

Indeed it now appears, although no one can be sure, that the acceptable rate of return for foreign investment is between 12 and possibly 15 per cent. Thus belief is based upon the rumoured existence of a *neibu* regulation at the highest government level, and it seems that China is becoming more rather than less opaque in its dealings with foreigners. An unnamed source is quoted as saying that '[a]ll Beijing's obsession with the rate of return for foreigners and the limits of foreign ownership are a direct consequence of the Goldman deal' (*Far Eastern Economic Review* 1994: 75).

Whether or not that interpretation is correct, it seems to be the case that the administrative regulations applied by central state planners to business will inevitably result in a common set of criteria for decision-making, thus creating inflexibility and imposing a common set of criteria as part of the package offered to investors from the perspective of state planners. This is the antithesis of the open-ended flexibility that lies within the structure of a civil society's rules and the ability of rules to deal with the unpredictable, including, for example, the rates of return on investments whether foreign or otherwise.

A further example of the interests of the state planners and the mothers-in-law of government versus the business interests of the 1990s' foreign investor is found in China's foreign exchange rules of January 1994 concerning the unification of the yuan. Prior to 1994, provincial institutions such as Guangdong Investment Trust Corporation (GITIC) provided guarantees at the provincial level that foreign exchange would be made available for projects involving the need for hard currency. Since the end of 1993, such guarantees have been forbidden by Beijing, although, for example, Shandong Investment Trust Corporation privately told foreign investors that it could still offer guarantees despite such measures from Beijing. Once again, it is impossible to check whether a special authority may have been given at the provincial level or whether Beijing's State Administration for Exchange Control has relaxed the rules temporarily and, if so, when and if the rules will be tightened again. From the Western perspective, it cannot be said that the officials' internal point of view and their understanding of the cohesiveness of the legal system in China are working in favour of the foreign investor.

Finally, one more example which highlights the lack of transparency in China's legal system and has serious consequences for international business and its expectations from the legal system. Joseph Fu, a tax partner with Deloitte Touch Tohmatsu, described China's structural tax reforms of January 1994 as a well-written law with

> insufficient guidance, although there are lots of tax notices being given to tax practitioners. In the law everything is clearly written such as appeal procedures. But in practice you'd better not follow the law or else it may upset the tax officers and may hinder your next deal with the officers. In China power is tightly grasped in the hands of the administration. And if the interpretation of tax rules is transferred to others, say the judiciary system, it is a transfer of powers.
> (*South China Morning Post* 20 September 1994)

Hence the same law is applied throughout the country but without any system of precedent that is familiar to the Western perspective.

Furthermore the interpretation of the rules depends on the domestic tax inspectors' views of directives as supplementary provisions to the existing regulations from higher ranking government departments to junior officials.

The implications for a management philosophy go far deeper than the difficulty of discovering what the law is in China and the difference between a law, a published regulation and an internal *neibu* statement. There can be no transparency in the Western sense without a coherent belief in the fundamental importance of the rule of law, and despite arguments that the term has become meaningless thanks to ideological abuse and over-use (Shklar 1987: 1), it had a crucial cultural impact on the management philosophy of those involved in business in China. It connotes assumptions about transparency, regularity and restraint, and requires constant re-assessment by those who seek to impose it as the basis of their political and legal philosophy in the culture of international business.

CONCLUSION

Three important characteristics underlie the international business community's assumption that law matters and these may serve as the basis for distinguishing the different management approaches to rules and legal procedures. The first characteristic is government by law that depends primarily on 'a stable and independent legal culture of interpretation' (Krygier 1990: 642). The second is government under law that depends upon a 'legal/political culture in which it is understood that even very high political officials are confined and confineable by legal rules and legal challenge' (Krygier 1990: 643). The third characteristic concerns rights, and focuses on the individual a concept that is so profoundly important to the idea of a civil society. The question for an international manager is therefore not only who makes the rules, but who interprets the rules and who enforces them? The development of Western style civil society as a key factor of business and its evolution needs to examine why the convergence of Western and Sinicized philosophies may require more than an insistence by the United States negotiators on transparency in the regulatory framework. It requires a fundamental shift towards *consensus ad idem* on the importance of the rule of law in the conduct of business dealings and that this lies at the very heart of the various self-interests of the international community in all its commercial transactions.

APPENDIX

Translation of *neibu* State Council document concerning the ideas for strengthening, development and market management of the telecommunication business:

Opinions for strengthening the management of the telecommunication business market

In order to meet the requirements of the reform and Open Door Policy and the socialist modernization construction, and to abide by and serve the central task of economic construction better, the telecommunication section must concentrate on developing a united, complete, and advanced national communication network. At the same time, it must exploit the potentials of the professional communication networks sufficiently, activate the motivations of the related departments, and speed up the development of the communication business.

In the recent years, the operation of part of the telecommunication business has been opened to society. Currently such openly-operated telecommunication businesses include: radio paging business, 800MHz cluster telephone business, 450MHz radio mobile communication business, domestic VSAT communication business, telephone information service business, computer information service business, electronic mail box business, electronic data exchanging business, visual graphics and texts business, and other telecommunication businesses approved by the state council or the national telecommunication ministry.

In order to maintain the normal communication order, to protect the communication security and service quality of the nation and the customers, and to create an environment for fair competition, the management of the openly-operated telecommunication business market must be strengthened. For such a purpose the following opinions are proposed:

1 A system of application and a system of operation licence will be applied to the openly-operated telecommunication business. For such businesses operating inside a province, an autonomous region, or a directly-administered city, the local telecommunication bureau will deal with their application, examination and approvement, and issue the operation licenses. The results must be reported to the telecommunication bureau for putting on record. For the businesses involved in the transprovincial (autonomous regional, directly-administered municipal) operations, the telecommunication ministry will deal with their application, examination and approvement, any working units or individuals must not take part in the operation of the above telecommunication businesses. The telecommunication ministry will draft and issue the implementing methods for the application system and operation licence system, accordingly. For the working units which are already operating the above telecommunication businesses, related supplementary procedures will be produced.

2 According to the corresponding authority of examination and approvement, any units applying for the operation of telecommunication businesses must go to the Telecommunication Ministry or the local Telecommunication Bureau to apply for the operation licence, and use

that licence to get the usage frequency approved by the radio administration section; only then can the operation be started.

3 For the sections and units approved to operate the above telecommunication businesses, regional blocks should not be created. These sections and units must abide by the nation's communication-related policies, laws and regulations. They must accept the industrial management, supervision and examination of the communication administration section, guarantee the telecommunication service quality, implement the nation's fee-collection policies and related fee-collection standards strictly, pay taxes according to the laws, protect the legal rights and benefits of the customers. In their business operations, these sections and units must not intervene in the normal operation and construction of the national public telecommunication network and other professional communication networks.

4 The national communication administration section must create an environment of fair competition for the telecommunication enterprises and other enterprises involved in the operation of communication businesses. In accordance with the principles of usage with proper compensation and mutual benefit, telecommunication enterprises at different levels must coordinate with each other, basing their arrangements on the conditions of supply and demand, to provide the basic equipment and routes to meet the business requirement of the units with operation licences approved by the national communication administration sections, so as to ensure better telecommunication services for society by such units.

5 Foreign investors must not operate or take part in operating telecommunication business inside our country. The various foreign groups, enterprises, individuals, and foreign-funded enterprises established in China, including wholly-owned foreign enterprises, Sino-foreign equity or contractual joint ventures, are not allowed to operate or take part in operating wired or radio communication business of the public and professional communication networks inside China. Any method of attracting foreign investment into such operations are prohibited.

6 The Telecommunication Ministry and Telecommunication Bureaux in various provinces, autonomous regions, and directly administered cities must supervise and examine the situations regarding implementation of the above regulations. The telecommunication enterprises and other units involved in the operation of telecommunication business which violate the above regulations, will incur different degrees of punishment such as warning, public criticism, forcing to correct in a certain period, forcing to stop operation, confiscating the illegal operational income, administrative fine, and revoking the operation licence. Telecommunication sections at different levels are not allowed to exploit private benefits by taking the advantage of issuing the operation licence; serious punishment will be imposed once such case are found.

If the above opinions are suitable, please transfer to various areas and sections to implement.

(Telecommunication Ministry 30 June 1993)

REFERENCES

Agence France Report 1993 'China carries the day at human rights conference' Ohio: Lexis. Nexis Mead Data Central Inc. 3 April.

Asian Wall Street Journal 1993 'Rule of no law' 16 December.

Asian Wall Street Journal 1994 'Foreign companies resist hefty Chinese surcharges' 7 February.

Bureau of National Affairs, Inc. 1993 'Press summary of Uruguay round agreement issued 14 December 1993', *Daily Report for Executives* 17 December.

Chen, K. 1994 'Multinational move to preempt entry by rivals', *South China Morning Post* 16 February.

Eliot, T.S. 1948 *Notes towards the definition of culture*, London: Faber & Faber.

Far Eastern Economic Review 1994 14 April: 74–75.

Fukuda, J. 1989 'China's management tradition and reform', *Management Decisions* 27(3): 45–49.

Haley, J.O. 1991 *Authority without power*, Oxford: Oxford University Press.

Jayawickrama, N. 1990 'Human rights exception no longer' in G. Hicks (ed.) *The broken mirror: China after Tiananmen*: 345–368, London: Longman.

Krygier, M. 1990 'Marxism and the rule of law: reflections after the collapse of communism', *Law and Social Inquiry* 15: 633–663.

Lloyd, Lord 1985 *Lloyd's introduction to jurisprudence*, London: Stevens & Sons.

Massey, J. 1993 '301: The successful resolution', *The China Business Review* 9–11 December.

People's Daily 1993a 'The radio administrative regulation of the People's Republic of China order from the State council and Central Military Commission of the People's Republic of China' 11 September.

People's Daily 1993b 'Resolution of the NPC Standing Committee to revise the 1985 Accountancy Law' 31 December.

Seligman, A. 1992 *The Idea of a Civil Society*, New York: Manhattan.

Shiu Yun Ma 1994 'The Chinese discourse on civil society', *The China Quarterly Review* 137: 180–193.

Shklar, J. 1987 'Political theory and the rule of law', in A. Hutchinson and P. Monahan (eds) *The rule of law: ideal or ideology* 63: 1–24, Toronto: Carswell.

South China Morning Post 1993 28 November.

South China Morning Post 1994a 4 January.

South China Morning Post 1994b 18 January.

South China Morning Post 1994c 3 February.

South China Morning Post 1994d 7 February.

South China Morning Post 1994e 15 February.

South China Morning Post 1994f 16 February.

South China Morning Post 1994g 20 September.

Stewart, S. 1992 'China's managers', *The International Executive* 34(2): 165–179.

— (with Paula Delisle) 1994 'Hong Kong Expatriates in PR China', *International Studies of Management and Organization* 24 (3) (in press).

Wong, Kan Seng 1993 'Asians urge pragmatism on human rights', *Agence France Presse*, Ohio: Lexis. Nexis Mead Data Central Inc. 16 June.

Xinhua News Agency 1993, BBC Monitoring Summary of World Broadcasts, Far East/16 86 B2/3 10 May.

2 Overcoming barriers to technology transfers into China

Aimin Guo and Robert Akroyd

ABSTRACT

This chapter looks at technology transfers into the People's Republic of China from the point of view of barriers impeding their successful identification, negotiation, implementation and development. It argues that, by precipitating cumulative, latent failure (whether passive failure, through the indifference of one party, or active failure, as a result of a dispute involving both parties) such barriers are the major factor influencing decisions and, hence, the design of management systems for decision making.

The staging of technology transfers is discussed in terms of strategic transactional decision making. A number of models, including two alternative five-stage models, were identified in the surveys and interviews, although subjectively perceived multi-stage transactions, on the one hand, and an inherent minimal three-stage transaction on the other, are by no means mutually exclusive. Five barriers were likewise identified as unevenly distributed amongst such stages. Such barriers, therefore, exist at all stages, but may exercise greater influence at one or other of them. Moreover, some of such barriers may be heavily open to influence from subjective perception. Hence, barriers at given stages may be objective and bilateral, or subjective and unilateral.

Accordingly, decision support systems for technology transfers need to be modelled as mechanisms for navigating such barriers, stage by stage, rather than as providing recipes for success. There is no clear safe route, either generally, or for particular transactions. In consequence, a five function cycle at each stage can be used to articulate particular disciplinary aspects integrally. Five disciplinary aspects likewise, were identified with the common function of locating, characterising and promoting the avoidance of barriers. While such aspects are in contact with potential barriers, however, they may need to be accessed randomly by a human user, who remains central to the system.

INTRODUCTION

The object of the research was to build, test and improve one or more possibly alternative models for operational decision making as the potential basis for a computer-based decision support system, accessible to both cultures in this process. A basic consideration would be the nature of the difficulties experienced by either party and their possible solutions (Contractor 1985: 23–50; Contractor and Lorange 1987; Campbell 1988; Ball *et al.* 1993).

CONCEPTUAL ELEMENTS OF DECISION MAKING IN TECHNOLOGY TRANSFERS

Technology transfer into China is a multi-faceted problem involving major conceptual elements, i.e. sequential stages, relating to content and time scale; barriers to technology transfer identified at each stage; operational functions, articulating aspects from stage to stage; and disciplinary aspects, identifying problem solving tools.

Sequential stages in technology transfer

Like all business transactions, technology transfers are a dynamic process, involving significant changes over a period of time, defined by the impedance of barriers to change. Such discernible stages, therefore, have different characteristics involving decision makers in characteristic issues. Such issues are a complex of staged barriers and a response involving operational functions and their associated disciplinary aspects. Perceptions of such stages vary. Initially the collaborating attentions had been able to recognize as many as eight and as few as three basic stages: Pre-transfer, Real transfer, and Post-transfer. A five-stage model was adopted as the basis for surveys of English and Chinese barriers:

1 Partner search
2 Proposal
3 Negotiation
4 Implementation
5 Further co-operation.
                    (Wionczek 1979; Atkinson 1984; Adler 1992: 449–466).

An alternative five-stage model suggested by a former Molin's chief executive with experience of Chinese technology transfer would be:

1 Motivation (i.e. China's natural or local enterprise need or foreign innovator or multinational company need)
2 Capitalisation (i.e. Chinese government funds, special development funds, or multinational company resources)
3 Negotiation (i.e. inputs, distribution of returns and control)

4   Execution (i.e. location, co-ordination and management)
5   Exploitation (i.e. licensing the actual transfer of knowledge and installation of support systems).

Staging, i.e. the recognition of types, rather than the times of key decision points, is a complex matter of diverse, informal perceptions forming the outcome of interaction between any barriers to technological transfer and any disciplinary aspects for their perception, evaluation and resolution. Its coherent, formal expression, however, is characteristically within the purview of the legal aspect, forming an expression of apparently legitimate effective power within a given hegemony and, hence, providing a minimal standard for legitimate exercise, or invocation, of such authority.

Common sense would suggest an irreducible minimum of four inherent stages in any transaction, by recognizing the process of negotiation as one of proposal and counter-proposal (supported by techniques for sincerity testing, delineation, areas of commonality and so on). Yet even this may be excessive, if further co-operation can be regarded merely as a process of renegotiation during, or on completion of, the implementation stage.

Success is avoidance of failure by surmounting the barriers. The staging, moreover, may be diverted if any associated barriers cannot be surmounted. Thus, failures may be relatively passive ones of indifference, or active ones of dispute. The latter case introduces stages of its own in the process of dispute resolution. Go back and return (or renegotiation) likewise takes on its own characteristic stages, perhaps analogous to further co-operation, where add-ons are employed in a new proposal.

Nor does time scale necessarily shed light on the problem. Success on the Chinese side, as might be expected at the present time, invariably meant continuation of the relationship, although this was less apparent to British respondents. Hence, the termination of an on-going relationship was open-ended. The Chinese also were found to invest longer in preparation and to allow a longer period for transition from stage to stage, at least ten years, for example, between the end of formal (but not informal) negotiations and further co-operation.

Nor would time scales necessarily be definable in the event of a failure. Passive failures, resulting from lack of interest by one party, may take years to become apparent, remaining amenable to revival by going back and making a fresh approach. Only in the case of active failures, involving a dispute which effectively terminates the transactional relationship, is the whole time scale apparent. It is, therefore, possible to speculate that case studies demonstrating failure to avoid particular barriers may offer clearer guidance than open-ended apparent successes containing an unidentified potential failure.

BARRIERS SHAPING THE DECISION SPACE IN TECHNOLOGY TRANSFER

Lack of success in a transaction is often caused by the cumulative failure to surmount barriers. These may be objective and real or subjective and imagined. Nevertheless, a number of barriers inherent in the transactional situation are definitive of decision points to go on (success), go back (reiterate), or go out (failure) at each of its stages.

Obviously, any business transaction involves the need for a perceptibly favourable balance, not only between the inputs and outputs for each party in isolation, but also between the inputs and outputs for one party compared with those for the other. In any given transaction it may be possible to generalize on likely areas of congruence and conflict distributed between different dimensions. The likely areas of congruence identified by Michael Wright of Molins plc were:

• access/service to domestic markets
• local optimization of products and services
• cash generation (in other words, the main outputs).

The likely areas of conflict were identified as:

• distribution of inputs/resources
• ownership of intellectual property rights
• management of technological and managerial discontinuities in the transferee business
• distribution of returns and competing taxation policies
• national versus local aims and objectives
• the transferee's ambitions for export-led generation of foreign revenue
• the transferee's potential for competitive autonomy (in other words, the main distributions).

Such basic issues are essentially those between any more developed and any less developed country except that China's relative size and speed of change hold out the real possibility of a reversal in such relationship within the next generation. In order to maximize the congruencies and minimize fields of dispute, a number of barriers must be overcome. Such barriers bear a close relationship to failure and success. There appear to be five major barriers:

1 an information barrier
2 a communication barrier
3 a decision-criteria barrier
4 an infrastructure barrier
5 a perception barrier.

Almost by definition, inherent barriers are likely to be of unequal significance at each stage. An indication of the relative importance attributed to them by British and Chinese executives at given stages is given in Appendix II.

Information barriers

Difficulty in sending or obtaining relevant technology transfer information represents an information barrier. Information transmission is a first step preliminary to identifying a prospective partner for technology transfer. For the receiver it is to identify an appropriate supplier; for the transferrer it is to send relevant information to the new market.

A Chinese company's difficulties are considerable. Chinese firms often have difficulty in identifying appropriate suppliers of new technology and promotions by UK companies fail to reach many Chinese firms. In Appendix I, Case (3) ZNP, one Chinese factory manager complained of how difficult it was to identify a potential foreign technology supplier. He had learnt from a Chinese technical publication several years before that a new manufacturing technology used in a UK company was what his factory needed, and had borne this in mind ever since, but he still did not even know the UK company's name and address. He kept trying to find out more about the company offering this technology, but only in 1993 had he been able to ask a personal friend to get more information in the UK. This is not an unusual case. In fact, this factory manager had been doing quite well in importing foreign technologies compared with the majority of Chinese managers. He first began to import foreign technology in the early 1980s, from West Germany, Japan and the US. The technology transfer projects were successful and his factory co-operated well with the foreign counterparts. His difficulty in identifying a technology supplier can be regarded as representative of many Chinese firms.

In the UK, the commercial information system includes the yellow pages, a public information centre, business directories, commercial organizations and associations, etc., all open to public use. For UK companies, the information barrier lies in the difficulty of promoting their new technology to the Chinese market. It is very difficult to find relevant information. One British managing director who had personally been successful in doing business in China, commented 'You can hardly find any yellow pages in China'. He pointed out that personal contact is one of the most effective approaches, quite different from information collection in the UK. It is also difficult for UK companies to make it clear to a Chinese firm what is on offer. Chinese firms do not have access to reliable suppliers as UK companies do, and as a result they have to be more self-sufficient than is usual amongst UK companies. In consequence, what Chinese firms assume to be included in an offer may well belong to the UK company's supplier and hence need to be bought separately. Misunderstandings about the real needs and what may be on offer pose the greatest threat of fast failure in technology transfer. The need is for effective information for clarification to both the transferee and the transferrer.

Communication barriers

The communication barrier refers to frustrations and misunderstanding caused by different systems of communication derived from both technological and cultural factors. The communication process is the means of getting to know the counterpart. For the transferrer, it is to know the real need of the technology transferee; for the receiver it is to know what is on offer from the transferrer. A communication barrier can lead to serious misunderstanding of what is the need or what is on offer.

The Chinese information system is not an open one comparable with that of the UK. In the UK, not only traditional postage, telephone and telex communication channels are widely available privately, but also mobile phones, fax and E-mail. These are as yet not widely available in China. Moreover, few open services are available for business use. The information flow, at both the formal and informal levels, is between government bodies and factories, organizations and personal contacts. Chinese managers are expert at using these channels. Effective information transmission is within the tight closed circle characteristic of the Confucian cultural infrastructure, albeit one which in other respects works exceptionally well.

As the 1991 Manchester survey pointed out (Ball, Zheng Rong and Pearson 1993), the Chinese communication system is a technically rather than a commercially oriented one, in contrast with that of the UK. In the UK, the information services are commercially oriented and information is presented in a form suitable for business uses. Commercial promotion is an important part of the information flow; hence, research, consultancy, financial services, insurance companies, legal firms, etc., are all very capable of providing commercial services. These functions are as yet in their infancy in China. Accordingly:

> Chinese industries have their own information systems: each industry has many state-level research institutes (some of them designated technical information research institutes) and each research institute is responsible for the development of certain products or technologies. Collecting information on new technology from outside China and conveying it to Chinese firms and government is one of their responsibilities.
>
> (Ball, Zheng Rong and Pearson 1993)

Market mechanisms have been introduced into research institutes under the pretext of economic reform and the development of a socialist market economy. Rapid changes in ownership and fund raising have been taking place, even in the intervening two years. Hence, purely state ownership has been changed into multi-form ownership, characterized by the co-existence of state owned, collectively owned, privately owned enterprise, as well as enterprises owned jointly with foreign investment. The management mechanism is being transformed into a system based on self-sustaining autonomous fund raising, and self-restrained autonomous management. As regards changes in fund raising, government funding has been reduced gradually (about 20 per cent per year). By 1988, 44.3 per cent of the R&D institutions in natural science became financially independent from government or had reduced government funding. In 1990, of the total science and technology funding, 30.05 billion yuan, the non-state allocation reached 16.39 billion yuan, accounting for 54.5 per cent, the first time that the non-state proportion exceeded the state proportion. Sixty per cent of the science and technology research institutions became financially independent from government. Research institutions are strengthening their ties with enterprises and establishing strong relationships with industrial firms. In 1990, a total of more than 10,000 enterprise groups were set up. These groups are scientific research–production–marketing integrations (consortia). Three thousand five hundred economic entities integrated with scientific research, production and business operation were set up by scientific research institutions. The Chinese Science Academy is being transformed into a new model: a top authoritative Chinese Academy of Science; a number of research institutes, science centres, and engineering research centres; a number of high technology companies or company groups joining domestic and international competition. All these changes in the science and technology administration imply movement away from a technically oriented towards a commercially oriented communications system. Moreover, China does not have a computerized telecommunication system. In the UK, the telecommunications system is computerized. In libraries and information centres, on-line information inquiries can be made; telephone and fax facilities are very convenient for information transmission. In China, however, communication of information usually requires personal visits and contacts. Success in obtaining relevant information depends to a large extent on finding the right person with whom to co-operate. Sending information to or obtaining information from so different a system is a daunting task at the beginning.

It requires an understanding of differences in establishing a communication channel between China and the UK. Effective communication requires each side to make any offer or need, or any other element of a technology transfer, clear to the other. The point is to understand the differences and identify the right person to communicate with. By understanding the differences between the two information systems and trying different ways of getting things done, however, an effective information channel can be built up. In the research project, for example, three different ways of obtaining information from Chinese counterparts were attempted before a fourth was successful:

1 co-operation with Chinese institutions
2 contacting Chinese companies directly
3 personal contacts
4 a personal visit.

(Leiberthal and Ocksenburg 1985: 24–31; Guo, A. 1988–92;
Guo, C.J. 1993)

The barrier also shows itself at a simpler level. One Birmingham software engineering company started to do business in the Chinese market. Their representative had been to China many times, but could not speak any Chinese. He said he found it very difficult to do anything without a translator, even eating in restaurants. Because many of the potential customers could not speak English well, it was impossible to create good relations with them, while some of those who could speak English better were not in positions of power to choose to buy from him. Other problems were that employees of a company would often make promises to buy from him, although they lacked the authority to make such a decision. This is related to the Chinese idea of 'face'. Compared with business in other countries the process in China was much slower, sometimes taking over a year. Often faxes would go unanswered. When a Chinese national was temporarily hired, it became much easier to make progress, as they could phone and speak directly to the people in power, and being from the same Chinese business background they could tell if the person they were speaking to was really in a position to fulfil promises. This contrasts sharply with the statement of a Japanese businessman in Beijing, 'I don't like a third person standing between me and the one I want to speak to'. As a result he was taking lessons in Chinese.

Decision criteria barriers

The decision criteria barrier refers to difficulties raised by having no common base for evaluating new technology, finance or other matters, such as different investment approval techniques and different pricing methods used in negotiation. It may also refer to deployment of difficult criteria for strategies and skills in negotiation.

Criteria for making decisions may involve everything concerned with the technology transfer. The decision criteria barrier is not merely a matter of strategy, or negotiation, but of the entire range of functions which influence the whole technology transfer process.

If the real need of the receiver is not met, there will be a failure in the technology transfer process. However, it is difficult for UK companies to know the real need of Chinese partners for new technology. This is determined by a number of factors. The main influences are: the government's technology import criteria; a Chinese firm's translation of the criteria into business practice; and funding resources. The government technology importing criteria place emphasis on new product production and development; decrease of the consumption of energy and raw material; better resource utilization, environment protection, product safety and management improvement; export and foreign currency earning; and the general advancement of science and technology in China. Chinese firms' translation of these criteria into business practice may differ not only from that of the would-be foreign partner, but from one firm to another: 'Is the technology one of the latest in the world?' 'Is it better than what we have now?' Is the technology unavailable in China?' and so on (Appendix I, Case 3, ZNP). One Chinese industrial firm manager expressed the ideal of new technology he wanted to buy in this way: 'If we can find production technology of a certain product which has potential in China's domestic market, and is not yet available, then we will buy this technology and produce that product.' It sounds vague to UK managers, but it is the Chinese manager's ideal choice. (This was a machine tool plant manager and managing director of an industrial group company in central China.) In Appendix I, Case 3, ZNP the real need of technology import is very definite: i.e. new manufacturing technology in that specific production area. The money supply will also affect the real need of technology import (Appendix I, Case 2, HDF). In one successful case, the real need for technology import was expressed as follows:

> In order to establish a modern industrial firm in a poor area in central China, the local government decided to set up a new factory by importing foreign advanced technology. They also managed to get a sum of foreign currency loan from an investment company.

Chinese firms' main concerns in a negotiation are derived from government technology import criteria, enterprises' interpretation of business practice, the development of a business system and the general economic and cultural situation. They represent generalized decision making criteria.

The meaning of technology advancement may be quite different from firm to firm in business practice. It may refer to the advancement of a manufacturing technology or just the advancement of the product which will be produced. In Appendix I, Case 3, ZNP, the Chinese firm needed a kind of manufacturing technology: the technology advancement here is the quality improvement and productivity of this manufacturing technology. In Appendix I, Case 2, HDF, the Chinese firm wanted to buy a refrigerator production line: here technology advancement mainly referred to the advancement of the product which would be produced. Is the product a new one? What is the market potential of the product? These are the main concerns. In this case, the Italian company IBERNA's newly released product (EL-20) was interpreted as the latest technology. In fact this is not the correct interpretation because the manufacturing technology may not be the latest technology. But in this situation, the product met the needs of the Chinese firm and this interpretation was very important in obtaining government approval of the project.

Chinese firms want to get advanced technology at a fair price. The price negotiation also represents an establishment of trust. The price one foreign company offers in a negotiation will be compared with other offers and the final cost of the deal. In Case 2, HDF, the Chinese firm received various price offers for a production line. The Italian company, IBERNA's offer of $3 million was regarded as an honest offer (compared with a Japanese company's offer of $6 million). Chinese firms anticipate differences between a first offer and the final price, according to the nationality of the company making the offer. A Chinese manager comments as follows:

> As regard to the price of technology import, generally the European and American companies will offer fair price to the technology, you can not expect much on price reduction in the final deal. The US company's offer is quite fair, the UK's, Germany's, Holland's are a little bit higher, but still fair. A Japanese company's offer may be much higher than a reasonable price. There could be considerable difference between a first offer and the final deal.

Prospects for long term co-operation may be valuable to Chinese firms in obtaining government approval. It is by no means always easy for Chinese firms to import technology from abroad, so they treasure their relationship with foreign companies and seek to establish long term co-operation.

The main concerns of the foreign company are assumed by the Chinese party to be limited to profitability and stability. These depend on the success of the project and hence on key Chinese decision makers. Rather than making these mere bargaining points, foreign companies will feel more secure if they can be convinced of the success of the project and develop trust in key decision makers. For example, in Case 2, HDF, the Italian company was principally convinced about China's market size. Subsequently, they were able to realize the capability of the key Chinese decision makers and so successfully carry out the project, secure in their understanding of the Chinese decision makers' power. In the negotiation process, disputes will be aroused and attitudes of each party thereby disclosed. Foreign companies should aim not only to get a paper deal, but also to satisfy the more important criteria for success; the strategic success of the project, obtaining the right key persons and the establishment of trust. These can only be achieved by regarding the process of negotiation as going before and far beyond the mere bargaining stage into the long-term relationship of the parties based on continuous monitoring and strategic review.

The Chinese negotiation team typically involves legal, commercial and technical expertise together with a (quiet) party official, who is likely to be the effective decision maker. The attitude towards bargaining was characterized as 'anything goes' by one British executive, in sharp contrast with their 'sacrosanct' commitment to its implementation. The time scale, not the transactual stages negotiated for, is likely to be at least ten years beyond agreement, four for implementation, six for experience and any additional for further strategic developments. The official encouragement of Chinese negotiators to adopt a far sighted, strategic approach is deliberate ('A superior person must have a far sighted goal, despite immediate worries' – ascribed to Confucius). The end product of negotiation is emphatically not a mere document, but an actual on-going relationship. The paper contract is for the authorities. Foreign parties are advised to get a preliminary commitment that their Chinese counterpart has appropriate authorization to contract with a foreign party. An initial memorandum of understanding should identify the main aims of the parties, set a timetable for completion of negotiations and allocate responsibility for preparing a detailed feasibility study and submitting it for internal approval, together with an undertaking that the parties involved have access to sufficient foreign exchange to complete it on that basis. A draft formal contract in Chinese and English forms the background to detailed negotiations in accordance with relevant legal, resource/financial, technological, managerial and cultural aspects. The completed draft, and any subsequent modifications, signed by the parties, including the Chinese party official, must be submitted for approval to all relevant authorities, who may require its amendment.

Infrastructure barriers

The infrastructure barrier refers to problems at pre- and post-implementation stages such as the new enterprise's compatibility with existing technology, systems and management, the operation and maintenance of new technology, sourcing of raw materials, personnel training, and so on. The category includes all situations in which logistic equipment and personnel factors in the parties' organizations involve problems of mismatch, updating and so on, not only for a new proposed venture, but for any changes proposed for an existing venture. Thus, although most obviously associated with the implementation phase, it also carries implications for further strategic involvement.

Putting infrastructures in place involves the realization of new technology, profitability, productivity, etc. Typically involving 3–4 years of complex bureaucratic, management and technological processes, in which to build and equip plant, take on and train a workforce, such implementation was described by Stephen Perry, chief executive of the London Export Company, as 'sacrosanct'.

Major difficulties for the Chinese side at an implementation stage are: the compatibility of new technology with an existing technology system; the need for improvement of poor management skills to meet the demands of new technology; and workforce training.

From a Western point of view in particular, both parties have a strong mutual interest in thorough joint exploration of possible mismatches, together with methods for circumventing them, and an appropriate division of responsibilities, especially at the negotiation stage. It is most important to clarify these areas for any would-be partner on the Chinese side who might be responsible for implementation, paying particular regard to relevancy, appropriate level and effective execution. Conversely, it may be necessary for the foreign partner to explore different methods of implementing the agreement thoroughly, including especially an appreciation of the strengths and weaknesses of the Chinese party's *guanxi* (informal personal network) based on Confucian stereotyped relationships.

Perception barriers

Perception/misperception barriers are those where, despite copious and accurate information, excellent communications, matching criteria for decision making and successful establishment of a technology transfer enterprise, a spontaneous atmosphere of harmony cannot be achieved. This is often, but need not be, a function of culture, and has effects at a societal, enterprise, or even individual executive level, especially in a key expatriate liaison role. This need not imply bad faith, or mistrust, merely an inability to develop a spontaneous feel for the concerns of the other party, so that no advance is effectively made beyond the mechanistic concerns of the original approach.

Perception barriers are of mainly strategic significance, affecting the establishment of a joint venture, its stability, productivity, quality, profitability and whether the parties eventually become collaborators, or competitors. If a perception barrier affects a proposed technology transfer in the early stages, its implementation will be wholly dependent on the parties' ability to clarify and, if necessary, rectify it at the negotiation stage. Where damaging perceptions survive into the implementation stage, however, they cease to be acute and, if unresolved, become chronic. Major opportunities, therefore, may be frustrated by such an inability to give meaning to the concerns of the other party. If that can be achieved, on the other hand, even intractable practical difficulties may be transcended. Thus, the Chinese party's perception of the foreign party's obsession with short-term profit to the exclusion of strategic influence, for example, may preclude any possibility for longer-term strategic co-operation, which could involve organizational dependence. Case 1, KONKA, however, provides an example of the converse situation, where both companies have established sufficient mutual confidence to proceed towards greater involvement, although the significance of the fact that the foreign partner was a Hong Kong company is uncertain. Clearly, commitment of the foreign partner to continuance/development of the relationship is one of strategic level.

Another perception may be any unstated fears of the foreign party that the Chinese enterprise is a potential competitor which would block their own involvement in a global strategic scale. With fundamental and far reaching strategic issues at stake, it would be surprising if one or the other of the partners did not regard it as being in its best interests to control the perceptions of the other. Such an approach merely perpetuates and institutionalizes the problem. Whilst retaining a proper sense of what may be due to prudence, both parties should work hard at removing such misperceptions. Good relations will thereby be preserved and opportunities maximized. Stephen Perry summed up the problem: 'The difficulty is to get each side to identify what they really want, i.e. to the other in the light of the real situation'.

OUTCOMES OF DECISION MAKING: SUCCESS, GO BACK AND FAILURE

Out of four technology transfers brokered by the London Export Company, and motivated by a desire for entry into the Chinese market, Stephen Perry, current chief executive, identified the Agmee Marles transfer as a failure, the Molins venture as a qualified success – the technology had been allowed to spread to unauthorized plants – and Tootal and Pilkington as strategic successes. What this might mean, however, was less apparent.

In a Chinese context, success is most conveniently defined widely as the absence of any failure which may be sufficient to inhibit continuation of the operation, although different criteria involving the fulfilment of policy objectives may apply to Western parties. Some firms may appear to exhibit spectacular success and it is essential to learn from the initiatives of highly entrepreneurial innovators, but these are likely to involve an innovative avoidance of barriers rather than some magic formula for success. Once learnt, moreover, these quickly pass into the general body of management practice. The scope for further innovation always remains in the human domain, at the centre of the decision system and beyond the scope for machine based support.

There are, therefore, three discernible levels of major success in transferring technology into China. The primary start level of success depends on the parties overcoming information and communication barriers to promote technology and get a first contract for its transfer approved by the Chinese authorities. Even such a primary level of success, therefore, depends on overcoming barriers throughout the first three stages of technology transfer, prior to conclusion of the negotiation stage. The middle implementation level of success depends on the parties overcoming implementation and co-operation barriers, in order to succeed in licensing intellectual property, redesigning the technology as necessary, training the personnel, encouraging target users to define their technological needs and developing a new market. The advanced strategic level of success depends on realizing the strategic potential of technology in a non-strategic geographic area, or entering new, less advanced markets in Asia and Africa with cheaper products in concert with Chinese partners, i.e. using the strategic and productive potential of advanced technology to its fullest extent. It follows that, where the cost outweighs the advantages of technology, this poses a major obstacle to strategic success in technology transfer.

Go back and return is an essential alternative to both success and failure, either as a result of immediate pressure, or as a strategic option. There is a sense in which this is the focus of an effective strategy. Hence, unlike failure and even success, this is a decision within the autonomy of the parties. Moreover, the extent of the go back to one or more earlier stages and the timing and character of any return are, likewise, under their control. Decision points related to such success, go back and return, or failure were identified as defining factors at every stage, although in practice, the transition from stage two to stage three of the five-stage model was seen as relatively easy. It is possible to speculate that continuous readiness to re-negotiate (go back and return) is the surest route to maximizing a party's interests with minimal risk. This, and its converse, provide alternative definitions of success and failure. It is best conceived in terms of continuous iteration of the functions allowing limited scope for backtracking, combined with the omission of the fourth function, except where interests are perceived as at a maximum with risk at a minimum. Accordingly, the decision making is conceived as a continual, if not continuous, process, with action being the exception rather than the rule.

Major overall failures have been observed by one British executive to fall into two broad groupings: type A, 'fast failures' and type B, 'slow failures'. Fast failure is limited to an inability to commence business in China. It includes failures in information, communication and negotiation, such as promotions by UK companies which fail to reach many Chinese firms so that no contract is made, or the inability to identify or get information on potential users of new technology, or negotiate a contract during a business trip to China. Fast failures, therefore, are almost entirely caused by information and communication barriers. Slow failure tends to refer to problems arising out of implementation, and possible strategic co-operation, such as a failure to obtain stable profit from the technology transfer, to identify and reduce the costs of competitive advantage, or to capitalize on the strategic potential of advanced technology. From a Chinese point of view, slow failure is particularly likely to involve unrealized strategic potential of new technology in maximizing productivity. From a foreign party's point of view it may be the inability to get stable long-term profit, or to realize a strategic goal of entering new markets in Asia and Africa using relatively less advanced technology generating cheaper products from the joint venture. Slow failures, therefore, are caused mostly by negotiation, implementation and perception barriers.

Looked at more logically, however, failure can be defined as an inability to progress beyond a given barrier as a result of shortcomings in the disciplinary aspect of the transaction showing themselves in the exercise of any function at a given stage. Regarded in this way, it can be observed that a congeries of minor failures triggered off by a disparate series of 'barriers' may accumulate in a dormant state, causing ineffectiveness in the working of disciplinary aspects, inefficiency in management functions culminating in failure at a major stage.

THE SEARCH FOR AN OPERATIONAL MODEL

The collaborators were able to identify two distinct types of tool available for the management of barriers to technology transfers. These have been labelled operational functions and disciplinary aspects, respectively, as a matter of convenience.

A number of cumulative, albeit discreet, operational functions can be perceived in business transactions as integrating and articulating the disciplinary aspects, both at each stage and, iteratively, from stage to stage. Such functions and aspects, therefore, are the principal means available to the parties whereby barriers to success are to be avoided, or otherwise. Although different transactions, environments, cultures and levels of competence give rise to considerable variation in any given case, each is present in some form in every transaction, including technology transfer. The authors were again able to identify five such functions operating iteratively at each stage, subject to limited backtracking: team building; research; operational planning; execution; and strategic review.

The content of transactions, such as technology transfer, moreover, can be represented in terms of analytical disciplines. The collaborators, likewise, found it convenient to identify five such aspects: a legal aspect, which, *inter alia*, determines the character and staging of the transaction; a financial, material and human resourcing aspect; the obvious technological aspect; an integrative managerial aspect; and the residuary socio-cultural aspect (Cohen and Pierce 1987). Clearly, these contain many sub- and cross-disciplines, some of which cross disciplinary boundaries.

A decision support system, therefore, would involve five key elements. It would need to represent (1) the stages of the transaction, together with (2) any barriers likely to be encountered at each stage, and (3) provide a mechanism for the operational functions to articulate (4), each disciplinary aspect to assist the user to progress beyond each barrier.

A number of exploratory models, multidimensional, sequential and even composite were considered and rejected. This process was particularly interesting as the microcosm of a two way technology transfer between Chinese and English collaborators, who recognized in themselves phenomena described by Trompenaas. Hence, the exploration admitted of two basic approaches potentially more accessible to one or other collaborator. It was agreed, however, that a common model should ideally attempt to satisfy both.

A totally new approach came with the realisation that what the collaborators themselves were trying to do, and hence by analogy the parties to a technology transfer, was in essence no different from fifteenth-century Chinese and Western merchants attempting to rendezvous along the Spice Route, using contradictory maps, exercising incompatible skills and with only the most primitive navigational equipment. What was needed, therefore, was a joint transactional navigation system – 'JOI TRANS NAV' perhaps.

If success is defined as the avoidance of failure, safe routes are defined by the progressive charting of barriers. Parties to technology transfer must at least

- share a common map, i.e. perception of stages in the transactional voyage
- exercise compatible/complementary functions
- practise interdisciplinary communication of aspects.

But the key to success lies in joint navigational equipment, i.e. integrated functional decision support capable of giving both parties warning of barriers, irrespective of which may be at a greater immediate risk. This might be provided by a common database of hazards, together with an agreed code of criteria, whereby new information can be communicated between the parties.

If the first phase were to be the development of a basic system as described, the second phase would involve identification of supplementary criteria for access (including levels of importance of barriers to functional aspects and functional stages) using additional case materials. A possible third phase might involve attempts to chart specifically safe routes from proven examples of successful barrier avoidance.

APPENDIX I

Case 1, KONKA

Chinese firm's name:	Shen Zhen Konka Electronic Company Ltd (KONKA)
Address:	Shen Zhen, People's Republic of China
Managing Director:	Mr Luo Yi Hong

The company and its development

KONKA is a joint venture company (China–Hong Kong) established in 1979. It is the first joint venture enterprise in the Chinese electronic industry. In 1991 and 1992 it was among the top 10 successful joint venture enterprises in China. Its export of colour televisions accounts for 20 per cent of the total colour television export of China. Its foreign currency income accounted for one third of the total foreign currency income of the Shen Zhen Special Economic Development Zone in 1991. KONKA was regarded as a successful joint venture by the State Council of China.

Technology advancement

During the 14-year development of KONKA, the two parties to this joint venture succeeded in getting their own interests satisfied from the successful co-operation. The Chinese party, Shen Zhen Hua Qiao Cheng Economic Development Company, got a modern electronic production company, stable foreign currency income, employment opportunity, etc. The Hong Kong party, Hong Kong Hua Electronic Company, got stable profit, expanded property, etc. These benefits are based on the successful business, which is a combination of competitive advantages of each party in the international competition. The competitive advantages moved from cheap labour to high productivity by technology advancement during the 14-year development.

The first stage of development, 1979–1986, was a combination of favourable investment and product technology. The Shen Zhen Special Zone was considered a favourable investment environment: cheap labour, low production costs, low tax rate, etc. The Hong Kong company provided product technology, electronic elements, and international market access. A labour intensive electronics production assembling line was set up. The Chinese party got a new electronics factory; the Hong Kong party got benefits from selling production equipment, selling electronic elements, and obtaining international market access.

The second stage (1987–1992) was the move from low cost advantage to high productivity advantage. The technology advancement rate was 20 per cent during these years. That is, 20 per cent of the production equipment was replaced by new technology every year. In contrast with state companies, employees' salaries were profit related. In 1992 the labour cost was seven times as high as it was in 1979, but the profitability was higher than it was in 1979. This was because productivity increased faster than the increase in labour costs. Corporate management culture was based on the Western model of a managing director and board of directors, rather than a party general secretary and committee. The company became a capital intensive, advanced technology based electronic production company. The Chinese party got profit, foreign income, employment, etc. The Hong Kong party got stable profit.

Case 2, HDF

Chinese firm's name:	He-nan Deep-Freezer Factory (HDF)
Address:	Min Quan Xian, He-nan Province, People's Republic of China
Manager:	Mr Chen Zuo Yu

Technology import

This factory is regarded by the State Council of China as a successful model of technology import. It is a newly built factory and the imported production line began to produce products in the same year of technology import. The product quality and profitability is at China's top level. This factory and its Italian partner are preparing to export their technology to Africa.

This is a successful technology import project carried out during China's economic expansion of 1984–1986 in poor areas of central China. The local government wanted to establish a new, modern industrial factory by importing foreign advanced technology, and managed to obtain a sum of foreign currency loan from a Chinese investment company. This is the first time the decision maker had imported foreign technology, and during this period of time more than 100 refrigerator production lines were imported to China. So the challenge was very high both in terms of international negotiation and in terms of domestic competition.

Successful points in negotiation

The successful points of this project were: the manner of negotiation, the terms of co-operation and the establishment of mutual trust. In choosing negotiating counterparts, they selected from most of the manufacturers in the world, contacted five company representatives in Beijing, and negotiated with the five foreign companies at the same time. The criteria were: the advanced state of the technology; the cost; and the promise of long-term co-operation.

An Italian company, IBERNA, was chosen because it fulfilled all these criteria, offering a new technology; low cost; and long-term co-operation. The product was a new one, as the model of deep freezer was newly developed in that year, and the Chinese firm's interpretation was: 'This is the latest technology'. The low cost was both in comparison with that of other foreign companies, and of the final price with the offer price. IBERNA's first offer was $3 million. Compared with a Japanese company's offer of $6 million, this was quite acceptable. The Chinese firm's interpretation of this was: 'IBERNA is a trustworthy company'. As for the long term co-operation, a 10-year technological and economic co-operation agreement was signed. Chinese firms value this very much.

Profitability and stability are the main concerns of foreign companies. In this case, IBERNA was convinced by the decision maker's capacity to carry out the project successfully. The Chinese manager had shown both his management skills and the strong support of the government. The foreign manager was impressed by China's market size. The confidence in profitability and stability was based on confidence in the success of the project, and on trust in the key decision maker.

Case 3, ZNP

Chinese firm's name: Zhong-Yuan Internal Combustion Engine
                         Components Factory (ZNP)
Address: Meng Xian, He-nan, People's Republic of
                         China
Manager: Mr Zheng Bing

Production and sales

ZNP is an engine components manufacturer specialized in cylinder liner production. Its production output in 1991 was two million sets of cylinder liners, the largest production output in China and the second largest in the world. Its products sell in both domestic and international markets.

Technology import

ZNP began to import foreign advanced technology in the early 1980s, from West Germany, Japan and the US. The technology transfer projects were an improvement in productivity and quality and reduced material consumption; the projects were successful and this factory co-operated well with its foreign counterparts.

Real need of technology transfer

The manager of this factory had learnt from a Chinese technical publication several years before that a new manufacturing technology was used in a UK company and had realised that it was what his factory needed. It was a kind of 'chromizing on thin steel wall' technology used in cylinder liner production to improve the quality.

Identifying an appropriate supplier

The manager had borne this in mind every since, and kept trying to contact the UK company, but only in 1993 had he been able to ask a personal friend to get more information in the UK.

APPENDIX II

Table 2.1: Perceived importance of barriers at given stages

Stage	Information	Communication	Decision criteria	Infrastructure	Perception
UK perceptions					
Partner search	***	***	**	*	*
Proposal	***	***	***	**	**
Negotiation	***	***	***	***	***
Implementation	**	***	***	***	***
Further co-operation	*	***	**	**	***
Chinese perceptions					
Partner search	***	***	*	*	**
Proposal	**	***	***	*	**
Negotiation	**	***	***	***	***
Implementation	**	***	**	***	***
Further co-operation	**	***	*	***	***

Note: * important
** very important
*** most important

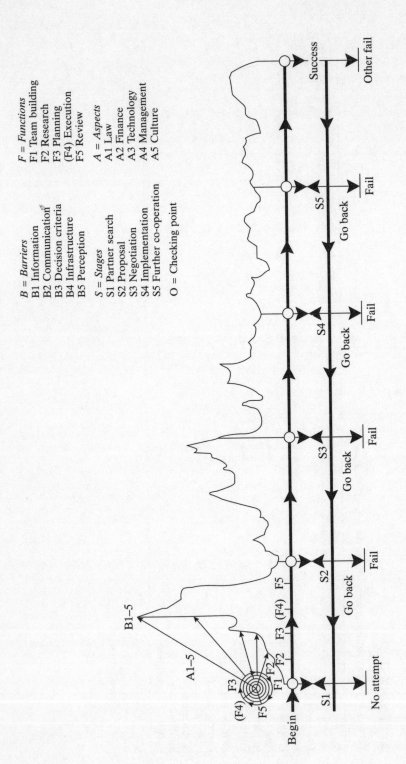

Figure 2.1 Conceptual model of decision support system for technology transfers in China

F = Functions
F1 Team building
F2 Research
F3 Planning
(F4) Execution
F5 Review

A = Aspects
A1 Law
A2 Finance
A3 Technology
A4 Management
A5 Culture

B = Barriers
B1 Information
B2 Communication
B3 Decision criteria
B4 Infrastructure
B5 Perception

S = Stages
S1 Partner search
S2 Proposal
S3 Negotiation
S4 Implementation
S5 Further co-operation

O = Checking point

REFERENCES

Publications in English

Adler, N.J. 1992 'Strategy Implementation: A Comparison of face-to-face Negotiations in the People's Republic of China and The United States', *Strategic Management Journal* 13: 449–466.

Atkinson, K. 1984 'Case Studies on Negotiation and Financing Joint Ventures', *China Update Conference*, Hong Kong: Institute for International Research.

Ball, D.F., Zheng Rong and Pearson, A.W. 1993 'Perceptions of United Kingdom exporters in transferring Technology into the People's Republic of China', *R & D Management* 23 January: 29–41.

Campbell, N.C.G. 1988 *A Strategic Guide to Equity Joint Ventures in China*, Oxford: Pergamon Press.

Cohen, J.A. and Peirce, D.G. 1987 'Legal Aspects of Technology Transfer in the People's Republic of China', *China Business Review* May-June, 14: 14–18.

Contractor, F.J. 1985 'A Generalized Theorem for Joint Venture and Licensing Negotiations', *Journal of International Business Studies* Summer: 23–50.

Contractor, F.J. and Lorange, P. 1987 *Co-operatives in International Business*, Lexington, Mass.: D.C. Heath.

Guo Chuan Jie 1993 'A Choice for the Future', Speech on the Future Development Model of Chinese Academy of Science, *China Science News* 25 May: 1.

Leiberthal, K. and Ocksenburg, M. 1985 'Understanding China's Bureaucracy', *The China Business Review* November-December: 24–31.

Mudu, C.N. 1990 'Prescriptive Framework for the Transfer of Appropriate Technologies', *Futures* November, 22: 932–958.

Mudu, C.N. and Jacob, R.A. 1991 'Multiple Perspectives and Cognitive Mapping to Technology Transfer Decisions', *Futures* November, 23: 978–997.

Trompenaas, F. 1993 *Riding the Waves of Culture*, London: Brealey.

Wionczek, M.S. 1979 'Measures strengthening the negotiation capacity of governments in their relations with transnational corporations', UN Centre on Transnational Corporations, UN, Agencies, Washington, DC.

Xueke, R. and Steward, F. 1992 'Reform of the Scientific and Technological Management System in China: An Overview', *Aston Business School Research Paper Series 9220*, Birmingham: Aston Business School.

Publications in Chinese

Guo, A. 1988 *Enterprise Profit Theory and Application*, Zhengzhou: He-nan People's Publishing House.

Guo, A. 1988 *Superior Business Administration*, Zhengzhou: He-nan People's Publishing House.

Guo, A. 1989 *Industrial Enterprise Production Management*, Zhengzhou: He-nan People's Publishing House.

Guo, A. 1992 'A Successful Export Oriented Joint Venture Enterprise – Shenzhen Konka Electronic Company Ltd', *Study Materials for Economists* 73, State Council of China, Beijing.

Guo, A. 1992 'Technology Import is the Way of Improving Enterprise Profit', *Study Materials for Economists* 74, State Council of China, Beijing.

Guo, A. 1992 'Economic Reform and Enterprise Transform Management Mechanism', *Reform and Theory* 4.

Guo, A. 1992 'The Integration of Planned Economy and Market Regulation', *Journal of He-nan Finance and Economics College* 2.

3 In search of complementary assets

Co-operative strategies and knowledge seeking by prospective Chinese partners

Jiatao Li and Oded Shenkar[1]

ABSTRACT

This chapter focuses on the hitherto neglected perspective of the local partner during the preliminary phase of the decision to form a Chinese-foreign venture. By exploring the intentions of Chinese firms which seek foreign investment, it becomes possible to identify and assess the managerial, marketing and technological skills those firms seek from prospective foreign partners. It is also possible to discern to what extent the desired skills are related to the local partners' own skills, to the intended venture characteristics, namely equity or contractual, and to the size of the investment.

The study shows that local partner skills largely determine the skills sought from foreign partners, providing support for the underlying principle of skill complementarity. Briefly stated, this principle suggests that a threshold of knowledge is a prerequisite for further requisition of skills in that domain. In other words, firms which do not possess a particular skill are less likely to seek it than firms which seek to supplement an already existing skills base.

The study also shows that Chinese state-owned firms were more likely to seek the transfer of managerial (but not marketing or technological) skills than non-state enterprises, possibly because of their dominance in the local market. In general, prospective Chinese partners were more likely to seek the transfer of management and marketing skills via an equity joint venture rather than a contractual one. For larger projects, local firms were more likely to seek transfer of management skills (rather than marketing and technological ones), perhaps due to the substantial capital requirement in such projects.

INTRODUCTION

International co-operative ventures (ICVs) have been studied in China in a similar fashion to the way they have been studied in other developing countries (e.g. Beamish 1985; Hladik 1985), namely from the point of view of foreign multinational corporations (MNCs). In contrast, the perspective of the Chinese parents has been neglected. The assets of Chinese partners, their strategic intent, and the assets they have sought to acquire via the establishment of a co-operative relationship (Contractor and Lorange 1988; Osborn and Baughn 1990; Tallman and Shenkar 1990, 1994; Parkhe 1993) were all but ignored.

The emphasis on the foreign party perspective implied that Chinese firms had no tangible or intangible assets to speak of, and that their strategy and interests had little or no bearing on the ICV formed. The dynamic, mutual process of give and take inherent to all ICV transactions was hence reduced to a unilateral strategy of foreign investors, extrapolated from post-formation data. The focus on the foreign partner not only distorted the realities of foreign direct investment (FDI) in China; it also preempted putting current theories on FDI to an accurate test of their applicability to the unique Chinese environment.

Relying on data from Chinese companies seeking foreign partners for ICVs, and building on an institutional analysis of the Chinese business environment at the time of the investigation, this chapter tackles such issues as the key sets of knowledge and skills prospective Chinese partners are seeking from foreign firms; the possible complementary effect of the skills base of the Chinese partner (in marketing, management and technology) on its partner seeking strategies; and the implications of the concept of complementary assets for the universal applicability of international co-operative venture theory.

SKILLS AND SKILLS BASE IN INTERNATIONAL CO-OPERATIVE VENTURES

Despite high instability rates, propensity for failure, and a complex governance structure (Morris and Hergert 1987), firms continue to engage in ICVs at a rapid pace. These prospective partners either seek to establish the independent entities known as equity joint ventures (EJVs) or aim to sign agreements regarding licensing, distribution and the like, known as contractual ventures (CVs) (Thorelli 1986; Osborn and Baughn 1990).

Three approaches are usually offered as to why firms form ICVs of either type. First, the transaction costs approach suggests that firms establish ICVs when the cost incurred is perceived to be lower than that involved in full integration of the given activity within the existing corporate hierarchy (Kogut 1988; Hennart, 1991). Second, the strategic behaviour approach suggests that firms establish ICVs to maximize profits via improved competitive position (Friedmann and Kalmanoff 1961; Contractor and Lorange 1988; Harrigan 1988; Gomes-Casseres 1989). Third, the learning approach suggests that firms form ICVs to acquire the vital knowledge they lack or to rent such knowledge to others.

Building on these three approaches, ICVs can be considered vehicles designed to join together complementary skills and know-how. While ICVs sometimes bring together partners making similar contributions, e.g. sharing the capital investment in a new project, they frequently form vertical quasi integration, with each partner contributing one or more distinct elements in the production and distribution chains. Thus, their inputs are complementary (Contractor and Lorange 1988). Harrigan (1985) argues that ICVs are more likely to succeed when partners possess complementary attributes such as missions, resources and managerial capabilities, since such complementarity creates a strategic fit in which the bargaining power of the venture's sponsors is evenly matched.

A long-term, mutual need binding partners together is another signifi-cant variable associated with ICVs' success. Such needs have been classi-fied by Beamish (1984) into readily capitalized items: human resources, market access, government/political, and knowledge needs. In his study, managers of successful MNC ventures rated local management and knowl-edge (e.g. familiarity with the local culture, knowledge of the political system) as key ingredients in their long-term success. In contrast, MNCs with low performing ventures did not fulfil any long-term needs for their partners, who they felt could not provide advantages, and had formed the venture only because full foreign ownership was illegal or impractical. Local general managers, on the other hand, wanted their ventures to be successful in the long run, while in the short term hoping to gain raw material supply and technology or equipment from the parents.

In the next few pages, we briefly present two major considerations in the ICV preferences of prospective local partners:

(a) The existence or absence of a knowledge base on which imported knowledge is to be built; and
(b) the type of skills sought as a function of their transferability.

Other considerations, in particular those unique to the Chinese environ-ment, as well as such variables as local parent ownership and project size, will be considered later in this chapter.

Knowledge base and complementarity in ICV formation

The transaction cost approach suggests that firms transact in a way that minimizes the sum of production and transaction costs (Williamson 1975; Kogut 1988; Hennart 1991). The decision to form an ICV assumes that the added costs of interfirm coordination should reflect management perceptions that one or more partners can be selected who will enhance the venture's competitive position. Benefits from a prospective partner's contribution might occur throughout the entire range of a venture's value chain. However, management may hierarchically rank those activities and focus its attention on a few key activities which affect overall operations most decisively (Davidson 1982; Geringer 1991). The more skills and assets such as patents, technical know-how, financial resources, experienced managerial personnel, and access to marketing and distribution systems can contribute to a co-operative venture, the greater the likelihood that their possessors will be selected as a venture partner (Awadzi 1987).

In the typical manufacturing ICV where assets are complementary, the major contributions of the MNCs comprise manufacturing technology, product know-how, patents, business expertise, technical training, and management capabilities. The local partner, in turn, commonly contributes capital, management, knowledge of the domestic market and environment, and contacts with the government, financial institutions, local suppliers, and labour unions (Dymsza 1988). A successful ICV creates synergies which produce a premium exceeding the partners' pooled resources.

To date, however, research on ICVs in developing countries has largely ignored the skills base of the local partners, with the possible exception of their relationships with local authorities and the ability to 'get things done' in the host environment. Here, however, it is proposed that familiarity with the local environment can be translated into significant contributions in the management of local enterprise and domestic marketing. Furthermore, the skills base of the local partners is an important determinant of partner seeking strategy which is likely to affect the level and types of skills the local partners are looking for among potential foreign firms.

We suggest that complementarity is not likely to materialize unless a certain threshold of self-skills is in place. In other words, firms that completely lack a given skill are less likely to seek the transfer of skills in that category from their partners. The necessity for a skills base is related to the concept of 'absorptive capability' (Cohen and Levinthal 1990) of local partners for new skills. The absorptive capability is defined as a firm's ability to acquire, evaluate, assimilate, integrate, diffuse, deploy and exploit knowledge. These information management capabilities affect firms' ability to learn (Ghoshal 1987) and are what makes firms effective 'repositories of embedded knowledge' (Badaracco 1991). The embeddedness of the underlying processes will limit transferability of tacit organizational knowledge, but at the same time be the source of inimitability and consequently, sustainability of rents. The firm's ability to process, integrate and deploy new flows of knowledge closely depends on the relatedness of such knowledge to the existing stock of knowledge, that is, the skills base of the firm. Therefore, transfer of a foreign firm's technology, management and marketing skills will be less successful if the local firms do not have the necessary skills base or absorptive capability.

Structure of co-operative venture

Each of the two major ICV types has typical advantages and disadvantages. Equity Joint Ventures (EJVs) provide joint ownership and control over the use of assets and production (Kogut 1988) and are effective in bypassing market inefficiencies. Equity control and sharing in the profits or losses also serve to align the interests of parent firms, reducing the opportunism that may arise in contractual ventures (CVs) (Hennart 1988), and eliminating the need for complex *ex ante* specification of ongoing activities and behaviour. EJVs also allow for a superior monitoring mechanism, since owners are typically entitled to access independently verified financial information and are able to observe operations directly (Osborn and Baughn 1990).

Among the disadvantages of the EJV are shared ownership and joint decision making arrangements which make it cumbersome to manage and slow to react to new opportunities. Compared to CV arrangements, the EJV is more difficult to establish, terminate, and fundamentally change (Harrigan 1988). Thus, the EJV's potential for protection and control may be offset by substantial administrative costs (Osborn and Baughn 1990) and a requirement for give and take which limits its strategic flexibility vis-à-vis CV arrangements (Harrigan 1988). Given joint ownership (and control) rights and the mutual commitment of resources, the situational characteristics best suited for an EJV are high uncertainty regarding specifying and monitoring performance, and a high degree of asset specificity.

Undoubtedly, the 'typical' advantages and disadvantages of both EJVs and CVs as well as the value of given knowledge assets can be altered in a given investment environment. In the following pages, we take a brief look at China's investment environment at the time of this study, and its possible impact on the processes considered so far.

THE BACKGROUND FOR INTERNATIONAL CO-OPERATIVE VENTURES IN CHINA

ICVs were first established in the People's Republic of China in 1979. The number of ICVs quickly mushroomed from the six ventures established during the first year to 5, 945 ICVs approved in 1988, the year the data for the present study were collected, and to 48,000 in 1992. In 1993 alone, China attracted over US\$ 20 billion in FDI.

The foundations for China's investment environment during 1988 were laid in 1986, when a new phase of FDI policy was enacted by the Chinese government. Known as the Provisions of the State Council for the Encouragement of Foreign Investment, or The 22 Articles, it shifted the focus of investment from real estate and tourism to light manufacturing. By 1988, fully 85 per cent of foreign investment projects involved manufacturing (US-China Business Council 1990). In the same year, the Chinese government designated energy, construction, chemicals, metallurgy, machine and equipment, process control, electronics and computers as priority areas for foreign investment (Pearson 1991).

As part of its new approach in 1986, the Chinese government created important incentives for export-oriented as well as 'technologically advanced' enterprises, to which it granted such incentives as tax holidays, a guaranteed supply of raw materials, and easier access to bank loans (Pearson 1991; Nyaw 1993). Having been frustrated by the transfer of whole assembly lines and sometimes whole plants during the early investment years, the government now saw ICVs, and in particular EJVs, as having the potential to disseminate technology much more effectively. Such preferences were particularly salient in cities like Shanghai, whose authorities were quick to bestow the status of 'an export-oriented enterprise' and the benefits associated with it on selected ventures as a way of improving the competitiveness of local products and producing the foreign exchange necessary for the importation of raw materials and capital goods, in particular advanced technologies. These policies created an additional impetus for Chinese firms to seek foreign partners with the appropriate skills to complement and augment their own.

At the same time, the Chinese authorities fully recognized in 1986 that local firms have had key assets of their own to bring to the match, which was one reason why wholly owned foreign ownership has been permitted. Besides the aforementioned advantages of familiarity with the local environment and domestic marketing knowledge, Chinese firms possessed important technological assets. Although many Chinese firms, especially state enterprises, were using obsolete technology, quite a few were already manufacturing export-quality goods in 1988, sometimes as suppliers to foreign companies. The Chinese firms were also quite proficient in certain intermediate technologies which foreign firms were no longer familiar with. These skills, we suggest, were likely to affect the skills sought from foreign co-operation, and therefore the selection of prospective foreign partners.

KNOWLEDGE SEEKING BEHAVIOUR AMONG CHINESE PROSPECTIVE PARTNERS

The investment preferences reported in this section are derived from 90 proposed projects promoted by the Shanghai Foreign Investment Development Agency of the Municipal Government of Shanghai (1988). The project lists utilized were published and promoted in order to guide foreign investment in Shanghai and help foreign and Chinese investors choose the right investment projects.

One of China's largest and most dynamic cities, Shanghai is not necessarily representative of the foreign investment patterns in China at large; however, it has been a locus for much of the investment coming into the country and hence a major case of such investment.

In the following pages, the knowledge seeking behaviour of prospective Chinese partners is analysed. The impact of the skills base of these local firms is considered with reference to the skills sought as well as the structure of the proposed co-operation. Differences among various types of Chinese firms are also taken into account.

Chinese partner skills and foreign skills sought

From the perspective of Chinese partners, it is important to know whether the foreign firm is interested in using China's cost advantage to serve its domestic and foreign market, which was in line with the objectives of the local government; or rather in targeting the Chinese domestic market which Chinese firms (particularly state-owned) tended to monopolize at the time (Wang *et al.* 1991). A second major point of interest for Chinese partners was whether the proposed project facilitated the transfer of foreign technology along with management and marketing expertise, which the Chinese government looked to ICV foreign partners to provide.

Following the earlier developed concept of skill complementarity, we assumed that local companies were more likely to seek transfer of skills from foreign partners when they already have a skills base in the respective area. Indeed, we found that local companies were more likely to seek transfer of skills from foreign partners when they possessed a certain skills base in the respective areas. Thus, the local partner was more likely to seek transfer of management skills from foreign partners when the local partner itself was in a position to contribute technology, management, or marketing skills to the co-operative venture (see Table 3.1).

Table 3.1 Knowledge seeking of Chinese local partners

	Contributions sought from prospective foreign partners		
	Management skills	Marketing skills	Technology
Local partner factors			
Contributions			
Management skills	***	***	***
Marketing skills	***	***	***
Technology	***	***	***
Ownership structure			
State-owned enterprises	**	*	*
Intended ICV characteristics			
Structure			
JV	**	**	*
Size			
Total investment	**	*	*

Note: *** Significant
   ** Marginally significant
   * Non-significant

The pattern seems to be consistent for the transfer of marketing skills and technology from foreign partners. For example, firms which completely lacked a management skills base were not likely to seek the transfer of those skills from a foreign partner. While this may seem contrary to the very idea of complementarity, one should keep in mind that a lack of knowledge in a given area may preclude seeking skills in that area, as firms are unable to pinpoint their needs or realize an effective learning process.

Venture structure preferences in the Chinese context

Two benefits of the EJV which were unique to China in 1988 were its ranking as the most desirable vehicle by the government, with the concomitant benefits of such standing, e.g. preferential access to subsidized and scarce components and materials (Chu 1986); and the existence of a relatively complete and coherent framework of rules and regulations governing the establishment and operation of this type of ICV alone (US-China Business Council 1990). In contrast, a legal framework governing CVs was promulgated only in March 1988 (Pearson 1991), and hence was not tried and tested at the time the firms in this study articulated their intentions. This reality created a situation unique to China: while CVs are typically considered a better defence against opportunism, it seems that the opposite was true in China. Thus, the existence of a legal framework for EJVs but not for CVs reduced, for both foreign and local EJV partners, the relative opportunism of one's partners as well as the government's and otherwise reduced the unpredictability inherent in foreign investment in a transitional economy. It also created an environment more conducive to the learning process which was certainly more essential for the Chinese than for the foreign partners.

EJVs typically provide a hedge against the uncertainty characterizing foreign operations for firms with very limited understanding of and experience in foreign markets. In line with the transactions cost argument, an equity position may be perceived by the Chinese parents as protection against opportunism on the part of the foreign parent. More importantly, however, an EJV is probably considered a more effective learning vehicle for local firms seeking entrance to foreign markets for the first time because this mode of governance typically allows for prolonged co-habitation of managerial and technical personnel from the two parties. This is particularly true for skills which are more tacit, intangible and ill-structured, and hence more difficult to specify. In the context of the present study, skills seem to be very specific in the technological arena, but less so in marketing and particularly in management which are embedded in complex organizational routines (Kogut 1988).

The very long negotiation period typical of such ventures in China (e.g. Pearson 1991) increased the transaction costs of embarking on that option, and exposed both partners to the actions of competitors as identified in the strategic behaviour perspective. Second, even the fairly comprehensive legislation on EJVs did not fully address termination and liquidation issues. Together with restrictions on the withdrawal of registered capital during the life of the contract, the potential for profit on the part of the foreign investor has diminished. From the point of view of the Chinese partner, however, this was hardly a drawback. Rather, it enabled the local firm to hold its foreign partner hostage without having to reciprocate, making the EJV potentially more attractive. A third drawback of EJVs was the requirement of a minimum investment (unnecessary in the case of CVs) and flexibility in asset allocation and management. Such flexibility was sometimes desirable for both foreign and Chinese partners but for different reasons. While the foreign partner wanted to ensure productivity and profitability by controlling the production process, Chinese partners, who were less concerned with knowledge transfer, sometimes sought to channel unproductive excess personnel to the venture so as to improve the competitiveness of the parent firm at a time when profitability pressure was beginning to build up.

On balance, then, it appears that while Chinese firms seeking knowledge transfer had added incentives to seek EJVs, many of the typical drawbacks of that form did not apply to their situation. This was particularly true for local firms seeking the transfer of tacit knowledge, for whom a CV would not have allowed the intense interaction which is necessary for significant exposure to and ingestion of information (Vernon and Wells 1986; Pisano 1988). Therefore, we suspected that local companies were more likely to seek transfer of management, marketing skills and technology from foreign partners via an EJV rather than a CV.

We found that the structure of co-operative ventures significantly affects the transfer of specific skills from foreign partners; in particular, that local partners were more likely to seek transfer of management and marketing skills in an EJV than in a CV (see Table 2). However, the need for the transfer of technology from foreign partners was not affected by the structure of the co-operative venture, suggesting that Chinese partners in both EJVs and CVs were likely to seek the transfer of technology from foreign partners. In addition, certain co-operative structures such as licensing agreements are specially designed for transfer of technical know-how. Finally, the results also show that for larger projects, local firms tend to seek the transfer of management skills from foreign partners, perhaps because of the substantial capital requirement in such projects. Capital was hard to come by in China in 1988, and having a foreign party with an equity position provided access to a number of customized financing channels which the Chinese parent may have wanted to tap. However, the size of investment in the venture did not show significant effects on transfer of marketing skills and technology.

The ownership factor: state-owned versus non-state enterprises

State-owned enterprises and non state-owned enterprises are different in organization and operation, and their objectives and strategies are often dissimilar. The non state-owned enterprises in this study include both collective and township enterprises. In theory, collective enterprises are owned by communes (or their derivatives) and township enterprises by localities. In reality, however, the distinction between them is blurred and therefore we treat them as a single group in the present study. Throughout the reform period, collective and township enterprises continued to expand at the expense of state-owned enterprises. In 1988, collective and township accounted for 36.15 per cent of China's industrial output, up from 14.09 in 1970 (*China Statistical Yearbook* 1992). At least some of that growth may be attributed to the dislocations in the domestic market created by the decentralization drive occurring at the time, which collective and township enterprises rushed to fulfil. Being less stagnant than their state-owned counterparts, these firms had less need for learning via EJVs.

In addition to central government preferences, local governments also recognized the need to attract these two types of foreign investment and have announced favourable terms in their districts. In Shanghai, for example, the municipal government implemented a set of favourable terms in October 1986 to encourage foreign investment in export-oriented and technology-oriented enterprises. We should also note that at that point, Shanghai authorities were authorized to approve projects of up to 30 million US$ – the same level as Tianjin and significantly more than other large municipalities, including Guangzhou.

Finally, while both state and non-state firms may seek international partners in order to enhance their competitive position, state-owned enterprises – which are in essence extensions of government agencies – are more likely to conform to the explicit preference of both the central and the local authorities for transfer of foreign technology, management and marketing skills than companies belonging to the non-state sector. This preference stemmed from a belief that transfer of technology will enhance the commitment of the foreign partner while at the same time provide the government with a symbolic stake as well as actual control (Chu 1986; Pearson 1991).

Therefore, we assumed that state-owned companies were more likely than collective and township enterprises to seek transfer of management, marketing skills and technology from foreign partners for the co-operative venture. The results show that state-owned local firms were more likely to seek transfer of management skills from foreign partners than non-state firms. However, there were no significant differences between state and non-state enterprises in seeking the transfer of marketing skills and technology from foreign partners (see Table 3.1).

One explanation for the results is that large state-owned firms are more dominant in their domestic market and are hence more reluctant to risk sharing their dominance with a foreign rival. The reason for not seeking marketing skills may be that state firms already controlled domestic market and distribution channels. The lack of differences in technology may be due to the fact that both state and non-state local firms are seeking technology so that there is little variation in this dimension between the two organizational forms. The need for the transfer of management skills in state-owned firms, on the other hand, is consistent with the observation of problems in the management systems of state-owned enterprises. In addition, some collective and township enterprises are known to be spin-offs of state enterprises, which confounds the results. Finally, the finding may be peculiar to 1988, a time in which the state and non-state sectors were competing on more or less equal footing. Indeed, austerity measures announced in October 1988 and implemented largely during the following year have since undermined the position of collective enterprises by cutting back on their loans and increasing their tax burden (Shapiro *et al.* 1991; Pearson 1991).

SUMMARY AND CONCLUSION

Perhaps the most important conclusion of the present study is that skills complementarity is a more complex construct than has hitherto been realized in the current theories on foreign direct investment, and that its implications for partner preferences are far reaching. Transaction costs, strategic behaviour and the approaches have yet to consider the implications of a broader view of complementarity for their respective models. In assessing such complementarity, these approaches will be hard-pressed to consider China's institutional environment, and the skills possessed and sought by the Chinese and foreign partners during the rapidly evolving phases of China's business modernization.

Knowledge transfer is often a package including both the tangible embodiment of the technology and the associated tacit managerial know-how, the two of which cannot be separated for successful transfer (Teece 1981). The more complex and sophisticated the technology, the more desirable it becomes to pool complementary know-how in order to exploit it more effectively. Complementarity is therefore not only technological but is also manifested in the ability to bring together product and market knowledge, in effect leveraging respective strengths. That local companies which form EJVs rather than CVs with foreign partners are more likely to seek transfer of management and marketing skills than transfer of technology suggests that management and marketing skills may be more 'tacit' than specific technologies (e.g., patents). If this is the case, it may be useful to replace the current dichotomy of 'tacit' and 'non-tacit' skills with a continuum of competencies hierarchically ordered by the degree of transferability across organizational boundaries. The ranking on this continuum is likely to influence the choice of ICV type as well as other mechanisms, e.g. staff assignment, directed at achieving effective learning.

In further developing this line of thought, it may be useful to draw on the structural contingency theory, in particular Perrow's (1967) concept of 'non-analyzable material' and Fry and Slocum's (1984) classification of subject areas according to the extent to which task-relevant knowledge is pertinent and well understood. Thus, it may be argued that because technology is well defined, it is easier to transfer on contractual terms than marketing, and in particular managerial knowledge. A contingency approach would also suggest that the structure of the recipient organization is likely to affect the effectiveness of transfer. For instance, the highly specialized division of labour in the production realm in post-Cultural Revolution China facilitated the transfer of technologies because of the ready availability of staff who could evaluate needs, while the lack of professional managerial staff hindered the transfer of the less tangible skills in that area.

Moving into the current investment environment, a number of key questions remain open. Having accumulated a more solid knowledge base, as well as significant experience in ICV establishment and operation (Lyles 1987), are Chinese firms changing their skill and structure preferences? Are foreign firms, now more familiar with the local environment but also facing more competition, altering their preferences? A recent McKinsey survey of MNCs successfully committed to China shows that they have progressed far beyond the cautious experimental stage (Shaw and Meier 1993). Increasingly, they are focusing on managing their relationships with local partners and their 'mothers-in-law'; decision making authorities that sit above these operating local partners such as government commissions and bureaux and industrial associations. Recent data also show that the increase in wholly foreign owned subsidiaries as well as in EJVs has been proportionately higher than the increase in CVs. Traditional post-formation data can be misleading, however, in that it may reflect changing bargaining power positions rather than changing preferences. Only a first hand study of investment intentions can provide more clues.

NOTE

1 The authors gratefully acknowledge support provided by the Center of International Business Education and Research, University of Hawaii.

REFERENCES

Awadzi, W.K. 1987 *Determinants of joint venture performance: A study of international joint ventures in the United States*, Unpublished doctoral dissertation, Louisiana State University.

Badaracco, J.L. 1991 *The Knowledge Link*, Boston, MA: Harvard Business School Press.

Beamish, P.W. 1984 *Joint venture performance in developing countries*, Unpublished doctoral dissertation, London, Ontario: University of Western Ontario.

Beamish, P.W. 1985 The characteristics of joint ventures in developed and developing countries, *Columbia Journal of World Business* 20(3): 13–19.

China Statistical Yearbook 1992 Beijing: China Statistics Press (in Chinese).

Chu, Baotai 1986 *Foreign investment in China*, Beijing: Foreign Languages Press.

Cohen, W. and Levinthal, D.A. 1990 Absorptive Capability: A New Perspective on learning and innovation, *Administrative Science Quarterly* 35(1): 128–152.

Contractor, F. and Lorange, P. 1988 'Why should firms cooperate? The strategy and economic basis for co-operative ventures', in F.J. Contractor and P. Lorange (eds) *Co-operative Strategies in International Business*, Lexington, MA: Lexington Books.

Davidson, W.H. 1982 *Global strategic management*, New York: Wiley.

Dymsza, W.A. 1988 'Successes and failures of joint ventures in developing countries: Lessons from experience', in F. Contractor and P. Lorange (eds) *Co-operative Strategies in International Business*, Lexington, Mass.: Lexington Books: 403–424.

Friedmann, W.G. and Kalmanoff, G. (eds) 1961 *Joint international business ventures*, New York: Columbia University Press.

Fry, L.W. and Slocum, W. 1984 'Technology, structure, and work group effectiveness: A test of a contingency model', *Academy of Management Journal* 27(2): 221–246.

Geringer, J.M. 1991 'Control and performance of international joint ventures', *Journal of International Business Studies* 22(2): forthcoming.

Ghoshal, S. 1987 'Global strategy: An organizing framework', *Strategic Management Journal* 8: 425–440.

Gomes-Casseres, B. 1989 'Ownership structure of foreign subsidiaries: Theory and evidence', *Journal of Economic Behavior and Organization* 11: 1–25.

Harrigan, K.R. 1985 *Strategies for joint venture success*, Lexington, Mass: Lexington Books.

Harrigan, K.R. 1988 'Joint ventures and competitive strategy', *Strategic Management Journal*, 9: 141–158.

Hennart, J.F. 1988 'A transaction costs theory of joint ventures', *Strategic Management Journal* 37: 483–497.

Hennart, J.F. 1991 'The transaction costs theory of joint ventures: An Empirical Study of Japanese Subsidiaries in the United States', *Management Science* 37: 483–497.

Hladik, K.J. 1985 *International joint ventures: An economic analysis of US-foreign business partnerships*, Lexington, Mass.: Lexington Books.

Kogut, B. 1988 'Joint ventures: Theoretical and empirical perspectives', *Strategic Management Journal* 9: 319–332.

Lyles, M. 1987 'Common mistakes of joint venture experienced firms', *Columbia Journal of World Business* 22(2): 79–85.

Morris, D. and Hergert, M. 1987 'Trends in International Co-operative Agreements', *Columbia Journal of World Business* 22(2): 15–21.

Nyaw, M.K. 1993 'Direct foreign investment in China: Trends, performance, policies and prospects', in J.Y.S. Cheng and Maurice Brosseau (eds) *China Review 1993*, Hong Kong: The Chinese University Press.

Osborn, R.N. and Baughn, C.C. 1990 'Forms of interorganizational governance for multinational alliances', *Academy of Management Journal* 33(3): 503–519.

Parkhe, A. 1993 ' "Messy" research, methodological predispositions, and theory development in international joint ventures', *Academy of Management Review* 18: 227–268.

Pearson, M.M. 1991 *Joint ventures in the People's Republic of China*, NJ: Princeton University Press.

Perrow, C. 1967 'A framework for the comparative analysis of organizations', *American Sociological Review* 32: 194–208.

Pisano, G.P. 1988 *Innovation through markets, hierarchies and joint ventures: Technology strategy and collaborative arrangements in the biotechnology industry*, Unpublished PhD dissertation, Berkeley, CA: University of California.

Shanghai Foreign Investment Development Agency 1988 *Requirements and introduction of projects list for foreign investment in Shanghai as guided by Shanghai municipality*, Shanghai.

Shapiro, J.E., Behrman, J.N., Fischer, W.A. and Powell, S.G. 1991 *Direct investment and joint ventures in China*, NY: Quorum.

Shaw, S.M. and Meier, J. 1993 'Second generation MNCs in China', *The McKinsey Quarterly* 4: 3–16.

Tallman, S.B. and Shenkar, O. 1990 'International co-operative venture strategies: Outward investment and small firms from NICs', *Management International Review* 30: 299–315.

Tallman, S.B. and Shenkar, O. 1994 'A managerial decision model of international co-operative venture formation', *Journal of International Business Studies* 25: 91–113.

Teece, D.J. 1981 'Multinational enterprise: Market failure and market power considerations', *Sloan Management Review* 22: 3–17.

Thorelli, H. 1986 'Networks: Between markets and hierarchies', *Strategic Management Journal* 7: 37–51.

US-China Business Council 1990 *US Investment in China*, Washington DC: The China Business Forum.

Vernon, R. and Wells, L.T. 1986 *The economic environment of international business*, Englewood Cliffs, NJ: Prentice-Hall.

Wang, R.L., Wang, C. and Gong, Yingrong 1991 'Enterprise autonomy and market structures in China', in O. Shenkar (ed.) *Organization and Management in China 1979–1990*: 23–33, Armonk, NY: M.E. Sharpe.

Williamson, O.E. 1975 *Markets and hierarchies: Analysis and antitrust implications*, New York: Free Press.

4 Market entry and development in China

The experience of companies selling industrial goods and projects[1]

Ingmar Björkman

ABSTRACT

The choice of how to organize sales and marketing in foreign markets is a crucial one. This chapter describes the operational modes used by 24 Finnish companies engaged in marketing and sales of industrial goods and projects in China. Perceived characteristics of the various operational forms used by these companies are described. The companies covered by the present study tended to use several operational modes. There was a clear trend towards more direct involvement in China. Most of the sampled companies followed closely the kind of sequential adaptation of gradually more advanced operational modes proposed by the Uppsala Internationalization Process Model (Johanson and Vahlne 1977). The experiential knowledge of managers involved in the China business typically triggered a gradual expansion of the companies' presence in China itself. Underlying factors were the decentralization of economic decision making in China and the particular socio-cultural Chinese setting, both of which were seen as favouring a local presence in the country itself. A majority of the sampled companies made decisions to establish offices and/or joint ventures in China in 1993 or early 1994. Interviews indicate that many executives then suddenly thought that a strong corporate presence in China was a necessity; the emergence of this 'institutionalized myth' (Meyer and Rowan 1977) seems to have contributed to the surge in establishments that took place in 1993–94.

INTRODUCTION

For companies entering foreign markets, the choice of how to organize sales and marketing operations is a crucial one. Companies may choose among a variety of operational modes, ranging from company-external modes (such as using different kinds of distributors or agents) to company-internal modes (e.g. own sales persons who only occasionally visit the market in question; or the establishment of a local unit). Also, intermediate forms can be used (for example, jointly owned units). Earlier research has tried to explain the organizational modes that exporting companies have chosen in foreign markets (see e.g. Anderson and Coughlan 1987; Klein and Roth 1990), and numerous attempts have been made to explain the sequence of organizational modes in overseas markets (for a review, see Johanson and Vahlne 1990). Though considerable research has been carried out on these issues, a review of the literature indicates that no clear consensus has emerged concerning how to explain the choice of organizational mode in foreign markets. We know that organizational modes tend to have certain pros and cons which vary depending on local market, industry and company characteristics, but it is nevertheless not clear, based on the literature, which organizational modes companies will use in, say, a culturally, institutionally and geographically distant country such as China. Neither is it clear which theoretical framework will be most suitable for analysing why companies choose to use certain organizational modes. This chapter draws on ideas from an experiential learning perspective (Johanson and Vahlne 1977; Levitt and March 1988), an economic perspective (cf. Young *et al.* 1989), and an institutional perspective (Meyer and Rowan 1977; DiMaggio and Powell 1983).

Only about a decade ago, in the early 1980s, Chinese decisions to import large-scale products – such as infrastructural development projects, machinery for the manufacturing industry, and large consultancy projects – were made by the central ministries. Reforms of the Chinese economic system have changed this situation. Research (e.g. McGuiness *et al.* 1991) suggests that decision making has become more decentralized, that the final users of the products tend to be actively involved in the purchasing process, but that provincial and central authorities still take part in the process. Anecdotal evidence also suggests that domestic and overseas Chinese consultants and middle men may play important roles. Thus, the rapid changes taking place in China recently (and, to complicate the picture further, changes occurring at a different pace in different parts of the country), have significantly changed the roles played by the Chinese actors participating in purchasing decisions.

How have foreign companies, over time, handled their sales and marketing operations in China? Although research has been carried out on some facets of contemporary marketing in China, on negotiations in particular, there is a paucity of scholarly work on the organizational modes utilized by Western companies in China. With the exception of studies of the equity distribution in foreign investment enterprises (e.g. Hu and Chen 1993), the only paper that I have been able to find is a case study by Easton and Li (1993). Further, little research has focused specifically on sales of industrial goods and projects. The aim of this chapter is to increase knowledge of Western companies' foreign market entry and development in China. The following questions are posed:

1 Which operational modes are used?
2 What characterizes these operational modes in the Chinese context?
3 Which changes have taken place over time in the use of operational modes?
4 How can the companies' use of operational modes be explained?

The remainder of the chapter is structured as follows: first, the empirical study is described, followed by a short discussion of some of the crucial issues facing western companies involved in industrial sales in China. The subsequent section presents the organizational forms used by the companies, and subsequently some characteristics of the operational modes used by the Western companies in the present sample are presented. Then, changes over time in the use of operational modes are described, and a preliminary attempt is made to explain the choices companies have made. In the closing section of the paper some suggestions for future research are forwarded.

THE STUDY

This chapter reports on some of the initial findings from an on-going research project on industrial and project sales in China. The data reported here was gathered through personal interviews with representatives from Finnish companies selling industrial products to China. The sample covers virtually all the largest Finnish exporters to China. In large industrial groups, each individual company (or division) was chosen as the level of analysis (cf. Turnbull 1987). The study relied on two different approaches to data gathering:

1 In-depth longitudinal studies were conducted of three companies involved in the sales of industrial products or projects to buyers in China. Multiple interviews were conducted in Europe, Hong Kong and China. Data was collected on, among other things, the organization of sales and marketing, and in-depth descriptions of two sales in the sampled companies: their first one in China and their most recent one. One company (which in this chapter is called *Alpha*) was studied in considerable depth. In this company interviews were conducted with seven employees, in China, Hong Kong, and Finland. Two main informants have been interviewed more than once, one of them five times over a period of one year. In the two other companies (*Beta* and *Gamma*) three interviews have been done.
2 Single or multiple interviews were carried out in 21 other companies. The companies represented different industries and different types of products. Data was gathered in Europe, Hong Kong, and China. The focus was on the organization of the sales and marketing work, and on the characteristics of the company's latest sales contract. The respondents were also asked to compare the focal process with earlier

ones, and to elaborate on why there were differences between the processes.

There were mainland Chinese, overseas Chinese and Westerners among those interviewed. When the companies were contacted, they were asked to suggest a person who was personally involved in developing and carrying out the company's marketing and sales in China. The companies were promised anonymity. Typically, the interviewees in East Asia had the position of general manager, business area manager, or sales/marketing manager. The interviewees based in Europe were typically responsible for exports to China. With one exception, all interviews were taped. A loosely structured interview guide was used during the interviews.

SOME CHALLENGES FACING WESTERN COMPANIES IN CHINA

The field work as well as extant research (e.g. McGuiness *et al.* 1991) indicate that Western companies selling industrial goods in China are facing at least three different challenges: how to obtain information about potential orders in China; how to influence the Chinese decision makers so as to win business deals; and how to handle the implementation of the orders that they receive in China. Although foreign companies face these challenges in all markets, arguably they are particularly difficult to handle in China.

How to obtain information about possible customers and up-coming purchases was commonly viewed as a difficult task. Furthermore, due to the decentralization of economic decision making in China, this task has become even more difficult during the last few years. For major governmental infrastructural projects, there were sometimes official lists available from which it was possible to get information about forthcoming tenders. Occasionally, the Chinese buying organizations used newspaper and trade journal advertisements to spread information about tenders. Well-known companies were sometimes contacted by the prospective buyers and asked to submit price quotations for a certain order. The typical situation, however, was that Western companies had little information about potential customers. For many companies it was difficult to get information about which the potential buyers were, and where they were located. For instance, a company exporting machinery to China was unable to obtain a satisfactory list of Chinese companies operating in the industry in question. Sometimes it was possible to buy this kind of information in Hong Kong, for example, but not even this information was seen as totally reliable.

Concerning very large orders, it was common practice among the Chinese buyers to arrange public tenders. As elsewhere (cf. Ahmed 1993; Bansard *et al.* 1993), if exporters managed to influence the specifications of the tender they were in a better position to win the final deal. Domestic or foreign experts, e.g. consultants appointed by international financial institutions, sometimes took part in the process leading up to the final business deal. To the extent that the exporters were able to influence these experts, they had an advantage over their competitors.

How to influence the Chinese decision makers so as to win business deals was of course a crucial question. Companies that had good *guanxi* (relationships) with the 'right' people were seen to have a big advantage. The respondents sometimes referred to a certain province as 'belonging to company X' because this company had good friends who controlled purchasing decisions within that province. It was viewed as very difficult to break into an existing friendship between a representative for a foreign producer and Chinese employees on the buyer's side. However, even if the central decision maker was the friend of another company, it was sometimes possible to win business deals. The reason for this seemed sometimes to be related to the personal benefits of the decision maker (typically that the person would be invited on an inspection tour overseas; if he or she had already visited the 'friend's' factory, it was difficult to obtain a visa to go there again). Sometimes it seemed to be the outcome of an agreement among the Chinese decision makers that the friend of another company was allowed to win at least one business deal. Further, the authority relationship between different Chinese organizations seemed sometimes unclear, changed over time, and varied depending on the characteristics of the business deal (in particular, how it was financed, and what the size of the contract was). The general perception, however, was that if you managed to develop a good personal relationship with the central decision maker you had a good chance of winning business deals controlled by this person.

Companies selling to China had of course noticed the importance of *guanxi*, and therefore attempted to develop relationships with people believed to influence the purchases. To provide decision makers with personal favours of different kinds was a common way to develop friendships, but the existence of and importance of non-instrumental relationships were stressed by many respondents. Competitors from different parts of the world had thus developed friendships with Chinese employees in the central ministries in Beijing, with government officials at the provincial and local levels, and with persons within the buying organization itself. Different producers sometimes also had different friends within the same Chinese organization. Consequently, companies competing for the same deal tried to pull their *guanxi* with different participants on the Chinese side.

In spite of the perceived importance of *guanxi*, the respondents stressed that, with a few exceptions (usually concerning orders in South China), suppliers who were not able to compete in terms of technical quality and price had scant chances of winning business deals in China. Most of the industrial buyers were state-owned organizations, which were controlled by higher-level authorities. Commonly there existed centrally approved lists of suppliers, and the supervising organization obtained information about the contracts that were signed. Therefore, at least for large projects, the buying organization would only sign contracts which were competitive in comparison with those signed by other Chinese organizations.

The third, somewhat smaller challenge was how to implement the orders that had already been obtained. There were, among other things, a number of practical issues to take care of in connection with overseas shipments. The respondents told a number of stories of instances when there had been problems in the implementation phase, the result of which had been considerable costs to the exporter and/or reduced future business possibilities for the company. The challenge was thus to handle the implementation smoothly. The geographical and cultural distance between company headquarters in Scandinavia and the customers in China exacerbated this problem. In project sales, a change in personnel in the transition from the negotiation to the implementation phase was a potential source of additional problems as new personal relationships had to be established, and because foreign newcomers often showed a lack of understanding of the Chinese context.

Different ways to organize the company's operations were found to have certain advantages and disadvantages in terms of the ability to meet the challenges discussed above. Different operational modes also differed in terms of investments, variable costs, the extent to which the company learnt how to operate in China, and in the parent organization's control over the China operations. The next section describes the operational modes used by the sampled companies.

THE OPERATIONAL MODES USED BY THE SAMPLED COMPANIES

Table 4.1 describes the operational modes used by, or in the process of being installed by the companies in this study. Most companies had their own units in either Hong Kong or China. There was also a bias towards companies with extensive Chinese sales in the sample. A representative sample of Finnish companies selling industrial goods and projects to China would surely rely more heavily on indirect and direct export from Europe than the companies in the present study (cf. Easton and Li 1993).

Only six out of 24 companies had neither an own unit nor a joint venture in China. Additionally, in at least two companies the respondents stated that a China unit would probably be established before long. It must also be noted that, with only three or four exceptions, the companies relied quite heavily on sales people from headquarters and/or production units in Europe. If the participation of these people is paid attention to, all the

Table 4.1 Operational modes used by the companies included in the study
($n = 24$)

Mode	Number
Own unit, China; own unit, Hong Kong	5
Own unit, China	4
Own unit, China; own unit, Hong Kong; JV, China	3
Own unit, China; JV, China	2
Foreign representative(s)	2
Own unit, China	1
Own unit, China; foreign representative(s)	1
Own unit, China; JV, China; local representative(s)	1
JV, China; foreign representative	1
Own unit, Hong Kong	1
Own unit, Hong Kong; foreign representative	1
Own unit Hong Kong; foreign representative(s); own unit, Singapore	1
Foreign representative(s); own unit, Singapore	1

sampled companies used more than one operational mode for their
Chinese marketing and sales.

CHARACTERISTICS OF DIFFERENT OPERATIONAL MODES

Table 4.2 describes different ways to handle sales and marketing in China.
The characterization of each organizational mode has been done by the
author based on information provided by the respondents.

Space constraints prohibit an in-depth discussion of each organizational
form, but the following section gives a short description of some of the
main characteristics of the various operational forms. Several kinds of
external operational modes are discussed first, followed by a presentation
of intermediate and company-internal modes.

External operational modes

A distinction when it comes to the role of external operational modes can
be made between ad hoc middle men, personal agents, and foreign or
local representatives.

All companies reported that ad hoc middle men had contacted them,
often in Hong Kong but also in China or elsewhere in the world. The
middle men promised that they were able to help the exporter reach a
certain business deal provided that they were paid a commission. These
middle men ranged from well-established trading companies to individuals
and persons representing 'post box' companies in e.g. Hong Kong.
Sometimes middle men offered to take care of the whole sales process
themselves, sometimes technical and commercial negotiations were to take

Table 4.2 Some central characteristics of the operational modes used by Scandinavian companies selling industrial goods and projects in China

	External				Intermediate		Internal			
	Ad hoc middle men	Personal agents	Foreign representatives(s)	Local representative(s)	Information brokers	Joint venture	HQ sales people	Local employees	Rep. office with expats office	Hong Kong office
Compensation	commission	commission	commission	commission/ mark-up	commission (plus own salary)	profit distribution	salary	salary	salary	salary
Customer information	medium– high	medium– high	low–high	high– very high	medium– high	medium– high	low	medium– high	medium– high	low– medium
Communication capabilities	medium– very high	medium– very high	medium– high	high– very high	NA	medium– very high	low– medium	medium– high	low– high	low– high
Product knowledge	low	low– medium	low– medium	low–high	very low	medium– high	very high	low–high	medium– high	high
Implementation abilities	low	low	low–medium	medium– high	very low	medium– high	medium– high	medium– high	medium– high	medium– high
Investments	none	very low	very low	low	very low	high– very high	low– medium	low– medium	high	high
Variable costs	medium–high	medium	medium	medium	low	low–high	medium	very low	low	medium
MNC knowledge development	very low– medium	low	low–medium	low	medium– high	medium– high	medium– high	low–high	medium– high	low– high
MNC control	low	low	low–medium	low	medium– high	medium– high	high	medium	medium– high	medium– high
Other	–	–	–	–	–	goodwill; low trade barriers	–	–	shows commitment	tax advantage; convenience for expats; communication

place between the Western exporter and the Chinese buyer. Offers to help the exporter obtain the order were also presented during on-going negotiations. Especially in large projects there were several middle men offering their services, everybody promising that they had good connections with the decision makers in China. Occasionally the Chinese foreign trade corporation wanted one of its overseas offices to act as 'agent' during the process. For the sellers it was difficult to know the real ability of the middle men to influence the purchasing decisions. In other words, the connection between the middle men and the Chinese decision makers was often unclear. The Mainland or Hong Kong-Chinese staff members usually judged whether or not to use the middle men. This decision was also influenced by factors such as the seller's own *guanxi* (compared to that of its competitors), and its competitiveness in terms of price and product qualities. The commission payment to the middle men was commonly labelled as a consultancy or agency fee, for which the exporter obtained a regular receipt.

The exporters varied considerably in their perception and their approach to middle men. Some companies viewed middle men as a convenient way to obtaining information about potential customers. Viewed in this way, using middle men can be seen as an alternative to developing one's own information network within China. Accepting the offers presented by middle men in Hong Kong might thus help the exporter win orders in China with little of one's own involvement there. Some Western companies believed that using middle men might sometimes help the company win a certain business deal. The exporter also avoided getting involved in the illegal practices that sometimes seem to be part of doing business in China. The Western company typically knew very little about to whom the consultancy fee was paid. In most export deals, the formal export contract was signed with a governmental Chinese foreign trade organization. However, in some instances, the buyer requested the exporter to sign the export contract with a particular company in Hong Kong or somewhere outside China. This overseas company would then charge a commission, something that the governmental foreign trade organization otherwise would do.

Most companies tried to avoid the middle men. They insisted that they would negotiate with the final customer themselves rather than let a Hong Kong company, for example, handle contacts with the buyer. Several different arguments were presented by the respondents in favour of this strategy. First, they avoided the extra consultancy fees that the middle men charged, which among other things increased the price that the buyers had to pay for the product. Second, they believed that by having direct contact with the buyers they would in fact have a *better* chance of reaching a deal. Their perception was that the Chinese buyers very much preferred to buy directly from the Western producer, and involving middle men (unless, of course, it was known that the middle men had own connections with the Chinese decision makers) might therefore have a negative effect on their chance of getting the order. Third, they avoided situations in which they would actually compete with their own middle men for a certain business deal.

Some companies used officially appointed representatives. Such representatives seemed most commonly to work on a commission basis, but some would also take title to the product. Some of the exporting companies in our sample used either representatives based in Hong Kong (but often with offices on the mainland), domestic Finnish trading houses with offices in China, or a Japanese trading house. One company had started to develop a network of domestic Chinese representatives. The trend seemed to be in the direction of the latter. A couple of other exporters with a large potential number of customers in different parts of China were considering the establishment of domestic Chinese representative networks, and the respondents mentioned several competitors who were in the process of appointing local representatives. The main perceived advantage with such a network was the *guanxi* of the local representatives in their regions. The *guanxi* of potential representatives with important decision makers was therefore an important issue when deciding whether to appoint a sales representative for the company. Information about potential representatives was typically obtained from 'personal friends who knew the company'.

The main advantage of using non-Chinese representatives in China was their experience and connections in China (compared to those of the Finnish exporters), while the reluctance on the part of the Chinese buyers to deal with representatives and the commissions charged by representatives were important drawbacks. The Chinese buyers preferred to deal directly with the Western exporters, several of the respondents believed. One advantage of using the Japanese trading house was to improve the likelihood of winning projects financed by Japanese soft loans.

A few companies used domestic or overseas Chinese personal agents. One company relied heavily on a consultant, who had excellent personal connections to Chinese decision makers. A drawback with this organizational solution was the dependence on the consultants, who were in a position to profit from their strong bargaining position. Also, there was limited *guanxi* development on the part of the Western company. Another company was in the process of appointing a handful of Chinese individuals who would work as sales representatives in different parts of the country. They were going to operate on a commission basis, governed by a one-page contract. The sales representatives would try to obtain relatively small orders, while the company's own employees would take care of the bigger deals.

Intermediate organizational modes

The role of an information broker was primarily to provide the exporter with information about potential customers in China. Given the size of the country, in many industries it was impossible for the company to cover a sufficient number of potential Chinese customers. One solution was for sales people to try to develop a network of people in different parts of the country who knew them personally, and knew the company and the products it was offering. Mainland or Hong Kong Chinese sales people took care of the development of this kind of network. According to the respondents, it would be close to impossible for a Westerner to develop and maintain such networks. The network was very much linked to the sales person himself, and it was unlikely that it could be transferred to another employee.

Sales people tried to develop this kind of network by extensive travelling in China, and by attending trade fairs and exhibitions. By subsequently keeping in touch with the people they met at different occasions, they tried to maintain a broad network of people who knew whom to contact in case they obtained information about up-coming purchases. The information broker then informed the sales person about the possible customer. The contact to the potential buyer was taken either directly by the sales person or, sometimes, through the introduction of the information broker to an employee of the buyer. Provided that the business deal materialized, the information broker was paid a certain personal commission. The commission was not based on any contracts, but rather on the trust that the exporter's sales person had been able to establish with the person acting as information broker. This person did not have relationships which enabled him significantly to influence from which supplier the buyer would purchase the product.

The situation was different when the Chinese collaborator was in a position to directly or indirectly influence the purchase decision. It was common practice to try to establish close contacts with people in the State Planning Commission, in the ministry responsible for the industry in question, and in industrial design institutes. Contacts were maintained regularly with such 'friends' in the Chinese bureaucracy. The foreign companies provided the friend with up-dated information about the company's products and the industry in general. In turn the companies hoped to obtain valuable information and to make decision makers and Chinese experts more favourable towards their products.

To establish a joint venture in China typically meant considerable investments. The management problems of joint ventures in China are well documented in the literature (Child 1991; Björkman 1994), and were mentioned by Western respondents in the present study as well. On the other hand, the potential advantages were significant, too. Local partners often had the *guanxi* needed both to obtain information about potential orders and to help the company to win them. The strong local presence also facilitated the implementation of orders. Perhaps most importantly, production localization was a must in several industries in which the Chinese authorities accepted only foreign suppliers that had a certain local content in their products. Licensing, co-production and joint venture manufacturing were alternative ways to comply with the localization requirements.

Internal organizational modes

Most companies engaged people from the European or North American marketing and/or production units in sales and marketing work in China. These people had up-to-date knowledge of the products, the investments in the Chinese market were relatively low, and if the people remained involved in the China business for a long period of time they gradually acquired some knowledge of Chinese business conditions. On the flip side, their chances of acquiring information about up-coming orders were limited, their knowledge of how to do business in China was, at least initially, very limited, and the implementation of received orders was costly and/or cumbersome without a corporate presence in China.

Local presence within China was perceived as instrumental in several different respects. First, to obtain information about, and, in particular, to handle relationships and contacts with prospective buyers. Usually, the number of prospective buyers was relatively large and it was difficult, if not impossible, for sales people situated in Hong Kong or Europe to establish and maintain contacts with them. As noted earlier, the seller had to confront the substantial problem of how to obtain information about potential deals and how to get in touch with the potential buyers. One's own unit in China was perceived as instrumental in helping the company to obtain such information. By employing Chinese people from the industry in question – often from organizations with which they had been negotiating – the exporting company obtained employees in China with *guanxi* to buyers and/or governmental organizations. Speaking Mandarin as well as the local dialect facilitated communication with people in the business. Let us use the *Alpha* case as an illustration.

In connection with sales negotiations in China, Alpha's Western sales manager was approached by one of the participants of the Chinese company who said that he would like to work for the manager in China. The sales manager liked the idea of having somebody in China to take care of practical issues, and an agreement was reached with the Chinese person's work unit. Later on, three additional people were employed by Alpha in the same geographical area, and two in two other Chinese cities. No formal unit was established in China. The Chinese employees handled a range of issues, ranging from taking care of travel arrangements to discussing Alpha's products with potential customers. Over time, they started to get more and more involved in the sales negotiations. They often served as local interpreters for the European sales people who came to China for technical and commercial negotiations, but increasingly they also handled the initial stages of relationship building and sales work themselves.

Second, the implementation of deals was facilitated by having a local unit in China. When supplying machinery, for example, to a Chinese buyer, there were many things that could go wrong. *Alpha*, for example, had a number of problems with its first export order to China. Some parts were missing, some were broken, and there were thus a number of things to take care of locally in China. Although the company finally managed to complete the order in a satisfactory manner, there were staggering costs in keeping foreigners in China for a period of several months. His experience of the problems involved in this initial order was the reason why *Alpha's* sales manager a couple of years later accepted the offer to employ a Chinese person. Shortly afterwards, there was another event that further strengthened his conviction that local employees were needed in China. A Chinese buyer received three engines, one of which was painted with a different paint. The Chinese employee solved the problem by buying some paint, and then quickly repainting the machine with the help of some local people. A problem which might have led to a bad reputation for Alpha had been solved quickly and at a very low cost.

Third, a local unit was instrumental in the process of developing and maintaining good relationships with the central authorities. Even if the role of the central authorities was diminishing in the early 1990s, it was still seen as an important advantage to have good friends in the ministry responsible for the industry in question. Thus, one of the aims of one's own unit in Beijing was to handle such relationships. This was the case even if the end buyers were in other parts of the country. Bank connections were also viewed as important.

The staffing of the units in China varied considerably. With one exception, the representative offices had at least one foreign manager present in China. Companies with a liaison office in China relied on domestic Chinese employees. Two companies employed Chinese people without any formally established presence in China. Regardless of the operational mode that was utilized, there was a clear tendency towards higher use of domestic Chinese in the sales and marketing work. To employ domestic Chinese was perceived to have several different advantages. First, costs were only a fraction of those of an expatriate manager. Second, the Chinese employees were able to pull the *guanxi* that they had prior to being employed by the foreign company. Third, the serious cross-cultural communication and interpretation problems encountered by non-Chinese were avoided. This was a considerable advantage during negotiations, where experienced foreign managers usually relied on the judgment of the Chinese employees concerning how to respond to suggestions made by the Chinese decision makers or third parties.

You must be extremely patient, listen to things that are completely ridiculous. They are telling you this for one good reason, which might not be apparent, but you have to find it out. . . . I am very well helped by our Beijing people, who ... negotiate 24 hours per day ... through different third parties. This is where the real negotiation is. In China, there is the problem of face. If you want to say something to the other one, you cannot tell it straight to him. Instead you talk to this guy, you talk to this guy ... who says 'don't go that way, because that is not the way to do it; if you accept this, we would be in position to accept this'. That's the way it is. Before we had the Beijing people we probably missed some deals. ... It's absolutely mandatory to have that. We were silly not to understand that.

According to the Western managers, one problem with the Chinese employees was that they tended not to take initiatives and to avoid making decisions themselves. A similar behavioural pattern has also been found in research on Chinese-Western joint ventures (Child 1991; Björkman 1994). Consequently, foreign managers believed that it was necessary to have a foreign manager leading the Chinese operations either from within China or from a unit situated in Hong Kong. Both the Chinese and the Western respondents saw other advantages in letting Western managers take part in sales and marketing: it gave face to the customers and showed that the foreign company was committed to the customer, and the Chinese buyers tended to trust the technical knowledge of the Western managers. However, these advantages could be attained also with managers stationed outside of China.

CHANGES OVER TIME

There was a clear trend over time towards more direct involvement by the companies within China itself. Three development patterns can be identified in the data material:

1 Several companies had started their Asian operations in e.g. Singapore, from which they handled all Asian markets. In the late-1980s or early 1990s they had established an office in Hong Kong, typically as a regional headquarters but in at least one company in order solely to take care of the Chinese market. These companies had then handled their Chinese operations from their Hong Kong office. Over time the Hong Kong employees had noticed the advantage of having some kind of presence within China itself, and had therefore employed their own Chinese personnel in China. Finally, in 1993 or early 1994 they had decided to establish a full representative office in China and/or increase the presence in China in some other way (e.g. through a joint venture). This pattern was followed by nine companies. The story of *Alpha* illustrates a fairly typical sequence.

Some 15 years ago Alpha made an agreement with a Hong Kong company to work on a case-by-case basis. At this point the Singapore unit was responsible for sales in Asia. This arrangement with the Hong

Kong company was later turned into a full agency agreement. Eventually, the company decided to establish an own subsidiary in Hong Kong. Another measure was to employ first one Chinese person, and subsequently some other local people to take care of various kinds of practical arrangements in China. Over time, the work of these Chinese employees became more and more sales oriented; potential and existing customers visited their office, and the employees stayed in touch with people in the industry in order to obtain information about up-coming orders. Finally, a decision was made to establish a representative office at one location in China. At other locations, the company employed local employees. At the same time, the company started to investigate whether to commence local production in China.

2 A second pattern was to get directly involved within China itself without first establishing an own presence in Hong Kong. This was done by nine companies. The companies in this group were more diverse in how they had developed their organizational presence within China. Five companies had used one or several foreign representatives in China, most of them for a quite long period, before either establishing a manufacturing joint venture or a representative office. Three firms (two of which belonged to the same group) had started immediately with a sales office in China before obtaining their first order. Finally, one company had sold extensively to China, mostly via Hong Kong traders and representatives, before a decision was made to set up a China representative office.

3 A third group consists of six companies that mainly used foreign representatives, a Hong Kong or a Singapore unit for their China sales and marketing. At the point of data gathering, two of them were considering the establishment of a China unit. Among the remaining firms, one had developed a network of information brokers, one used own sales people from the Hong Kong unit to reach the relatively few potential customers that the company had in China, and two used their representatives, middle men and their own sales people extensively.

None of the companies reported a withdrawal from operations in China. Three companies had either ceased or scaled down considerably their Hong Kong operations after increasing their own operations on the mainland.

ANALYSIS

The companies in the present sample followed quite closely the 'traditional' sequence of market entry modes predicted by the so called Uppsala Internationalization Model (Johanson and Vahlne 1977). With only one notable exception (a group that established a sales office prior to obtaining the first order in China), the companies moved gradually from low commitment organizational forms to higher commitment ones. The results are at odds with recent research which has indicated that companies quite often deviate from the process of only gradually increasing their operations in a foreign market (see e.g. Hedlund and Kverneland 1984; Turnbull 1987; Björkman and Eklund 1991; Lindqvist 1991). A plausible explanation is that the psychic distance is so great between Scandinavia and China that decision makers – facing considerable uncertainty and lack of knowledge of the Chinese market – are reluctant to jump directly to high commitment operational modes. Several of the cases support this conjecture.

Several companies with Hong Kong units had over time increased – albeit slowly – their presence within China. Comments made by the respondents indicate that the changes had been problem-driven (cf. Cyert and March 1963). When trying to handle sales and marketing within China itself they had noticed that there was a need for a representation on the mainland. This had materialized, although only on a limited scale. For instance, within Alpha the general manager of the Hong Kong unit had tried to persuade corporate top management that investments within China were necessary. However, it was not until the autumn of 1993 that top management approved such investments.

Suddenly in 1993 and early 1994, a majority of the sampled companies made decisions to establish a China representative office and/or joint ventures in China. While only seven of the sampled companies had a China unit at the beginning of 1993, by the summer of 1994 11 additional firms had established their own units in China. This also concerned some companies with relatively limited sales volume in China. How can this be explained? It is not a direct consequence of the decentralization of the Chinese economic system; this was started already during the 1980s, although it did accelerate from 1992. In my view, a neo-institutional explanation is very plausible.

The Finnish business community experienced a strong China boom starting during the latter half of 1992. In late 1992, but especially during the winter and spring of 1993, a number of China seminars were arranged in Finland. Orders obtained by Finnish companies received considerable publicity in the press, and members of the tightly structured Finnish business community found a new discussion topic for the sauna evenings. It became an 'institutionalized myth' (Meyer and Rowan 1977) that China was the place to be if you wanted to make money during the rest of the twentieth century. Although the other Asian markets also received some attention, China was by far the number one issue. Several very senior business delegations travelled with Finnish ministers to China on sales trips. Successful companies with their own China units were viewed as forerunners. Within the sampled companies there were increased expectations from top management for business unit managers to develop their China business. All of a sudden, it was not difficult to convince top management about the appropriateness of investments in China. The problem was rather for business unit managers to find the time to develop the China operations.

The Uppsala Internationalization Process Model has been criticized for not providing a sufficient explanation for why and when companies shift from one operational mode to another, and for not specifying the conditions under which the model may apply (Andersen 1993). The findings in the present study suggest that the explanatory power of the Uppsala Internationalization Process Model can be increased by supplementing it with insights from the institutionalization perspective. In situations with high psychic distance and uncertainty concerning the 'correct' market entry strategy, the emergence of institutionalized myths is likely to trigger changes in operational modes. Thus, even if corporate decision makers still perceive that there is a high psychic distance, companies are likely to mimic the market entry behaviour of companies seen as successful (cf. DiMaggio and Powell 1983).

As described in Table 3, six out of 24 companies had neither a sales nor a manufacturing unit in China. An attempt was made to analyse the difference between the two groups in terms of some of the variables typically used for analysing the choice of market entry mode:

- the company's international experience (operationalized as number of foreign units)
- the company's size (i.e. turnover)
- the number of 'serious' competitors that the firm had in China (as judged by the respondents)
- the number of (potential) Chinese buyers (as judged by the respondents)[2]
- the typical size of individual deals in China
- total sales in China.

None of these variables was statistically significant (at $p < = 0.10$, double tailed t-tests). With a sample only consisting of $6 + 18$ companies this is perhaps not particularly surprising, and additional research on larger samples is obviously needed. For example, there was a slight tendency for companies with limited sales in China to be less likely to establish their own units within China.

CONCLUSIONS

This chapter has described how Finnish producers of industrial goods and projects have responded to the challenges of how to obtain information about potential orders in China; how to influence the Chinese decision makers so as to win business deals; and how to handle the implementation of the orders that they receive in China. Different ways of organizing the company's operations were seen to entail certain advantages and disadvantages in terms of the company's ability to meet these challenges.

The companies covered by the present study tended to use several operational modes in China. There was a clear trend towards more direct involvement on the part of the Western companies in China. The companies expanded their sales networks in China through own employees but also through the use of various kinds of representatives. Concomitantly, the companies, especially those with a long track record in China, started to give Chinese employees a more important role in their business undertakings. It seems that the experiential knowledge of managers involved in the China business typically triggered a gradual expansion of the companies' presence in China itself. Underlying factors were obviously the decentralization of economic decision making in China and the particular socio-cultural Chinese setting, both of which were seen as favouring a local presence in the country itself. Similar expansion strategies seem to be found also among companies producing and selling consumer goods in China (Osland 1993).

The sampled companies followed closely the kind of sequential adaptation of gradually more advanced operational modes proposed by the Uppsala Internationalization Process Model (Johanson and Vahlne 1977; 1990). While recent studies in other markets have suggested that it is currently fairly common to use advanced operational modes when entering new markets (e.g. Turnbull 1987; Björkman and Eklund 1991), the present study suggests that a different pattern can be found in China. The extremely high psychic distance between China and Finland has probably contributed to this pattern. Suddenly in 1993 or early 1994, a majority of the sampled companies made decisions to establish a China representative office and/or joint ventures in China. Interviews indicate that a strong corporate presence in China became a must, an institutionalized myth (Meyer and Rowan 1977) within the Finnish business community. The emergence of this myth seems to have contributed to the surge in establishments that took place in 1993–1994.

Finally, it needs to be pointed out that this chapter is only an early attempt to analyse the data that has been gathered so far in an on-going research project. Additional survey data from a considerably larger sample will permit some statistical analysis. Further, there are several ideas that will be pursued. For instance, the case studies indicate that the personal experience of the decision makers is an important indicator of the market entry strategy that the company chooses. There is also some indication that the action of major competitors as well as the expectations of Chinese government officials occasionally influence companies to invest in China. The relationship between governmental actions and the strategies of the Western companies is seen as a particularly fruitful area for future investigations.

NOTES

1 Thanks to Nicola Lindertz and Annika Vatanen for their help with some of the data collection. The research has been partly funded by Hans Bangs Stiftelse and by the Finnish Ministry of Trade and Industry.
2 To estimate the potential number of customers was for several respondents somewhat difficult. This difficulty was partly due to the question of who the buyer was (the end-user or some of the governmental organizations involved), partly due to the fact that the situation in China was changing so rapidly and, consequently, the number of *potential* buyers might increase very rapidly. The respondents' estimate concerns the *current* situation.

REFERENCES

Ahmed, M. 1993 *International marketing and purchases of projects: interactions and paradoxes*, Helsinki: Publications of the Swedish School of Economics 49.
Andersen, O. 1993 'On the internationalization process of firms: A critical analysis', *Journal of International Business Studies* 24: 209–231.
Anderson, E. and Coughlan, A. 1987 'International market entry and expansion via independent and integrated channels of distribution', *Journal of Marketing* 51: 71–82.
Bansard, D., Cova, B. and Salle, R. 1993 'Project marketing: beyond competitive bidding strategies', *International Business Review* 2: 125–141.
Björkman, I. 1994 'Running head: role perceptions and behavior among Chinese managers', in S. Stewart (ed.) *Advances in Chinese Industrial Studies* 4, JAI Press.
Björkman, I. and Eklund, M. 1991 'Entering foreign markets: an analysis of the market entry modes used by Finnish direct investors in Germany', in H. Vestergaard (ed.) *An enlarged Europe in the global economy. Proceedings of the 17th Annual conference of EIBA* 15–17 December: 791–820, Copenhagen.
Bond, M.H. and Hwang, K.K. 1986 'The social psychology of Chinese people', in M.H. Bond (ed.) *The psychology of the Chinese people*: 213–266, Hong Kong: Oxford University Press.
Child, J. 1991 'A foreign perspective on the management of people in China', *International Journal of Human Resource Management* 2: 93–107.
Cyert, R. and March, J.G. 1963 *A behavioral theory of the firm*, Englewood Cliffs, NJ: Prentice–Hall.
DiMaggio, P.J. and Powell, W.W. 1983 'The iron cage revisited: institutional isomorphism and collective rationality in organizational fields', *American Sociological Review* 48: 147–160.
Easton, G. and Li Zhi Xiong 1993 'The dynamics of export channels – a case study of exporting from the UK to the People's Republic of China', paper presented at the *9th IMP Conference* 23–25 September, Bath.
Hedlund, G. and Kverneland, Å. 1984 *Investing in Japan – the experience of Swedish firms*, Stockholm: IIB/Stockholm School of Economics.
Hu, M.Y. and Chen, H. 1993 'Foreign ownership in Chinese joint ventures: a transaction cost analysis', *Journal of Business Reseach* 26: 149–160.
Johanson, J. and Vahlne, J.-E. 1977 'The internationalization process of the firm – a model of knowledge development and increasing market commitments', *Journal of International Business Studies* 8(1): 23–32.
Johanson, J. and Vahlne, J.-E. 1990 'The mechanism of internationalization', *International Marketing Review* 7(4): 11–24.
Klein, S. and Roth, V.J. 1990 'Determinants of export channel structure: the effects

of experience and psychic distance reconsidered', *International Marketing Review* 7(5): 27–38.

Levitt, B. and March, J.G. 1988 'Organizational learning', *Annual Review of Sociology* 14: 319–340.

Lindqvist, M. 1991 *Infant multinationals: the internationalization of young, technology-based Swedish firms*, Stockholm: IIB/Stockholm School of Economics.

McGuiness, N., Campbell, N. and Leontiades, J. 1991 'Selling machinery to China: Chinese perceptions of strategies and relationships', *Journal of International Business Studies* 22: 187–207.

Meyer, J.W. and Rowan, B. 1977 'Institutionalized organizations: formal structure as myth and ceremony', *American Journal of Sociology* 83: 340–360.

Osland, G.E. 1993 'Successful operating strategies in the performance of US-China joint ventures', paper presented at the *Second conference on joint ventures in East Asia* 16–17 December, Bangkok.

Turnbull, P.W. 1987 'A challenge to the stages theory of the internationalization process', in P.J. Rosson and S.D. Reed (eds) *Managing export entry and expansion*, New York: Praeger.

Young, S., Hamill, J., Wheeler, C. and Davies J.R. 1989 *International market entry and development: strategies and management*, Englewood Cliffs, NJ: Harvester Wheatsheaf.

Part II

The challenge of managing international enterprises in China

5 Conflict management in US-Chinese joint ventures

An analytical framework

Elizabeth Weldon and Karen A. Jehn

ABSTRACT

Managing conflict can be difficult in any work group, but it can be particularly difficult when two cultures are involved. In this Chapter we describe
a study of conflict management in US-Chinese joint ventures designed to
improve our understanding of intercultural conflict in bicultural teams.
An inductive technique (multidimensional scaling) is used to uncover the
dimensions underlying strategies used by American and Chinese managers
to manage conflict with same-culture (intracultural conflict) and different-
culture managers (intercultural conflict). This study contributes to a theory
of intercultural conflict management by

(a) providing information about the impact of individualism-collectivism,
    low- *vs* high-context communication, and facework on conflict man-
    agement behaviour, because Americans and Chinese differ on these
    three dimensions of cultural variability;
(b) uncovering dimensions of conflict management behaviour that are
    relevant to both cultures (i.e., etic constructs), if they exist;
(c) uncovering culture-specific dimensions (i.e., emic constructs) that
    contribute to a complete understanding of differences across cultures;
(d) testing the hypothesis that managers behave differently when involved
    in intercultural compared to intracultural conflict.

US-CHINESE JOINT VENTURES

Effective intercultural interaction is important to the success of US-
Chinese joint ventures. Members of the bicultural board of directors must
work together to guide the venture, and members of the top management
team, American and Chinese, must work together to run the firm
(Davidson 1987; Hendryx 1986a). Unfortunately, intercultural interaction
is problematic in many joint ventures, because the Americans and Chinese
are unable to resolve their differences. For example:

The Chinese and Americans [at Beijing Jeep] had been trying to coexist and adapt to one another, but it wasn't easy. Both sides found that the cultural differences were even greater than either had expected before the joint venture opened its door.

(Mann 1989: 199)

Similar problems were reported at Babcock & Wilcox Beijing Company (B&WBC), another manufacturing joint venture (Grub and Lin 1991). In both joint ventures, dislike and mistrust polarized the groups and threatened the survival of the firm (Mann 1989; Grub and Lin 1991). 'Workers [at B&WBC] evaluated Chinese managers by a simple standard: whoever quarreled with Americans the most aggressively would be considered [a] comrade in arms, and whoever cooperated with the Americans would be nicknamed "Er Gui Zi" (fake foreigners)' (Grub and Lin 1991: 194). 'The atmosphere [at Beijing Jeep] became so tense that even the most trivial business dealings between the American and Chinese became bogged down in charges and countercharges' (Mann 1989: 180).

In some international joint ventures these problems can be eliminated by assigning responsibility for operations to one partner (Wright 1979; Peterson and Shimada 1978), or using informal arrangements to remove one group of managers from the decision making loop, as sometimes happens to American managers in Japanese firms operating in the US (*Chicago Tribune* 1992). These strategies can be used when one party has all the technical and managerial information necessary to run the firm. Or, cultural differences could be reduced by assigning ethnically similar managers from the American firm to the joint venture (Beck *et al.* 1990).

Unfortunately, these solutions will not work in most US-Chinese joint ventures. First, the American partner may not employ Chinese-Americans or ethnic-Chinese managers who are qualified to run a foreign joint venture. Second, in most US-Chinese joint ventures, neither partner has all the information necessary to run the firm. The Americans contribute technical and managerial skill (Hendryx 1986b; Zhang 1987), and the Chinese contribute an understanding of the firm's political and economic environment. Therefore, managers in US-Chinese joint ventures must learn to work together as a team.

INTERCULTURAL CONFLICT MANAGEMENT

Unfortunately, there is no comprehensive theory of intercultural conflict management that can be used to improve interaction in US-Chinese joint ventures. Before a theory can be developed, two issues must be addressed. First, cross-cultural differences in conflict management behaviour must be identified. It is important to study cross-cultural differences, because conflict is a culturally defined and regulated event (Sillars and Weisberg 1987). That is, each culture defines what constitutes conflict and the appropriate behaviours for dealing with it (Hocker and Wilmot 1991). Second, the distinction between intercultural and intracultural conflict management must be explored. Cross-cultural studies focus on intracultural conflict management (members of the same culture are involved), whereas intercultural conflict involves members of different cultures. As Adler and Graham (1989) point out, theories of cross-cultural differences should not be applied to intercultural interaction without testing the assumption that people behave similarly with domestic and foreign colleagues.

An understanding of these two issues will contribute to a theory of intercultural conflict management that considers cross-cultural differences in conflict management behaviour and differences between intercultural and intracultural conflict. In the next section, we review existing theory and research focusing on cross-cultural differences in conflict management, and explain why this work provides little useful information about these differences. Following this discussion, the distinction between intracultural conflict management behaviour and intercultural behaviour is discussed. After these two issues are addressed, a study of intracultural and intercultural conflict in US-Chinese joint ventures is described.

Cross-cultural differences in conflict management

Existing theory and research focusing on cross-cultural differences in conflict management behaviour examine the links between dimensions of cultural variability and conflict management. Jehn and Weldon (1992), Trubisky *et al.* (1991) and Lee and Rogan (1991) have described the impact of individualism-collectivism on conflict management behaviour. Ting-Toomey (1988) and Ting-Toomey *et al.* (1991) describe the impact of facework, and Weldon (in press) and Ting-Toomey (1985) consider communication style.

Individualism-collectivism is an important dimension of cultural variability (Parsons and Shils 1951; Kluckhohn and Strodtbeck 1961; Triandis 1986), because it provides a key to understanding the norms and values that govern social relationships and social exchange (Triandis *et al.* 1988). In a collectivist society, social relationships and group welfare dominate individual needs and desires. As a result, behaviour is influenced more by social norms and social obligations than by personal desires (Triandis 1986); co-operation and social harmony are emphasized (Waterman 1984) and individual effort and achievement are expected to contribute to the collective good (Laaksonen 1988). In contrast, in an individualistic society, people value autonomy, assertiveness, competition and individual achievement, and personal satisfaction and growth are important (Triandis 1986). These differences in cultural values are believed to influence attitudes towards conflict and conflict management behaviour (Jehn & Weldon 1992; Trubisky *et al.* 1991; Lee and Rogan 1991).

Face is 'the public self-image that every member of a society wants to claim for himself/herself' (Brown & Levinson, 1978: 66). Facework is the social behaviour used to create and support one's face (Goffman 1967). Because the relative importance of self and group differ in individualistic and collectivistic cultures, the characteristics of an appropriate face and the nature of facework also differ. In a collectivistic culture, facework is used to present the self as an appropriate member of the social network, and people are expected to help others maintain a similarly appropriate face. In contrast, in an individualistic society, facework focuses more on maintaining one's personal identity with little concern about helping others maintain theirs (Ting-Toomey 1988). Ting-Toomey (1988) and Ting-Toomey *et al.* (1991) suggest that differences in facework have important implications for conflict management behaviour.

Communication style can be described along a dimension called *high- vs low-context* (Hall 1976). In a high-context culture, 'most of the information [to be communicated] is either in the physical context or internalized in the person, while very little is in the coded, explicit, transmitted part of the message' (Hall 1976: 79). In contrast, in a low-context society, 'the mass of the [communicated] information is vested in the explicit code' (Hall 1976: 79).

Communication in high-context and low-context cultures differs in four important ways. First, communication in a low-context culture is explicit and direct (Gudykunst and Ting-Toomey 1988). In contrast, in a high-context culture, communication is implicit, and the receiver must invoke the context to interpret the message (Gudykunst and Ting-Toomey 1988). Second, communication in a low-context culture is sender-oriented (Gudykunst and Ting-Toomey 1988), whereas communication in a high-context culture is process-oriented. In sender-oriented communication, the speaker and listener are assigned distinct roles and the burden of communication is placed on the sender. It is the speaker's responsibility to make the listener understand. In process-oriented communication, the roles of the speaker and the listener are highly interdependent, and the burden of communication is shared.

Third, in high-context cultures people are more tolerant of silence during conversation, they use silence strategically, and they place more emphasis on non-verbal cues (Gudykunst and Ting-Toomey 1988). In a low-context culture, talk is more important than non-verbal information and silence is avoided. Fourth, people in high-context cultures adopt a role-oriented style. Role-oriented communication emphasizes the social roles that the participants hold and different scripts are invoked depending on role relationships. As a result, interaction is formal and ritualistic. In contrast, people in low-context cultures use a personal style. A personal style emphasizes personal identity over social position. Because role relationships and status differences are less important, communication is less formal and often more intimate (Okabe 1983). Weldon (in press) and

Ting-Toomey (1985) link conflict management behaviour to low- *vs* high-context communication style.

Links to conflict management behaviour

The problem with this literature is not the choice of these dimensions for consideration. All have been recognized as important dimensions of cultural variability that explain how values and behaviour differ across cultures (Kluckhohn and Strodtbeck 1961; Goffman 1967; Brown and Levinson 1978; Hofstede 1980; Triandis 1986). And, as these descriptions suggest, it seems that these dimensions of cultural variability would influence conflict management behaviour.

Instead, the problem centres on the way that conflict management behaviour is conceptualized, and the way it is measured in studies of cross-cultural differences. In each case, a theory of conflict management behaviour developed in the West is adopted. These theories focus on dimensions that differentiate strategies of conflict management: the extent to which the style shows concern for self; shows concern for others; focuses on getting the problem resolved quickly (issue-oriented) or maintaining social harmony (relationship-oriented); reflects a willingness to deal with conflict or a desire to avoid conflict; and reflects a direct approach to managing conflict or an indirect approach. These dimensions of conflict management behaviour are then linked to dimensions of cultural variability. Individualism, low-context communication and self-oriented facework are believed to produce a direct, solution-oriented conflict management style reflecting concern for self, whereas collectivism, other-oriented facework and high-context communication are believed to motivate avoidance and produce indirect, relationship-oriented styles reflecting concern for others.

Researchers test these predictions by linking dimensions of conflict management behaviour to specific conflict management styles (or strategies), selecting samples from cultures that differ on dimensions of cultural variability, and administering questionnaires designed to measure these styles. Jehn and Weldon (1992) administered the Thomas-Kilmann questionnaire (Kilmann and Thomas 1977), which measures five styles, and predicted that people in collectivistic cultures would use accommodating and avoiding more often than those from individualistic societies, and individualists would use competing, compromising and collaborating more than collectivists, because the former are attempts to avoid conflict and the latter are direct, confrontational styles. Trubisky *et al.* (1991) and Ting-Toomey *et al.* (1991) administered the Rahim Organizational Conflict Instrument (Rahim 1983), which measures the same five styles, and made similar predictions. Lee and Rogan (1991) administered the Organizational Communication Conflict Instrument, which measures three styles, and predicted that solution-oriented and controlling strategies would be used more in individualistic cultures compared to collectivistic, because these strategies are direct or self-oriented, whereas nonconfrontational strategies would be used more in collectivistic societies, because these are indirect. In each case, results produced mixed support for predictions. More detailed descriptions of these studies are provided in Table 5.1.

Table 5.1: Cross-cultural studies of conflict management behaviour.

Study	Sample	Measure of conflict management behaviour	Predictions	Results
Jehn and Weldon (1992)	American and Chinese managers were asked to describe their typical conflict management style	Thomas-Kilmann Conflict Mode Instrument (Kilmann and Thomas 1977)	Chinese use compromising, accommodating and avoiding more than Americans. Americans use competing and collaborating more than Chinese	Scale scores calculated according to instructions showed that Americans used compromise more than the Chinese. Scale scores based on factors from intracultural factor analyses showed that Chinese managers typically use accommodating strategies, whereas US managers typically use collaborating and competing styles
Lee and Rogan (1991)	Bank employees in Korea and the US were asked to consider a recent disagreement and describe their behaviour	Organizational Communication Conflict Instrument (Putnam and Wilson 1982)	Americans use solution-oriented and controlling strategies more than Koreans; Koreans use nonconfrontational strategies more than Americans	Koreans used solution-oriented more than Americans; Americans used controlling and nonconfrontational more than the Koreans

Table 5.1: cont.

Study	Sample	Measure of conflict management behaviour	Predictions	Results
Ting-Toomey et al. (1991)	American, Japanese, Chinese, Korean and Taiwanese students were asked to describe strategies they would use to ask a class-mate to redo his/her part of a class project	Rahim Organizational Conflict Instrument II (Rahim 1983)	Americans will use dominating and integrating more than the Japanese, Koreans, Taiwanese and Chinese, who will use obliging, avoiding and compromising more than the Americans	Americans used dominating more than the Japanese and Koreans, but not more than the others. Americans used integrating more than the Japanese, but not more than the others. The Chinese and Taiwanese used obliging more than the Americans, but the others did not. The Taiwanese used avoiding more than the Americans but the others did not. The Chinese used compromising more than the Americans but the others did not
Trubisky et al. (1991)	American and Taiwanese students were asked to describe strategies they would use to ask a class-mate to redo his/her part of a class project	Rahim Organizational Conflict Instrument II (Rahim 1983)	Taiwanese use obliging and avoiding strategies more than Americans; Americans use dominating, compromising and integrating more than Taiwanese	Taiwanese and American students were equally likely to use a dominating strategy; Taiwanese were more likely to use obliging, avoiding, integrating and compromising strategies than Americans

Critique of theory and research

This approach to the conceptualization and measurement of cross-cultural differences in conflict management style has three shortcomings that limit the value of this research. First, when a theory is transported across cultures the researcher assumes, implicitly or explicitly, that the constructs in the theory are etic constructs. Etics are culture-free or universal aspects of the phenomenon that can be used for direct comparisons across cultures (Berry 1980). When constructs are assumed to be universal, but they are not, a misleading explanation for behaviour may be produced (Triandis 1980). Second, emic constructs important to an understanding of the phenomena in the new culture are not included in the theory. Emics are culture-specific aspects of a phenomenon that are necessary to an understanding of the culture's indigenous conception of the phenomenon. When emics are ignored, an incomplete understanding of the phenomenon in the new culture will be produced (Berry 1980).

Third, applying a psychological measure developed in one culture to another creates three problems: the psychometric properties of the measure may differ across the two cultures; emics operating in the new culture are not included in the measure; and etic dimensions may be measured improperly in the new culture. This third concern is particularly important when descriptions of behaviour are used to measure the constructs of interest, because similar activities do not always have similar functions in different cultures (Frijda & Jahoda 1966). Thus, the functional equivalence of the measure across cultures is suspect.

There is reason to worry about all these issues in this body of work. First, these theorists and researchers offer no evidence that the constructs used to compare cultures are in fact etic constructs. That is, there is no evidence that the distinctions used to differentiate conflict management behaviour in the West are useful for understanding conflict management behaviour in other cultures. Second, these theorists and researchers made no attempt to discuss or measure emic constructs. Therefore, constructs necessary to an understanding of conflict management behaviour in non-Western cultures are ignored. Third, measures of conflict management behaviour developed by researchers in a Western, individualistic culture (i.e., the United States) were applied to Eastern, collectivist societies. Thus, the cross-cultural equivalence of these measures is suspect. In fact, there is evidence that they are not equivalent.

First, the functional equivalence of the items is not established. For example, silence is used to measure avoidance behaviour on the Organizational Conflict Communication Instrument administered by Lee and Rogan (1991). Although silence might reflect a desire to avoid conflict in individualistic, low-context cultures, it does not necessarily reflect avoidance in all cultures. In a high-context culture, silence may be a natural part of dealing with conflict. Second, there is evidence of psychometric inequivalence. Although Lee and Rogan (1991) performed separate intra-cultural factor analyses, and these analyses produced three factor solutions in each culture (presumably the same solution), the correlations between the factors differed across the two cultures. The factor representing a nonconfrontational style was positively correlated with the solution-oriented factor in the Korean sample, but a negative correlation was found for Americans. This difference violates the assumption of psychometric equivalence, and raises questions about the psychological equivalence of the constructs, because these results suggest that a nonconfrontational strategy contributes to a solution in Korea, but does not contribute to a solution in the United States. Trubisky *et al.* (1991) checked the internal reliabilities of the scales on Rahim's questionnaire and found them to be equally reliable in the two cultures. However, correlations between the scales were not reported. Jehn and Weldon (1992) performed intracultural factor analyses for the Thomas-Kilmann questionnaire and found different factor solutions in the two cultures. Ting-Toomey *et al.* (1991) performed a pancultural principal components analysis. Although a five factor solution that is quite similar to Rahim's was discovered, a pancultural analysis cannot be used to draw inferences about the similarity of factor structures across cultures. Moreover, estimates of internal consistencies for the different scales varied across cultures, ranging from 0.59 for the Chinese on the compromising scale to 0.84 on the dominating scale for the American sample. Thus, in each study, the assumption of metric equivalence must be questioned.

Together, these shortcomings suggest that this research provides little useful information about cross-cultural differences in conflict management style. To produce useful information, the ethnocentric assumption that Western theories and measures of conflict management behaviour can be applied in any culture must be discarded, and an inductive search for etic dimensions of conflict management behaviour and emic constructs must be conducted. Discovering true etics allows meaningful comparisons across cultures on a set of common dimensions, and the discovery of emics contributes to a full understanding of each culture.

Intercultural interaction

Once cross-cultural differences are discovered, their relevance to inter-cultural conflict management can be tested. It is important to conduct these tests, because cross-cultural differences in intracultural conflict management may not generalize to intercultural conflict. That is, people may use different strategies to manage conflict when a foreigner is involved.

Studies of social categorization and intergroup relations show that people group others on the basis of salient characteristics, and they create stereotypes of people who are different from themselves (Tajfel and

Turner 1986). This research also shows that stereotypes tend to favour the ingroup (Messick and Brewer 1983). The group that the categorizer feels similar to and identifies with is called the 'ingroup' and other groups are called 'outgroups'. Outgroup members are believed to be less attractive, less capable, less trustworthy, less honest, less co-operative, and less deserving than members of the ingroup (Messick and Mackie 1989; Kramer 1991). As a result, people behave differently towards outgroup members. People working in bicultural teams might therefore be expected to use different strategies to manage conflict with their cultural compatriots compared to foreigners.

PROPOSED RESEARCH INTO CONFLICT MANAGEMENT

As the preceding analysis suggests, a programme of research focusing on cross-cultural differences in intracultural conflict management and differences between intercultural and intracultural conflict should be performed. This research must include a search for

1 etic dimensions of intracultural and intercultural conflict management behaviour;
2 emic constructs necessary to understand intracultural and intercultural conflict management in different cultures;
3 differences in the etic and emic constructs used to understand intracultural compared to intercultural conflict management behaviour.

The study described here is a first step in that programme of research. It compares intercultural and intracultural conflict management in US-Chinese joint ventures, by identifying the strategies used to manage each type of conflict. US-Chinese joint ventures were chosen for this study because the United States and China differ on important dimensions of cultural variability, and intercultural conflict is common in US-Chinese joint ventures (Mann 1989; Grub and Lin 1991). The United States is an individualistic culture (Hofstede 1980), and Americans use a low-context communication style (Ting-Toomey 1985) and self-oriented facework (Ting-Toomey *et al.* 1991). In contrast, China is a collectivistic culture (Ho 1976; Li 1978), the Chinese use a high-context communication style (Weldon in press), and facework includes a concern for others (Ting-Toomey *et al.* 1991). Thus, this study contributes to our understanding of how these dimensions of cultural variability influence conflict management behaviour and provides an opportunity to study intercultural conflict.

Method

In this study, multidimensional scaling is used to uncover the dimensions that characterize the behaviours that American and Chinese managers use to manage intracultural and intercultural conflict. Multidimensional scaling

(MDS) is a quantitative inductive technique used to uncover the dimensions underlying a social phenomenon (Kruskal and Wish 1978). Thus, with MDS, etic and emic dimensions of conflict management can emerge from the data.

Our MDS analysis includes four steps. The first three are now complete. In Step 1, American and Chinese managers working in China were asked to describe two conflicts they had experienced recently, one involving a same-culture manager (intracultural conflict) and another involving a different-culture manager (intercultural conflict). To ensure thorough descriptions the interviewer prompted the respondent to answer five questions:

1 'What was the conflict about?'
2 'Who was involved?'
3 'What caused the conflict?'
4 'What did you do to deal with this conflict?'
5 'If the conflict was resolved, how was it resolved? If not, what is its current status?'

All the respondents interviewed in Step 1 were currently working in or had recently worked in a US-Chinese joint venture or the Chinese operation of an American firm. All had frequent interaction with different-culture managers. Although some of our American colleagues who are familiar with China believed that Chinese managers might be reluctant to discuss conflict, because it is a sensitive issue there, this was not the case. The Chinese social scientist who interviewed the Chinese managers found them willing to participate. Many of the conflicts described in Step 1 involved problems commonly found in American organizations. For example, one conflict centred on the size of a pay rise; another involved an argument about promotion; and another involved people who were jealous of perquisites enjoyed by some people in the firm. However, others were peculiar to US-Chinese operations. For example, American managers complained that the Chinese do not recognize the importance of deadlines and schedules; that the Chinese are not proactive and will not take risks; that the communist party representative at the firm often has more power than the Chinese managers; and that the hardship of working in China creates chronic stress, which exacerbates intercultural conflict. The Chinese managers complained that Americans do not try to understand and learn from the Chinese; that the American management style is too abrupt; that Americans fail to recognize the importance of relationships; and they overemphasize the importance of formal rules and regulations. These complaints are consistent with those found in other US-Chinese operations.

Perhaps the most interesting finding involves American intracultural conflict. Most reported little conflict among themselves (although every American could report an intracultural conflict) and believed that conflicts with other Americans were less emotional, easier to resolve, and more likely to be ignored, compared to conflicts with Chinese. While this difference might be explained by cultural similarity, which reduces conflict and makes it easier to resolve, one American attributed this difference to the fact that the American community in China is small and close-knit. American managers live in close proximity (often in the same hotel) and they socialize outside work. As a result, the Americans cannot afford to fight among themselves.

In Step 2, American and Chinese research assistants read the conflict scenarios generated in Step 1 and rated them on clarity, completeness and succinctness. Scenarios that scored high on all three dimensions were selected and the research assistants were asked to verify that each was a good example of conflict. This step was taken to identify scenarios experienced as conflict in both cultures. In most cases, research assistants agreed that these scenarios described conflict, showing that the experience of conflict is similar in at least some ways for Americans and Chinese. From these scenarios, two were selected, one generated by a Chinese manager and one generated by an American, and an intercultural version and an intracultural version of each scenario was produced, as shown below.

Intercultural and intracultural versions of the conflict scenarios used in Step 3[1]

Scenario 1

Intracultural An American manager was in a meeting and his American colleague and his colleague's employees agreed to set up a warehouse for the manager. When the manager arrived at the warehouse with four trucks and four drivers, nothing was ready. His colleague had privately convinced his employees not to do it because the manager was on temporary assignment and not important.

Intercultural An American manager was in a meeting and his Chinese colleague and his colleague's employees agreed to set up a warehouse for the manager. When the American manager arrived at the warehouse with four trucks and four drivers, nothing was ready. His Chinese colleague had privately convinced his Chinese employees not to do it because the American manager was on temporary assignment and not important.

Scenario 2

Intracultural An American manager has an American colleague who is as old as he is. The manager feels the colleague is competing with him secretly (inwardly, on the sly). The colleague stole some of the manager's ideas which they had previously chatted about. The colleague then went to their boss and said that they were his ideas. One time the colleague gave the manager an old computer reference program even though the colleague had the new version (which the manager found out later). It would have saved the manager tremendous time and effort if the colleague had given him the new version.

Intercultural An American manager has a Chinese colleague who is as old as he is. The manager feels the colleague is competing with him secretly (inwardly, on the sly). The colleague stole some of the manager's ideas which they had previously chatted about. The colleague then went to their boss and said that they were his ideas. One time the colleague gave the manager an old computer reference program even though the colleague had the new version (which the manager found out later). It would have saved the manager tremendous time and effort if the colleague had given him the new version.

In Step 3, another sample of American and Chinese managers read one of the intercultural and one of the intracultural scenarios and described how he or she would behave in that situation. Half of the Americans and half the Chinese read the intercultural version of Scenario 1 and the intracultural version of Scenario 2. The other half read the intracultural version of Scenario 1 and intercultural version of Scenario 2. The order of presentation (intercultural *vs* intracultural) was counterbalanced. This procedure has several advantages over other methods that might be used to collect descriptions of conflict management behaviour. First, asking people to respond to prepared scenarios allows us to hold the content of the conflict constant when cross-cultural and intracultural *vs* intercultural comparisons are made. Second, using two scenarios allows us to test the generalizability of our results across two situations. The interviewer recorded their responses, and afterwards asked the respondent whether the story was an example of conflict. Their responses confirmed our earlier check.

In Step 4, another sample of American and Chinese managers will be asked to read the responses to the scenarios generated in Step 3, rate how similar they are to each other, and then list the criteria they used to make these ratings. The similarity ratings will be submitted to a classical metric multidimensional scaling analysis (Young and Lewyckyj 1979) to determine the number of dimensions necessary to describe the similarities and differences among the responses.

Four MDS analyses will be performed for each scenario. One will analyse American responses to the intracultural version of the scenario; another will analyse American responses to the intercultural version; one will analyse Chinese responses to the intracultural version; and one will analyse Chinese responses to the intercultural story. In addition, the attributes used by the respondents to make their similarity ratings will be correlated with dimensions from the MDS solution, using the regression technique described by Forgas (1979). These correlations are used to interpret the meaning of the dimensions. We will interpret the American analyses, and a Chinese social scientist will interpret the Chinese results.

The dimensions identified in the American intracultural analysis will be compared to those identified in the Chinese intracultural analysis to uncover cross-cultural differences in intracultural conflict management styles. The American intracultural analysis will be compared to the American intercultural analysis, and the Chinese intracultural analysis will be compared to the Chinese intercultural analysis, to determine how intracultural conflict management differs from intercultural conflict management in each culture. The two intercultural analyses will be compared to see how intercultural conflict management differs across the two cultures. Canonical correlations (Cliff 1987) and qualitative interpretations will be used to make these comparisons.

Using these data, we can determine

(a) how strategies used by Americans to manage conflict with other Americans differ from strategies used by Chinese managers to manage conflict with other Chinese (cross-cultural differences in intracultural conflict management);
(b) whether strategies used by Americans to manage conflict with Chinese, and strategies used by Chinese to deal with Americans, are different from those used in same-culture interaction (how intracultural conflict management differs from intercultural conflict management in each culture);
(c) whether strategies used by Americans to deal with the Chinese differ from strategies that Chinese use to deal with Americans (cross-cultural differences in intercultural conflict management).

This information will contribute to a better understanding of intercultural conflict management and provide information that improves intercultural interaction in US-Chinese joint ventures.

NOTE

1 These scenarios were written for American managers. For the Chinese managers, the main actor was always Chinese.

REFERENCES

Adler, N. and Graham, J.L. 1989 'Cross-cultural interaction: The international comparison fallacy?' *Journal of International Business Studies* 20: 515–537.
Beck, J., Beck, M., Ritchie, J. and Tsui, F. 1990 'Mainland manufacturing: Bridging the cultural gap', *Exchange* Spring: 2–7.
Berry, J.W. 1980 'Introduction to methodology', in H. Triandis and R.W. Brislin (eds) *Handbook of Cross-cultural Psychology*, Boston, MA: Allyn & Bacon.
Brislin, R.W. 1980 'Translation and content analysis of oral and written materials', in H. Triandis and R.W. Brislin (eds), *Handbook of Cross-cultural Psychology*, Boston, MA: Allyn & Bacon.

Brown, P. and Levinson, S. 1978 'Universals in language usage: politeness phenomenon', in E. Goody (ed.) *Questions and politeness: Strategies in social interaction*: 56–289, Cambridge: Cambridge University Press.

Chicago Tribune 1992 'Japan firms in US make efforts to fit in', 13 January, section 4: 1.

Cliff, N. 1987 *Analyzing multivariate data*, New York: Harcourt Brace Jovanovich.

Davidson, W. 1987 'Creating and managing joint ventures in China', *California Management Review* 29: 77–94.

DeVos, G. and Ross, L. 1975 'Ethnicity: Vessel of meaning and emblem of contrast', in G. DeVos and L. Ross (eds) *Ethnic identity*: 363–390, Chicago: University of Chicago Press.

Forgas, J.P. 1979 'Multidimensional scaling: A discovery method in social psychology', in C.P. Ginsburg (ed.) *Emerging strategies in social psychology research*: 253–288, New York: Wiley.

Frijda, F.W. and Jahoda, G. 1966 'On the scope and methods of cross-cultural research', *International Journal of Psychology* 1: 110–27.

Goffman, E. 1967 *Interaction ritual: Essays on face-to-face interaction*, Garden City, NY: Doubleday.

Grub, P.D. and Lin, J.H. 1991 *Foreign direct investment in China*, New York: Quorum Books.

Gudykunst, W. and Ting-Toomey, S. 1988 *Culture and interpersonal communication*, Newbury Park, CA: Sage.

Hall, E. 1976 *Beyond culture*, New York: Doubleday.

Hendryx, S. 1986a 'The China trade: Making the deal work', *Harvard Business Review* July-August: 75–84.

Hendryx, S. 1986b 'Implementation of a technology transfer joint venture in the People's Republic of China: A management perspective', *Columbia Journal of World Business* Spring: 57–66.

Ho, D.Y.F. 1976 'On the concept of face', *American Journal of Sociology* 81: 867–884.

Hocker, J.L. and Wilmot, W.W. 1991 *Interpersonal conflict*, Dubuque, IA: W.C. Brown.

Hofstede, G. 1980 *Culture's consequences*, Beverly Hills, CA: Sage.

Jehn, K. and Weldon E. 1992 *A comparative study of managerial attitudes toward conflict in the United States and the People's Republic of China: Issues of theory and measurement*, paper presented at the Academy of Management, Las Vegas, NV.

Kilmann, R. and Thomas, K. 1977 'Developing a forced-choice measure of conflict-handling behavior: The "MODE" instrument', *Education and Psychological Measurement* 37: 309–325.

Kluckhohn, F. and Strodtbeck, F. 1961 *Variations in value orientations*, New York: Row, Peterson.

Kramer, R. 1991 'Intergroup relations and organizational dilemmas: The role of categorization processes', in B. Staw and L. Cummings (eds) *Research in Organizational Behavior* 13: 191–228, Greenwich, CT: JAI Press.

Kruskal, J.B. and Wish, M. 1978 'Multidimensional scaling', in E.M. Uslaner (ed.) *Quantitative applications in the social sciences* (Series No. 07–001), Beverly Hills, CA: Sage.

Laaksonen, O. 1988 *Management in China during and after Mao: Enterprises, government, and party*, Berlin: Walter de Gruyter.

Lee, H.O. and Rogan, R.G. 1991 'A cross-cultural comparison of organizational conflict management behaviors', *The International Journal of Conflict Management* 2: 181–199.

Li, D. 1978 *The ageless Chinese*, New York: Scribner's.

Mann, J. 1989 *Beijing Jeep: The short, unhappy romance of American business in China*, New York: Simon and Schuster.

Messick, D. and Brewer, M. 1983 'Solving social dilemmas: a review', in L. Wheeler and P. Shaver (eds) *Review of Personality and Social Psychology* 4: 11–44, Beverly Hills, CA: Sage.

Messick, D. and Mackie, D. 1989 'Intergroup relations', *Annual Review of Psychology* 40: 45–82.

Okabe, R. 1983 'Cultural assumptions of East and West: Japan and the United States', in W. Gudykunst (ed.) *Intercultural communication theory*, Beverly Hills, CA: Sage.

Parsons, T. and Shils, E. 1951 *Toward a general theory of action*, Cambridge, MA: Harvard University Press.

Peterson, R. and Shimada, J. 1978 'Sources of management problems in Japanese–American joint ventures', *Academy of Management Review*: 796–804.

Rahim, A. 1983 'A measure of styles of handling interpersonal conflict', *Academy of Management Journal* 26: 368–376.

Sillars, A. and Weisberg, J. 1987 'Conflict as a social skill', in M.E. Roloff and G.R. Miller (eds) *Interpersonal processes: New directions in communication research*: 140–171, Beverly Hills, CA: Sage.

Tajfel, H. and Turner, J. 1986 'An integrative theory of intergroup relations', in S. Worchel and W. Austin (eds) *Psychology of intergroup relations*: 7–24, Chicago: Nelson-Hall.

Ting-Toomey, S. 1985 'Toward a theory of conflict and culture', in W. Gudykunst, L. Stewart and S. Ting-Toomey (eds) *Communication, culture, and organizational processes*: 71–86, Beverly Hills, CA: Sage.

Ting-Toomey, S. 1988 'Intercultural conflict styles: A face-negotiation theory', in Y. Kim and W. Gudykunst (eds) *Theories in intercultural communication*, Newbury Park, CA: Sage.

Ting-Toomey, S., Gao, G., Trubisky, P., Yang, Z., Kim, H., Lin, S.L. and Nishida, T. 1991 'Culture, face maintenance, and styles of handling interpersonal conflict: A study in five cultures', *The International Journal of Conflict Management* 2: 275–296.

Triandis, H. 1980 'Introduction to handbook of cross-cultural psychology', in H. Triandis and R.W. Brislin (eds) *Handbook of Cross-cultural Psychology*, Boston, MA: Allyn & Bacon.

Triandis, H. 1986 'Collectivism vs. individualism: A reconceptualization of a basic concept in cross-cultural psychology', in C. Bagley and G. Berma (eds) *Personality, cognition, and values: Cross-cultural perspectives of childhood and adolescence*, London: Macmillan.

Triandis, H., Bontempo, R., Villareal, M., Asai, M. and Lucca, N. 1988 'Individualism and collectivism: Cross-cultural perspectives on self-ingroup relationships', *Journal of Personality and Social Psychology* 54: 323–338.

Trubisky, P., Ting-Toomey, S. and Lin, S.-L. 1991 'The influence of individualism–collectivism and self-monitoring on conflict styles', *International Journal of Intercultural Relations* 15: 65–84.

Waterman, A. 1984 *The psychology of individualism*, New York: Praeger.

Weldon, E. in press 'Intercultural interaction and conflict management in US–Chinese joint ventures', in S. Stewart (ed.) *Advances in Chinese Industrial Organization* 4, Greenwich, CT: JAI Press.

Wright, R. 1979 'Joint venture problems in Japan', *Columbia Journal of World Business* Spring: 25–31.

Young, F.W. and Lewyckyj, R. 1979 *ALSCAL–4: User's guide*, Chapel Hill, NC: Data Analysis and Theory Associates.

Zhang, X. 1987 'On the question of markers for the products of joint ventures in China', in R. Robinson (ed) *Foreign capital and technology in China*, New York: Praeger.

6 Linking management control and interpartner relationships with performance in US-Chinese joint ventures

Aimin Yan and Barbara Gray

ABSTRACT

This paper reports a study of the management control structures in US-China joint ventures. A conceptual framework for partner resource commitment, management control, interpartner working relationships, and venture performance is proposed. The relationships among these variables were empirically examined by using a comparative case study method and a quantitative analysis of a sample of 90 US-China joint ventures. The results of this study render strong support for the resource dependence argument concerning the determinants of management control in interorganizational alliances. It is evident that the partners' commitments of critical resources enhanced their bargaining positions in negotiations and, in turn, shaped the structure of management control they exercised in the venture. Accordingly, the pattern in which operational control over the venture is divided between the partners was found to have a significant effect on venture performance. The results also suggest that the working relationship between the partners has a profound impact on the venture's overall performance. Furthermore, the results depicted considerable differences between the American and the Chinese partners' strategic objectives. Whereas the former focused primarily on local market penetration, the latter aimed at the acquisition of advanced technology and management expertise as its foremost design.

INTRODUCTION

The Open Door Policy and economic reforms initiated in the early-1980s in China have stimulated a wealth of international business partnerships in the Chinese economy. The most recent statistics suggest that 167.5 thousand foreign enterprises have registered with and been approved by the Chinese government, half of which were operational by 1993. The cumulative actual foreign investment in these enterprises has totalled $121.6 billion. In 1993 alone, 83.3 thousand new international companies were formed in China with a total contracted capital of $110.9 billion and actual investment of $25.7 billion. These foreign enterprises contributed more than 11 per cent to 1993's national production of China and employed a work force of approximately ten million (Xu 1994). In 1994 China became the second largest country in the world (next to the US) for the absorption of direct foreign investment.

This rapid growth of co-operative arrangements in China, an overwhelming majority of which are equity joint ventures, presents a challenging opportunity to study international alliances in a new institutional context (Child 1991) and thus has caught the attention of Western management researchers. Current research, however, has limited its focus either to the macro political and economic environments in China for direct foreign investment or has only provided descriptive accounts for some individual joint ventures, typically in their initial stages. With the gradual knowledge accumulating in the West about how to do business in China and the rapid proliferation of Chinese joint ventures in the past decade, a greater interest in the implementation of joint ventures can be expected. For example, questions about how to structure and manage a joint venture in order to achieve the partners' strategic objectives are of particular concern. Little empirical research has been reported on how these joint ventures are structured and managed by the partners and how interpartner relational and structural characteristics impact the joint venture's overall effectiveness in achieving the sponsors' strategic objectives. Our research is designed to address these issues.

This chapter summarizes our findings from two studies, namely, a qualitative study of four joint ventures, and a quantitative analysis of 90 manufacturing joint ventures formed between the US and Chinese companies. The results of this study reveal a significant difference in the expectations and strategic goals of the American versus the Chinese sponsors. Whereas the American firms targeted the potential Chinese market and a profit objective, the overwhelming majority of the Chinese sponsors formed joint ventures to acquire the advanced Western technology and management expertise, as well as to pursue export opportunities for hard currency. Our findings also suggest that the contributions of critical resources by the sponsors to the partnership are the critical factor determining the level of management control they exercise in the joint venture. The management control structure was found to have a profound effect on the partners' success in achieving their strategic objectives. Moreover, the study generated strong evidence that the development and maintenance of a high quality working relationship between the partners in managing the joint venture contributed positively to the venture's performance.

In this chapter, we will first discuss the key concepts examined in this study, namely, strategic objectives, parent control, resource commitment, venture performance and interpartner relationships. Second, we will delineate the major characteristics of the joint ventures that participated in the qualitative and the quantitative studies, respectively. Third, a report will recapitulate the major results of this study. Finally, we will discuss the research findings in light of previous works on this subject matter and draw conclusions and implications.

CONCEPTUAL BACKGROUNDS

Partner strategic objectives

Joint ventures emerge as hybrid organizational forms which enable the participating firms to pursue certain strategic interests collectively while each still remains an autonomous entity. Through joint venturing, the partners achieve strategic objectives that they otherwise are not able to achieve if acting independently (Harrigan 1986). Yet, firms form joint ventures with very different expectations. Partner strategic objectives vary not only from one joint venture to another but also from one partner to another within the same alliance. Joint ventures have been used for a variety of purposes by the sponsors, e.g., for cost or risk sharing, as an alternative entry mode when wholly owned entry strategies are not possible, as a transitional form to phase out an unsuccessful wholly owned business operation, or simply for learning among the partners about each other's strategic competencies (Gray and Yan 1992).

Researchers have consistently pointed out that joint venture partners from developed countries have considerably different interests in entering alliances than those of their counterparts from developing countries, though a certain level of complementary attributes must be present between the two sets of interests. The partner from a developed country is usually seeking market expansion because of increasing saturation of the home market while the developing country partner typically expects to acquire new technology and/or to earn much needed foreign exchange. When local government is involved, the developing country partners may also be interested in creating new jobs and thus enhancing employment or in developing the local economy in particular regions.

In this study, we were able to develop a list of strategic objectives for each of the American and Chinese partners based on interviews and surveys. This inductively produced list reveals the motivations and expectations of the US and the Chinese partners respectively, in forming joint ventures. It also illustrates the potential complementarity between the two sets of objectives.

Parent control in international joint ventures

Parent control in joint ventures has been a problematic construct in the literature. First, managerial control and financial control were not always conceptually or operationally differentiated (Gray and Yan 1992). With very few exceptions (Killing 1983; Lecraw 1984), previous studies either equate equity contributions to management control or use the former as a proxy for the latter in analyses. Second, even when examining management control, inconsistent conceptualizations and measures have been used in empirical analysis, which make cross-study comparisons extremely difficult. Third, empirical results with respect to the determinants of parent control and its effects on venture performance have been inconsistent and thus highly inconclusive.

Geringer and Hebert (1989) viewed parent control in joint ventures in terms of three components: the scope of control (the areas of the joint venture's operation in which parent control is exercised), the extent of control (the degree to which the parents exercise control) and the mechanisms of control (the means by which control is imposed). In this study, we focused on the structure of managerial control exercised by the sponsoring organizations in influencing a joint venture's strategic decisions and regulating its important activities. We measured parent control on the following three key dimensions:

1 strategic control at the board of directors level;
2 operational control at the joint venture's general management level;
3 structural control imposed by the parents in forming the venture's organizational structure, processes, and operating routines.

We used the composition of the joint venture's board of directors as a measure of the strategic control each partner exercises in making important decisions for the venture. China's international joint venture law grants the venture's board of directors substantial power overseeing the venture, such as approving expansion projects, production and business programmes, the budget, distribution of profits, plans concerning manpower and pay scales, the termination of business, and the appointment of the key management personnel and their remuneration. Our case studies (Yan and Gray 1994) confirmed that the joint venture's board of directors exercised strategic, not just symbolic, control over the partnership. Operational control was reflected in the nomination of the key management personnel (general managers and deputy general managers) at the joint venture, and the extent of their authority. To assess structural control we compared the similarities of each parent's organizational structure and operational procedures to the joint venture's structure and procedures.

Partner resource commitments

Emerson (1962) argues that the dependence of one organizational unit on another gives rise to power and that dependence and power are directly but negatively related. Building on this notion, Pfeffer and Salancik (1978) suggest that the possession or control of critical resources constitutes power in interorganizational relations. In a joint venture setting, if a firm contributes a resource that its partner lacks but which is critical to the venture's success, this firm will gain power in and thus control over their partnership. Therefore, Harrigan (1986) argued that the relative bargaining power of the potential joint venture partners is determined by who brings what and how much to the venture.

In equity joint ventures the partners commit capital resources and jointly claim the ownership of the partnership. Equity joint ventures are different from other co-operative arrangements, such as marketing partnerships or technology transfer agreements, in that the latter represent pure contractual relationships in which no new, independent business entities are created. In equity joint ventures, however, the sponsors also contribute a variety of other types of resources, in addition to capital, in order to make the venture successful. Examples of such resources range from technology, management expertise, channels for raw material acquisition and output disposal (marketing), and access to government support, to business service support.

In the qualitative study we specified an array of resources, both capital and non-capital, that joint venture sponsors contributed to the partnership. We then examined the relationship between the partners' resource commitment and the level of management control they exercised. The effects of partner resource commitment on management control were then tested with the quantitative data as well.

Performance

Organizational performance has been a controversial concept because it can be examined and assessed from different stakeholders' points of view and few indicators of performance have been widely accepted. Performance evaluation becomes even more problematic in joint ventures because each participant in the partnership is likely to adopt idiosyncratic criteria. This is particularly true when the parents' strategic objectives diverge. Previous research reveals three major inconsistencies in performance assessment:

- whose perspective is used for performance measurement (that of one parent, two parents, or the joint venture's management)
- variation in performance measures, which may range from subjective judgments (e.g., partner satisfaction) to financial indicators (e.g., profitability)
- variation in performance measures used in different stages in the joint venture's development.

These inconsistencies make cross-study comparisons and generalizations about joint venture performance particularly problematic.

In this study, we adopted a multidimensional approach to performance and incorporated the perspectives of multiple players in the partnership.

We used each partner's assessment of the extent to which it had achieved its founding objectives as a measure of performance. This measurement is justifiable in that it reflects both partners' assessment regardless of the possible divergence between their expectations. Because most of the joint ventures in this study were still in the developmental stage, comparisons based on financial performance measures were not relevant.

Interpartner relationship

The interpartner relationship refers to the quality of co-operation and trust between the partners while co-managing the joint venture. Transaction cost theory suggests that since it is virtually impossible to specify all future contingencies at the time of drawing up a contract for interorganizational partnerships, mutual adjustment between the partners in executing the contract, as an informal control mechanism, should be installed to attenuate the costs potentially caused by opportunism engaged in by the partners (Williamson 1975). Development of a trustworthy interpartner relationship has been argued to be the most effective control mechanism in interorganizational alliances (Konig and van Wijk 1991; Faulkner 1994). Changing environmental circumstances (such as government policies, currency fluctuations, and market demands) as well as cross-cultural differences and dissimilar goals generate frequent conflicts between the partners. Therefore, the establishment of a positive interpartner working relationship becomes critical to the venture's operation. Interpartner co-operation, mutual adjustments, and renegotiations represent an inevitable solution to address unexpected challenges over time. As Davidson (1982) notes: 'Even more important than formal arbitration procedures, perhaps, is the nature of the relationship with the partner. A positive relationship that extends beyond legal, contractual commitments is the principal goal of any joint venture agreement' (Davidson 1982: 46). Previous research suggests that the partners' mutual commitment and interpartner trust are among the critical factors in international joint ventures. Bivens and Lovel (1966) note that 'the durability of a joint venture arrangement is enhanced when there is a spirit of give-and-take between local and foreign partners'; and Harrigan (1986) has observed that 'Alliances fail because operating managers do not make them work, not because contracts are poorly written'.

In this study, we argue that when the partners develop a high degree of consensus on the joint venture's mission, strategy and operating procedures, less co-ordination is needed. In this way, the overall efficiency of the venture can be enhanced. In addition, joint ventures with a trusting relationship between the partners are able to handle the inevitable conflicts better than those in which no interpartner trust is developed. In this study, data on the quality of the interpartner relationship were collected both in the interviews and in the surveys. Thus,

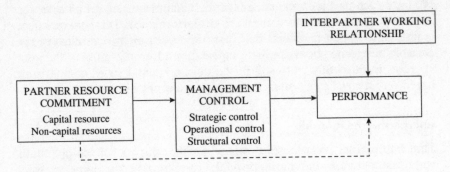

Figure 6.1 Relationships between partner resource commitment, control, interpartner relationship and performance in joint ventures

we were able to explore the effect of this relationship on venture performance.

Thus far we have discussed the major constructs and the relationships among them that we set forth to investigate. A conceptual framework that summarizes the above discussion and which guided our empirical investigation is offered in Figure 6.1. In the next section, we will describe our research methods and the sample of joint ventures we studied.

METHODS AND THE SAMPLE

The qualitative study

We collected both qualitative and quantitative data about US-Chinese joint ventures. In the qualitative study, we investigated four US manufacturing joint ventures in China in great depth. We limited our study to manufacturing partnerships because about 70 per cent of US joint ventures in China operate in manufacturing sectors (US-China Business Council 1990). Among these four ventures, one is a manufacturer of electronic office equipment and peripherals, one produces industrial control equipment, one manufactures a variety of personal hygiene products, and one is a pharmaceutical manufacturer. The key characteristics of the four joint ventures are summarized in Table 6.1.

We collected qualitative data through interviews and from archives. In-depth interviews were conducted with executives of both the US and Chinese partners and the managers of the joint ventures following a pre-designed interview protocol. Most of our informants (see Table 6.2) were personally involved in the initial negotiations for the joint venture or were members of the venture's management team in its early stages. All the interviews were conducted by the authors during the eight months between May 1991 and January 1992. In addition, archival data were collected for each partnership, including the highlights of the joint venture contracts, the joint venture's and the parents' organizational charts, corporate annual reports, published case descriptions and newspaper and magazine reports about the partnership.

The quantitative study

Data collection for quantitative analysis was carried out through a 12-page questionnaire prepared in both the English and the Chinese languages. The Chinese version of the questionnaire was prepared by the first author and back-translations were performed by three other bilingual scholars. The Chinese version of the questionnaire was mailed to the Chinese general manager or deputy general manager of the joint venture

Table 6.1 Major characteristics of the joint ventures in the qualitative study

Joint venture	OfficeAid	IndusCon	Daily Product	BioTech Ltd
Product	Electronic office equipment	Industrial process control	Personal hygiene products	Pharmaceuticals
Length of negotiation (years)	4	3	2	3
Formation	1987	1982	1981	1982
Total investment ($ million)	30	10	2.85	10
Equity share (% US/PRC)	51/49	49/51	50/50	50/50
Duration (years)	30	20	20	15
Product market	Mainly local; small % for export	Local, import substitution	50% for export	Mainly local; small % for export
Parents' objectives	US • Profit • Market share • Low-cost sourcing PRC • Technology and management • Export for ForEx	US • Business growth • Market penetration • Profit PRC • Import substitution • Manufacturing technology • Upgrade suppliers' technology	US • Learn how to do business in China • Establish credibility • Profit • Business expansion PRC • Profit • Export for ForEx • Technology • Growth	US • Market • Profit PRC • Technology • Learn management expertise • Business expansion

Table 6.2 Sources of data for the qualitative study

Joint venture	Interviewees
OfficeAid	Manager for business strategy of the US parent, member of the joint venture's board of directors, former head negotiator of the US team, and the first general manager of the joint venture
	Chairman of the board and general manager of the Chinese parent firm
	Deputy general manager of the joint venture, member of the joint venture's board of directors, former executive general manager and head negotiator of the Chinese partner
	Two department managers of the joint venture, one for marketing who was on the Chinese negotiation team and the other for quality control
IndusCon	Directing manager for international joint ventures of the US parent, member of the joint venture's board of directors, and former deputy general manager of the joint venture
	Deputy general manager of the joint venture, member of the joint venture's board of directors, former member of the Chinese negotiation team
	Manager of marketing of the joint venture
Daily Product	Regional general manager for China operation of the US parent, vice chairman of the joint venture's board of directors, one of the two members of the former US negotiation team, former second general manager of the joint venture
BioTech Ltd	Director of finance for the Asia-Pacific region of the US parent, and active participant in the joint venture negotiations
	Vice president of the joint venture, former member of the Chinese negotiation team
	Director for general administration of the joint venture

whereas the English version was sent to the American general manager or deputy general manager. The researchers received support in administering the questionnaire from the business school of a Chinese university and the municipal governments of several Chinese cities in which a large number of the targeted joint ventures were located.

Survey responses Responses were obtained from the executives of 96 US-China manufacturing joint ventures (response rate of 34.41 per cent). Of these 90 produced usable results. For 68 ventures (75.6 per cent of the sample), the respondents were top executives (the venture's chairman, president, general manager, or deputy general manager). For 13 ventures (14.4 per cent), the respondents were assistant general managers or chief staff members. For the remaining 9 ventures (10.0 per cent), a lower level manager or the general manager's secretary responded to the questionnaire.

From 27 joint ventures in the sample, two responses to the questionnaire were generated, typically, one from the Chinese general manager, the other from the expatriate general manager. Respondents from 55 joint ventures (61.1 per cent) had personally participated in the initial negotiations that led to the formation of the partnership.

Sample representativeness The 90 joint ventures in the sample were formed between 1981 and 1992 and are geographically located in 17 Chinese provinces. While all joint ventures in the sample are manufacturing or engineering partnerships, they fall into 12 industrial sectors (see Table 6.3). The majority of the joint ventures (71 per cent) operated within five industrial sectors: chemical materials or products, electronic components or equipment, light industry manufacturing, food processing and agricultural products, and miscellaneous industrial equipment.

Contractual characteristics The joint ventures in the sample varied considerably with respect to their contractual characteristics. They were formed between February 1982 and May 1992. The sample contains both very small and very large companies ($100,000 to $232,000,000 investments). They include a wide range of ownership structures (from 16 per cent to 90 per cent US ownership). Contract length varied from 10 to 50 years. (See Table 6.4 for descriptive statistics on the sample.)

In summary, this cross-sectional sample represents a wide range of US manufacturing joint ventures in China with respect to the industries represented, the years of formation, the geographical locations in China, the size of the partnerships, and the ownership structure between the foreign and the local partners. Thus, we are optimistic about the potential

Table 6.3 Industrial sectors represented in the sample*

Industry sector	No. of joint ventures	%
Chemicals	16	17.78
Electronics	14	16.56
Miscellaneous light industry	13	14.44
Food and agriculture	10	11.11
Miscellaneous industrial equipment	10	11.11
Metals	6	6.67
Medical	5	5.56
Building materials	5	5.56
Telecommunications	4	4.44
Engineering services	3	3.33
Resources	3	3.33
Transportation	1	1.11
Total	90	100.00

Note: *The categories are those suggested by the US-China Business Council (1990)

Table 6.4 Summary statistics for quantitative sample

Characteristics	Range	Mean	SD
Formation period	February 1982–May 1992		
Average age	1–10 years	5.66	2.14
Total investment	$10–$232.00 million	6.18	8.88
US ownership	16%–90%	43.85	14.66
Length of contract	10–50 years	17.00	6.70

generalizability of our research results, which are reported in the following section.

RESEARCH RESULTS

In this section we report the key results of this study. First we present some descriptive results regarding the joint venture negotiation, the pre-venture relationship between the partners, and partner strategic objectives. Thereafter we report our findings, based on our analysis of both the qualitative and the quantitative data, with respect to the relationships between partner resource contributions, management control structure, the inter-partner relationship, and venture performance, as depicted in Figure 6.1.

Negotiation

Time spent for negotiation Previous observers have pointed out that business negotiations with Asian country partners, particularly those from China or Japan, are significantly longer than most Western executives anticipate. Our data show that the average length of time that elapsed between the first contact among the partners and closing the deal (signified by signing the joint venture contract) ranged between two and 84 months with an average of 16.3 months (SD = 13.8). Generally, the larger the total investment, the longer the negotiation. This is understandable since the levels of complexity and financial risk increase exponentially as the venture's potential scale of operations increases. The fact that negotiations for a joint venture take an average of more than a year should not be a surprise given the geographical distance, radical differences in cultures, languages and political systems, and the lack of knowledge about international trade and business on the part of the Chinese, coupled with the lack of understanding of the Chinese political and bureaucratic systems on the part of the Americans. For the partnerships formed in the earlier years, high levels of political risks, mutual scepticism about intentions, the bureaucratic red tape, general lack of experience of the Chinese government as a match maker, and distrust between the would-be partners characterized most joint venture negotiations. For example, when the

American parent of OfficeAid, a high-technology electronic office equipment manufacturer, first contacted the central government in Beijing for a Chinese partner, it was matched with a shipyard in Wuhan, a city in an inner Chinese province. The dream of a partnership predictably dissipated because the local shipyard neither had any knowledge of international joint ventures nor had it produced anything electronic. Months had been wasted before the US company was eventually matched with a 'negotiable' local partner.

Means of first contact The most frequent means of initial contact among the potential joint venture partners included direct contacts with each other, arrangements made by the various agencies of the Chinese government, or matches arranged or mediated by third party brokers. Both our interview and survey data suggest that the use of government agencies for selecting a local partner was much more common for older joint ventures than for those that were formed more recently. As a matter of fact, all four joint ventures in our case studies were formed with the assistance of Chinese government agencies in selecting the local partner. Since 1987, partners were more frequently matched by third party brokers or by direct contact among themselves. While Chinese-Americans or various business agencies in Hong Kong have played a major role in bridging the gap between the US and the Chinese partners, in quite a few cases, the US partners in established joint ventures in China played third party roles in assisting newcomers to find a local Chinese partner. Other means of contact were also reported in this study, albeit they were used much less frequently. These included accidental meetings between executives, and connection through personal contacts, e.g., family relatives. Table 6.5 summarizes the details on the means of contact between partners.

Pre-venture relationship

Partners in more than half of the joint ventures in the quantitative sample (56.3 per cent) had no business relationships with each other prior to the

Table 6.5 Means of first contact between partners

Means of first contact	Frequency of use	%
Direct contact between partners	44	42.72
Via Chinese government	31	30.10
Via broker/middleman	23	22.33
Other	5	4.85
Total	103*	100.00

Note: *The total number exceeds 90, because several joint ventures reportedly used more than one means of contact joint venture negotiations. In three out of the four joint ventures in the qualitative study, the partners were strangers before the negotiations started and the relationship was initiated by making cold calls. This result should be expected because the adoption of the Open Door Policy in China is a matter of only a little more than a decade old. Before 1978, China very much represented a closed economic system and maintained few relationships with the Western business world. Nevertheless, 43.7 per cent of the participating joint ventures in this study were built on prior business relationships of various types between the partners, ranging from previous buyer-seller relationships to some sort of contractual partnerships, as indicated in Table 6.6. A majority of these partnerships were established in recent years.

Strategic objectives of the partners

Drawing on our case studies, as well as previous research on joint ventures, we compiled a comprehensive list of strategic objectives of potential joint venture sponsors. We provided this list in the questionnaire that we used to solicit quantitative data. Each respondent was asked to choose a maximum of four items on the list that best described the strategic expectations of each partner. These strategic objectives are summarized in Table 6.7 for the American and the Chinese partners, respectively.

The two dominant objectives for American firms included earning a profit and penetrating business markets in China. The leading strategic objective of the Chinese partner, however, was to acquire or to learn advanced Western technology. Earning a profit was the second most important goal. Our case studies, however, suggest that, until very recently, profitability was a goal much less important than technology to the Chinese partner. Acquisition of Western management expertise and promotion of export were also important objectives of the Chinese partners. Overall, the two sets of strategic objectives show more differences than similarities. However, because both partners regarded profitability as one of the most important goals, this convergence of strategic interests between the partners may have provided sufficient common ground for initial success. Moreover, a high level of complementarity between the two sets of partner objectives is also evident. The objectives of market penetration and business growth pursued by the US partner and the learning-oriented goals, i.e., acquisition of Western technology and management expertise, of the Chinese partner are in opposition but can be achieved simultaneously. As our interviewee at IndusCon's US parent noted, 'The joint venture represents a win-win situation. We have the technology and certain know-how. The Chinese partner knows how to make things happen in China. You put the two together right, it works.'

However, potential conflict between the partners' interests can also be

Table 6.6 Pre-venture relationships between partners

Pre-venture relationship	No. of joint ventures	%
No relationship	54	56.25
Buyer-seller relationships	14	14.58
Marketing agreement	6	6.25
Technology licensing agreement	3	3.13
R&D partnership	7	7.29
Other	12	12.50
Total	96*	100.00

Note: *The total number exceeds 90, because some joint ventures reported more than one type of pre-venture relationship between the partners

Table 6.7 Strategic objectives of partners

Strategic objectives of US partners	Frequency	%
Earn a profit in China	79	87.78
Penetrate the Chinese market	73	81.11
Pursue business growth	41	45.56
Develop a base for low cost sourcing	40	44.44
Establish presence in China	32	35.56
Build credibility and reputation	26	28.89
Establish a base to access Asia market	23	25.56
Learn how to do business in China	9	10.00
Others	2	2.22
Strategic objectives of Chinese partners	*Frequency*	*%*
Acquire/learn advanced technology	87	96.67
Earn a profit	70	77.78
Acquire/learn management expertise	61	67.78
Earn foreign exchange through export	47	52.22
Substitute import by manufacturing locally	42	46.67
Pursue business growth	23	25.56
Develop technology for Chinese suppliers/users	15	16.67
Others	4	4.44

observed between the two sets of objectives. For example, conflicts occurred in three of the four joint ventures in our qualitative study when the US partner was primarily interested in the local Chinese market (the second most important objective for the US partner) while the Chinese partner expected the joint venture to be a major vehicle for export (the fourth most important objective for the Chinese partner). Our data from these joint ventures suggest that mutual compromise between the partners served as a typical solution to such a conflict. A practical but viable strategy observed across cases was a joint decision between the partners that divided the joint venture's products into those designated for the Chinese market and those for export. Some Chinese sponsors perceived that their US partner was reluctant to export the venture's product because of the latter's concerns about potential internal competition within its own international networks. Some US firms, however, had to persuade their Chinese partners that the joint venture's products manufactured in China were not technologically competitive for global markets. Conflicts in partners' objectives could also occur in joint ventures whose US partner wanted a quick payback for investment whereas the local partner preferred to reinvest profits in the partnership.

Resource commitment and management control

Our in-depth case studies (Yan and Gray 1994) identified two categories of resources that joint venture partners contribute to the partnership: capital resource (equity investment) and non-capital resources, including technology, management expertise, local knowledge, raw material procurement channels, product distribution and marketing channels, and global service support. We saw a consistent, complementary pattern in both the qualitative and the quantitative studies with respect to the types of non-capital resource committed by the partners. Predictably, the US firms contributed more than their local partners in technology (product design, manufacturing know-how, and special equipment) and global support (technical, marketing, and maintenance services), while the Chinese partners contributed in the areas of knowledge about and skills for dealing with the local government and other institutional infrastructures.

One of the major objectives of this study was to investigate the relationship between the partners' resource commitment and the level of management control they exercise in the joint venture. Both our case studies and statistical analysis of the survey data suggest that there is a positive relationship between the two variables. Table 6.8 shows the relative levels of partner's resource commitment (both in capital and non-capital resources) and the extent of management control they exercised for each of the four case studies. The qualitative data reveal a consistent, positive relationship between resource commitment and the exercise of control. The quantitative data further confirmed the qualitative results (see Table 6.9). Capital resource commitment and two out of the three management control variables (strategic control and operational control, respectively) are positively correlated. The correlation between non-capital resource commitment and operational control and structural control, respectively, are also significant.

These results suggest that the contribution of capital resources by a partner enhances its management control over the venture at both the strategic level and the daily operational level. In other words, the more financial equity a parent company commits to the joint venture, in comparison with its partner, the more likely that this partner will exercise more control in making important strategic decisions for the venture and in

Table 6.8 Resource commitment, management control and performance in the qualitative study

Variables		OfficeAid		IndusCon		Daily Product		BioTech Ltd	
		US	China	US	China	US	China	US	China
Relative resource commitment	Capital (%)	51	49	49	51	50	50	50	50
	Non-capital	Higher	Lower	Equal		Higher	Lower	Approximately equal	
	Overall	Higher	Lower	Approximately equal		Higher	Lower	Approximately equal	
Management control	Strategic	Equal		Slightly lower	Slightly higher	Equal		Equal	
	Operational	Higher	Lower	Approximately equal		Higher	Lower	Slightly lower	Slightly higher
	Structural	Higher	Lower	Approximately equal		Higher	Lower	Approximately equal	
	Overall	Higher	Lower	Approximately equal		Higher	Lower	Approximately equal	
Venture performance		High	Low	High	High	High	High	High	High

Table 6.9 Descriptive statistics and Pearson Product-Moment Correlations (n = 90)

	Mean	SD	1	2	3	4	5	6	7
1 Capital resource commitment	1.07	1.17							
2 Non-capital resource commitment	1.22	1.37	.0703						
3 Strategic control	.82	.39	.6043**	.1673					
4 Operational control	1.43	1.23	.2747**	.3154**	.4546**				
5 Structural control	1.45	1.14	-.0278	.2113*	.2512*	.4679**			
6 Quality of working relationship	4.49	.96	.1994	-.0248	.1347	-.1792	-.3020**		
7 Pattern of performance	1.10	.44	.0396	.1220	.0093	.2859**	.0602	-.1766	
8 Overall performance	4.63	1.22	-.0410	.1566	.1125	-.0149	.0097	.4784**	-.1239

Note: * p < .05
      ** p < .01

running the venture's routine businesses. Similarly, the partners' commitment of non-capital resources also affects the level of management control they exercise over the venture's routine operation and its operational structure and processes. Overall, the structure of management control exercised by the parents depends on the pattern in which they commit critical resources – both capital and non-capital resources – to the joint venture.

Management control and performance

We were especially interested in the structure of management control exercised by the parents. Because power and control are associated with social relationships and thus are necessarily relative concepts, we examined parent control in joint ventures on an interpartner comparative basis. For example, for each joint venture in the case study, we were able to determine whether management control was shared relatively equally between the partners or exercised in an unbalanced, one-parent dominant pattern. Similarly, we also compared the extent to which each partner had achieved its strategic objectives. When both partners to a joint venture had achieved their objectives to a similar extent, we characterized the venture as having a balanced performance. Otherwise, when one partner had achieved its founding objectives while the other had not, the joint venture's performance was considered unbalanced.

Our qualitative study suggests that in two of the four joint ventures the parents exercised an approximately equal level of control, while in the other two ventures one partner exerted a higher level of management control than the other partner (see Table 6.8). With respect to performance, balanced performance was observed in three of the four ventures (see the last row of Table 6.8). For three of the four joint ventures (OfficeAid, IndusCon, and BioTech), a consistent and positive relationship is evident between the structure of management control and the pattern of performance. That is, a relatively balanced structure of control was associated with a balanced pattern of performance (high for both partners in IndusCon and BioTech) whereas an unbalanced management control was associated with an unbalanced performance (high for one partner while low for the other in OfficeAid). Only Daily Product does not fit this pattern of a positive relationship between control and performance. In Daily Product, management control was unequally shared between the parents, but performance was balanced, i.e., both partners achieved their most important objectives. A possible explanation for this anomaly can be derived from the effect of the interpartner relationship, which is described in the next section. The management control-performance relationship was further investigated in the quantitative study. Research results reconfirmed the relationship between operational control and the venture performance. This suggests that the more control a parent exercises, in comparison to the other partner, over the joint venture's routine operations, the greater the extent to which this parent is able to achieve its strategic objectives (see Table 6.9).

Partners' working relationship and overall performance

Further examination of the qualitative data for Daily Product suggested a critical factor that may have accounted for the relationship between control and performance, that is, the positive quality of the interpartner working relationship. The high level of trust and superior working relationship between the partners at Daily Product may have exerted a positive and direct effect on the venture's performance, which we will pick up in the next section.

To test this in our quantitative study, we correlated the quality of the partners' working relationship with an indicator of the venture's overall performance. This measure of performance was based on the joint venture's overall effectiveness in achieving both of its parents' strategic objectives. The relationship between the quality of the partners' working relationship and the venture's overall performance received strong support in both correlation analysis (see Table 6.9) and multi-regression analysis (R-square = .2060, Standardized Beta = .4663, $p < .01$). Thus, the quality of the working relationship among the partners can offset the negative effects of unbalanced control on performance.

Overall results

Overall, our empirical analyses rendered strong support for the model we proposed in Figure 1 regarding the relationships among the key variables. A series of multivariate analysis of variances were conducted to examine the relationships between partner resource commitment, management control, and performance at an aggregated level by treating each construct as a set of subvariables. The results support the proposed relationship between the partners' commitment of critical resources and the management control they exercise in the venture and the relationship between management control and performance. As we expected, no direct relationship was found between partner resource commitment and performance. As reported above, the positive effect of the interpartner working relationship on the venture's overall performance was supported by the multi-regression analysis. These overall results are summarized in Figure 6.2.

DISCUSSION AND CONCLUSIONS

This study suggests that the partners in the US-China joint ventures have very different objectives, though a high level of complementarity may exist between the partners' strategic expectations. However, our data show an increasing interest among the Chinese partners in monetary gains as well

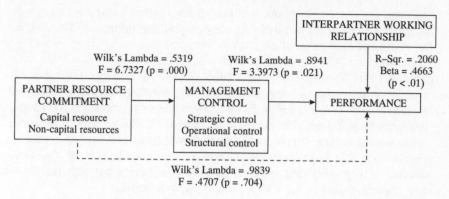

Figure 6.2 Results of multivariate analysis of the overall model

as in their quasi-political objectives, such as acquisition of high technology. This suggests that there may be greater convergence between the US and Chinese partners' objectives in the future. We predict that this tendency will continue as a result of the transition of China's economy towards a free market.

Our results regarding the relationship between partner resource commitment and management control suggest that capital investment or ownership is not the only vehicle through which the partners gain control. Non-capital resource contributions by the partners in a variety of expertise, skills, and capabilities also serve as important leverage tools in shaping the venture's control structure. While previous researchers (e.g., Harrigan 1986) observed that many firms strive for at least a symbolic majority of ownership in order to win control over the venture's routine operation, our results imply that potential joint venture partners need not depend solely on capital investment to gain management control. Our results corroborate previous findings that joint venture sponsors can gain management control disproportionate to their ownership (Killing 1983) through the input of non-capital resources.

The strong relationship between operational control and performance points to the potential for competition between the partners in co-managing the joint venture. In the literature, previous researchers tended to focus on the co-operative aspect of joint ventures and other forms of interorganizational arrangement while the potential competition between the partners has not received sufficient attention (Kogut 1989; Hamel *et al.* 1989). Our findings suggest that gaining management control enables a partner to manipulate the venture's operation to satisfy its own strategic interests. This result also implies that in order to assure the achievement of their goals, the partners should maintain an appropriate level of influence on the joint venture's operational decision making. By no means, however, are we encouraging potential joint venture partners to engage in power struggles for control. We suggest just the opposite. Our results regarding the strong positive linkage between the interpartner working relationship and the venture's overall performance suggest that trust and consensus building between the partners can greatly enhance the achievement of both partners' objectives even if control is disproportionately allocated. A co-operative and trustworthy relationship between the sponsors helps to gain shared understanding between them, to achieve smooth co-ordination among the venture's operational functions, and to create a context in which both partners' objectives are achieved. It seems only reasonable to predict that joint ventures in which both partners feel that their objectives are being met are most likely to endure.

This research investigated several key issues in managing and structuring international joint ventures in China. It provides empirical evidence that partner resource commitment to the joint venture is a key determinant of the structure of management control exercised by the parent firms. The research also offers support for the impact of management control structure and the interpartner working relationship on venture performance. Since previous research on parent control and interpartner relationships in Chinese joint ventures has been lacking, this study contributes to our understanding of the power interdependencies as well as the potential for competitive forces between the partners. Of particular interest for future research is how these interdependencies will change over time as the Chinese gain technological know-how and foreign investors gain experience of operating in China.

REFERENCES

Bivens, K.K. and Lovel, E.B. 1966 *Joint ventures with foreign partners*, New York: National Industrial Conference Board.

Child, J. 1991 *Managerial adaptation in reforming economies: the case of joint ventures*, paper presented at the Academy of Management Meeting, Miami Beach, FA.

Davidson, W.H. 1982 *Global strategic management*, New York: John Wiley & Sons.

Emerson, R. 1962 'Power-dependence relations', *American Sociological Review* 27: 31–41.

Faulkner, D. 1994 'The central importance of partner attitudes to the success of strategic alliances', paper presented at the British Academy of Management Meeting, September, Lancaster.

Geringer, J.M., and Hebert, L. 1989 'Control and performance of international joint ventures', *Journal of International Business Studies* Summer: 235–254.

Gray, B., and Yan, A. 1992 'A negotiations model of joint venture formation, structure and performance: implications for global management', in S.B. Prasad (ed.) *Advances in International Comparative Management* 7: 41–75, Greenwich, CT: JAI Press.

Hamel, G., Doz, Y. and Prahalad, C.K. 1989 'Collaborate with your competitors and win', *Harvard Business Review* January: 133–139.

Harrigan, K.R. 1986 *Managing for joint venture success*, Lexington, MA: Lexington Books.

Killing, J.P. 1983 *Strategies for joint venture success*, New York: Praeger.

Koenig, C., and van Wijk, G. 1991 'Interfirm alliances: the role of trust', in R.A. Thietart and J. Thepob (eds) *Microeconomic contribution to strategic management* Ch. 9: 1–16. North-Holland Elsevier: Advanced Series in Management.

Kogut, B. 1989 'The stability of joint ventures: reciprocity and competitive rivalry', *Journal of Industrial Economics* 2: 183–198.

Lecraw, D.J. 1984 'Bargaining power, ownership, and profitability of transnational corporations in developing countries', *Journal of International Business Studies* Spring/Summer: 27–43.

Pfeffer, J., and Salancik, G.B. 1978 *The external control of organizations*, New York: Harper and Row.

The US-China Business Council 1990 *Special report on US investment in China*, Washington, DC: China Business Forum.

Williamson, O.E. 1975 *Markets and hierarchies: analysis and antitrust implications*, New York: Free Press.

Xu, Y. 1994 'Sanzi qiye: Zhongguo jingji xin sheng zhang dian' (Foreign investment firms: The new growth spots in China's economy), *China Daily* 5 April: 2.

Yan, A., and Gray, B. 1994 'Bargaining power, management control, and performance in United States-China joint ventures: A comparative case study', *Academy of Management Journal* 37 (6): 1478–1517.

7 The management process of developing a Sino-British joint venture

Roy Rimington

ABSTRACT

This paper examines the management process of developing a Sino-British joint venture of which its UK partner – GPT Limited – is the UK's largest telecommunications equipment supplier. During the 1980s a need was identified to form a joint venture with a selected local partner, to serve as a vehicle for entering into the high potential Chinese marketplace. Key technology transfer elements are discussed including development of the organization along Western approaches; effective communication and performance measurement; training and development of human resources; development of effective Quality Management Systems; localization of material supply; and solutions to problems arising in the development of a joint venture. Additionally, key factors from the conception stage were the creation of an atmosphere of trust between partners and adherence to project time scales. The joint venture is now poised to enter the Chinese marketplace in earnest, and plans have been established to triple production, while at the same time moving the technology transfer mechanism to a higher stage.

HISTORY AND RATIONALE OF THE JOINT VENTURE

The joint venture to which this case study relates is called the Shanghai International Digital Telephone Equipment Co. Ltd (SIDTEC). The company was established in 1989, with the ownership being UK and Chinese. The UK partner is called GPT Limited. Prior to 1989, GPT had some limited success in distributing its products to China, but it recognized that a vehicle for increasing distribution was to form a joint venture and the location chosen was Shanghai. A partnership was formed between GPT Limited who would provide the technology, technical assistance and training; a state enterprise already established in telecommunications known as Factory 520, who would provide the factory with initial personnel and some equipment; and the China International Trust and Investment Corporation (CITIC), which would provide the Chinese equity. A loan-aid package was provided by the British government and the technology transfer stages were monitored by representatives from the Overseas Development Agency. The steps in the formation of the alliance are shown chronologically in Table 7.1.

Table 7.1 Development of events in the alliance

Date	Development
Up to 1989	GEC/Plessey Telecommunications having limited success in Chinese marketplace
1989	GPT Limited formed from GEC and Plessey Telecommunications
1989	Joint venture alliance formed between GPT Limited and Chinese partner
1990	First GPT Limited personnel go to China – general manager and a project manager
1991	Operation starts up with finished product shipped from the UK and tested in China (technology transfer stage 1)
1991	Chinese deputy general manager visits UK for six week training period
1992	Quality management systems to ISO 9002 commence development
1992	Sub-assemblies shipped from the UK for build up and test in China (technology transfer stage 2)
1992	Components only shipped from UK for product assembly and test in China (technology transfer stage 3)
1993	Programme to source materials locally within China and neighbouring countries commences
1993	ISO 9002 approval awarded by the Shanghai Quality Control Association
1993	ISO 9002 Approval awarded by the British Standards Institute
1994	First joint UK-Chinese board of directors meeting takes place in the UK
1994	Achievement award presented by the China Foreign Investment Enterprises Association
1995	Planned move to new factory in the Pudong Development Zone of Shanghai

The opportunities facing the joint venture are enormous within the rapidly developing telecommunications marketplace of China. By 1992, there were 32 million installed telephone lines, putting China in the top ten in the world in terms of lineage. Although the penetration is very small, with only 1.6 phones per 100 people, this is set to rise to 5 phones per 100 by the year 2000 and the associated lineage will rise from 32 million to 96 million by the turn of the century.

If China hits its target it will account for around 20 per cent of the world demand for telecommunications equipment by the year 2000. Other estimates have put this figure up to 30 per cent. Either way, that would make China a substantially bigger market than America or Germany and at least twice as big as Japan. In today's money, the Chinese would be

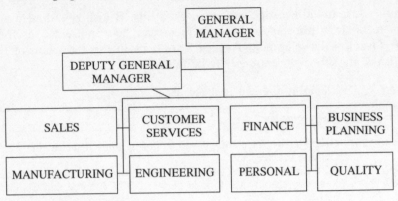

Figure 7.1 Organizational layout

spending between $30 billion and $75 billion on telecommunications equipment.

CHARACTERISTICS OF THE JOINT VENTURE

The products manufactured by the joint venture are private telecommunication switching systems and associated termination equipment, including end-user phones. The systems are called integrated services digital exchange (iSDX) which have already established a global marketplace reputation for high reliability from the UK production source. Products manufactured by the joint venture are distributed throughout China and customers include railways, mining, universities, car plants, government authorities' bureaux and hotels. Markets in the Pacific Rim countries are now being targeted.

Currently, the workforce numbers 250, with ages ranging mainly between 25 and 35. Many of the workforce have university education and in some cases have several degrees. This fertile combination of youth and intelligence provides an atmosphere of willingness to learn which contributed to a rapid passage through the stages of technology transfer.

The management is predominantly Chinese, but the general manager and a project manager are British. The organizational layout is shown in Figure 7.1 and follows a Western form of structure. Most of the managers have visited the UK for training.

The seven key elements shown in Figure 7.2 provided the framework of management objectives for the joint venture. For ease of recall, they may be termed the 'Seven Cs'.

- Control: To produce products in a controlled manner in a system based on ISO 9000 series Quality Management Standard which meets the requirements of cost-effective manufacturing and customer specifications.

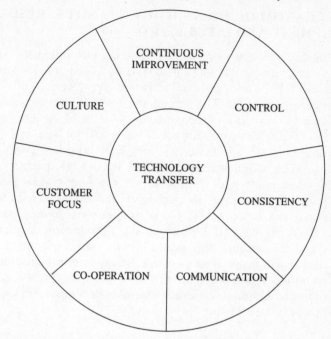

Figure 7.2 Model of the key elements in technology transfer

- Consistency: To produce products which do not vary from the initial approved sample in form, fit, function and cosmetic appearance.
- Communication: To ensure that effective channels of communication are established with external support, supply and associated functions. To carry out regular team briefings and management presentations.
- Co-operation: To ensure that a team spirit and understanding exists which extends throughout the organization(s) in the UK and China.
- Customer focus: To ensure that people fully understand the requirements of the next stage customer and other customers in the supply chain.
- Culture: To ensure that personnel involved in the establishment of the joint venture have an appreciation of the other partners' cultural background including language, and codes of behaviour.
- Continuous improvement: To ensure that a continuous improvement philosophy is pursued in products, processes and services to the best level achievable. By the monitoring and feedback by small action groups or formal reviews.

These elements contributed to a bonding process between the UK and Chinese partners and recognition of mutual requirements.

THE MECHANISM OF TECHNOLOGY TRANSFER, RESOURCE DEVELOPMENT AND INTERACTION

Initially, finished products were shipped from the UK and finally tested in the Shanghai factory. At this stage, final systems test equipment was established, and SIDTEC's test personnel trained under the guidance of GPT's test development manager. The second stage was to ship sub-assemblies – semi knocked down (SKD) components – for build up into complete systems. The third stage was to ship components only for hand and machine assembly and build up into systems – completely knocked down (CKD) components. With kitted material supplied by the UK partner, release inspection takes place and Certificates of Conformity are generated. Particular attention is given to packaging and customs requirements. At stages two and three, SIDTEC's personnel were trained under the guidance of a team from GPT which included production engineers, test engineers and the author, who assisted in the development of quality systems. The fourth stage is to purchase locally within China or neighbouring countries. Additionally at this final stage component assembly would progress to automatic onsertion assembly of components on printed circuit boards (Surface Mount Technology).

Training and development of human resources

At each stage of the technology transfer, personnel were sent from the UK to give training to SIDTEC personnel, as well as installation and commissioning of major pieces of production equipment. Additionally, transfer of documentation and software occurred with associated training. Selected SIDTEC personnel and customers of SIDTEC also visited the UK for training.

The training course material covers:

- Product appreciation
- Installation and servicing
- Software generation and control
- Manufacturing and test methods
- Management techniques
- Quality appreciation and ISO 9000
- Conducting internal and external audits
- Procedure and specification writing
- Customer focus.

SIDTEC has the facility for customer and installation training which gives courses on theory as well as hands-on product training.

Two important stages of training took place prior to build up of SKD Components (Technology Transfer Stage 2):

1 The Chinese deputy general manager was sent to visit the UK operation

for appreciation of product manufacturing, control systems and most importantly Quality Management Systems, including ISO 9000 series. Also during his training, process control was covered including Statistical Process Control using interactive video teaching methods.

2 The core group of personnel from the UK, mainly engineers numbering about six, including the author, undertook a 30-hour intensive course in Chinese language and cultural appreciation.

These two stages were intended to show a top level commitment to quality and standards to aim for, as demonstrated in the UK partner company, and for personnel who would be deployed to the joint venture for short periods assisting with the technology transfer stages to be adequately prepared in what might otherwise be a strange environment.

Communications and performance measurement

Effective communication links are now established between SIDTEC (Shanghai) and GPT (UK) by means of a dedicated project management team within GPT (UK) which provides on-going support to the joint venture. On a quarterly basis the board of directors (UK/Chinese) meet to review achievements against an agreed project programme and forward strategy. The first joint venture board meeting took place in the UK during July 1994. They are tough sessions but both sides have an opportunity in meeting each other to discuss and resolve the key issues for further development of the joint venture.

Of the workforce in SIDTEC, 10 per cent speak good English, 60 per cent speak some English and about 30 per cent do not speak English, but are being encouraged to develop this skill. Procedures and instructions used within SIDTEC which describe activities are straightforward, with simplicity being paramount, and people who use these documents are often involved in their formulation. In many cases a dual (English/Chinese) language is used. Measurements implemented at SIDTEC, which record commercial performance, material supply and customer support are regularly reviewed for action and form part of the GPT Business Metrics brochure.

Development and implementation of quality policy

From the start of technology transfer, emphasis was placed on developing an efficient Quality Management System and ensuring products were built and reached near 100 per cent first time pass rates at the final test stage. The Quality Management Standard GB/T19002-ISO 9002 was implemented across the company. The initial company's quality policy was:

1 To ensure that products manufactured (iSDX) at SIDTEC meet contractual requirements, meet local approvals and be built in an efficient/economic manner.

2. To ensure that quality systems which are involved in controlling products manufactured at SIDTEC are based on recognized standards, e.g. ISO 9002, which are ultimately approved by an international accredited organization.
3. To ensure that any complete or part product, intended for export outside China, meets the GPT requirements and individual country requirements, e.g. British Approval Board for Telecommunications (BABT) 340 specification for the UK.

A two-stage approach was adopted in the approval of systems to ISO 9002: 1987. First, contact was made with the Shanghai Quality Control Association as the Chinese registration body. A pre-assessment visit took place in December 1992. The formal assessment took place in April 1993 by representatives from Shanghai and observers from Beijing – the China State Bureau of Technical Supervision (CSBTS). Approval was formally granted in July 1993. The purpose of going initially for local Chinese registration was to give both the joint venture and Shanghai Quality Control Association a sense of ownership and at the same time measurement against a recognized international standard.

The second stage was to gain approval by an internationally recognized body. The British Standards Institute (BSI) was chosen, and in November 1993 an assessment took place jointly by representatives of the BSI (UK) and the Hong Kong Quality Assurance Agency. A satisfactory outcome was achieved, with the certificate of registration awarded in November 1993. It is worth noting that SIDTEC are the first telecommunications company in China to receive this recognition from the BSI.

Success came about through the involvement of everyone in the organization with training particularly given to personnel in procedure writing, auditing, supplier appraisal, documentation control and process control. Vulnerabilities were identified in each function either by external or self-auditing, and corrective action plans developed. Much work is currently being done in health and safety control.

Process control and product performance

Process control implemented in the joint venture includes Statistical Process Control (SPC) on all major processes and some manual operations. Prevention control includes static sensitive device protection and total productive maintenance, whereby operators themselves regularly maintain their own processes and, when required, carry out repairs. Some operators have toolmaking experience and can provide and repair jigs and fixtures. Operators are also responsible for inspecting their own work, completion of SPC charts and support improvement groups.

Localization of material supply

Currently, the joint venture is developing its local material sourcing base. Initially, an assessment of the potential supplier's premises and facility would take place. Such assessments would cover commercial, technical and quality requirements. Attention would be focused on whether the supplier exhibited a positive approach in becoming a 'partnership supplier'. If the potential supplier achieves a good result at this stage, samples are produced to the agreed specification. Such samples are submitted to an independent organization including GPT Limited (UK) for validation. Independent test houses such as the Singapore Institute of Standards and Industrial Research (SISIR) have also provided a service, particularly in fabricated metalwork, to validate construction, welding and paint finish. If samples achieve a positive result, initial orders would be placed with the provisionally approved supplier. It is emphasized that selected suppliers must have the potential to produce materials and components which ultimately meet world-wide standards.

FUTURE DEVELOPMENTS AND PROBLEMS TO BE SOLVED

The plans for future development of the joint venture from 1994 include:

* relocating to the new Pudong Economic Development Zone, Shanghai;
* extending the manufacturing facility to triple the output;
* moving technology transfer to automatic component onsertion (Surface Mount Technology);
* increasing the percentage of local material supply to a higher proportion.

There are a number of problems to be solved in the future, in particular:

* Localization: it is not possible to give exact dates when 100 per cent of the product will be manufactured in China. Many high-tech types of components will be sourced outside China for the foreseeable future.
* Standards and test: there is a growing need for China to establish independent test houses and recognize international standards. Currently, ministries, institutes and organizations within China, such as the China State Bureau of Technical Supervision (CSBTS) and the China Council of International Quality Assurance (CCIQA) are at the forefront of promoting these developments.
* Expatriate project support: when UK expatriates leave the joint venture and full hand-over takes place, it is hoped that a management control process would be in place. However, this stage is seen to be critical and close monitoring and support would be continued, albeit remotely from the UK.
* Joint venture developments: as the penetration into the Chinese marketplace accelerates, senior management decisions will have to take

place on the role of a single joint venture. Considerations will have to be given to extending the product portfolio, setting up a network of joint ventures in China and addressing marketplaces outside China including the Pacific Rim countries and ultimately the rest of the world.

- Transportation: there is a growing need in China to support businesses in the development of efficient transportation systems. As the supplier in-feed to the joint venture extends across China (currently commodities are sourced from Chengdu, Dalian and Shenzhen in China's extremities), and conversely as the joint venture customer base also extends, a threat is posed of time delays in the event of inadequate air, rail and road transportation.

CONCLUSIONS

Telecommunications is a growth industry in China, and the personnel within the joint venture SIDTEC are enthusiastic to develop. A strong team spirit and bond has been established with the UK partner, GPT Limited. Developments of the joint venture were planned in a number of specific stages, but they were implemented without complex, bureaucratic procedures. The core product (iSDX) as supplied by GPT Limited (UK) is already established in international markets. It has gained a reputation for good quality and reliability, and we can now see the same standards coming from the Shanghai joint venture.

Much has been achieved in a relatively short time scale within this joint venture. High levels of trust and commitment were established between the partners, and technology transfer stages were achieved in their planned time scales. High levels of commitment were given by all members of the joint venture in an enthusiastic approach. In-depth training and effective cross-cultural communication established the foundations for success. An internationally recognized Quality Standard (ISO 9002) was introduced, with positive acceptance across all personnel, resulting in approval by Chinese and internationally recognized bodies.

Experience in developing SIDTEC suggests a number of requirements for solving problems and contributing to the success of a Sino-foreign joint venture:

- There should be a mature, reliable core product, having good market potential, using proven production technology.
- From the outset of the joint venture it should be recognized that a well established Quality Management System will result in high product quality and reliability and cost savings.
- There should be a continuous improvement approach with people responsible for their own processes and resultant products, with deployment of TQM and SPC. This benefits from implementing procedures and specifications in a clear and concise format and developing an

already knowledgeable and skill based workforce through in-depth training.

- Suitable local commodity sources, with recognition of International Standards, need to be identified.
- Last but by no means least, there should be a mutual appreciation of cultural backgrounds, the establishment of an atmosphere of trust between partners, and an adherence to project time scales.

In addition to these elements and the 'Seven Cs' previously identified, the following are also considered important:

- Ensure that project time scales are agreed and maintained by both parties.
- Allow plenty of time for planning and preparation of the introduction and implementation of the technology transfer stages.
- Seek out the most suitable partner who is willing and committed to a long-term relationship.
- Ensure that the product or service is something that the country urgently requires.
- Ensure that the people selected have the commitment and qualifications to develop the enterprise.
- Be persistent in your approach, as the Chinese bureaucratic systems will delay the decision making process. Negotiations between partners can take a long time to finalize, so a high level of patience should be shown by the non-Chinese partner in order to develop a close relationship.

Part III

International activities of Chinese enterprises

8 International management strategies of Chinese multinational firms

Hai yan Zhang and Daniel Van Den Bulcke

ABSTRACT

Although the expansion of foreign owned enterprises within China has been very well documented, little is known about Chinese owned firms which are venturing abroad. This chapter tries to relate this new phenomenon not only to the expansion of multinational firms originating from developing countries in general, but also to the specific characteristics of the state owned Chinese firms. Aspects which are analysed are the motivation to invest abroad, the timing and route of the internationalization process, and the scope of the overseas business operations, as well as the entry mode, selection of location and partners, organizational structure, control system and management operations, etc. The empirical information was collected in China during August–September 1993 from about 16 large and middle sized Chinese firms and 31 of their overseas manufacturing subsidiaries.

INTRODUCTION

While a lot of attention has been devoted to the expansion of foreign owned enterprises in China since 1979, recent interest has extended to Chinese owned firms which are venturing abroad. This new interest is to be interpreted not only against the background of the growth of multinational firms originating from developing countries in general, but should also be linked to the specific characteristics of the Chinese state owned firms which are operating in an economic system in transition to a market economy.

This chapter intends to investigate strategic and managerial patterns of Chinese enterprises in the process of multinationalization, and is more particularly concerned with overseas manufacturing operations. The first part briefly sketches the evolution and growth of Chinese foreign direct investment and the attitudes of the Chinese authorities towards the internationalization of Chinese enterprises. The second part examines the main strategic and managerial characteristics of Chinese Multinational Enterprises (CHMNEs)[1], such as their motivation to invest abroad, the timing

and route of the internationalization process, and the scope of their overseas business operations, as well as their entry mode, selection of location
and partners, organizational structure, management control and operations, etc. This analysis is mainly based on empirical data collected via a
detailed questionnaire survey and personal interviews with Chinese
managers who are in charge of the internationalization of their respective
companies. In the third part of this chapter some differences and
similarities between CHMNEs and multinational enterprises from other
countries will be discussed. The literature about Third World multinationals and the multinationalization of state owned companies will be
referred to in the latter part of the chapter.

BACKGROUND

Chinese enterprises started to invest abroad during the early 1980s. While
the Chinese government in 1982 had approved less than 50 overseas non-
trade[2] subsidiaries, this number already surpassed 1,300 at the end of 1992.
The accumulated investment by Chinese investors abroad reached almost
US$1,585 million in that year. If the equity participation of the foreign
partners is included this amount increases to more than US$3,500 million
(Table 8.1). The major destinations of the Chinese accumulated foreign
direct investment (FDI) in non-trade activities at the end of 1992 were
the US (12.2 per cent of the total number of projects), Hong Kong
(8.6 per cent), the former Soviet Union (7.3 per cent), Russia after the
dissolution of the Soviet Union (6.3 per cent), Thailand (7.0 per cent),
Japan (5.2 per cent), Australia (4.7 per cent) and Canada (4.6 per cent)
(Chai and Tang 1993: 10).

Table 8.1 Chinese foreign direct investment in non-trade sectors (1982–1992)
(US$ million)

Year	Number of over-seas subsidiaries	Amount of Chinese investment	Amount of total investment	Average project size
1982	43	37.00	82.00	1.91
1983	33	13.00	8.00	0.24
1984	37	100.00	120.00	3.24
1985	76	47.00	88.00	1.16
1986	88	33.00	109.00	1.24
1987	108	410.00	1,373.00	12.71
1988	141	75.00	118.00	0.84
1989	119	236.00	325.00	2.73
1990	156	77.00	167.00	1.07
1991	207	362.00	760.00	3.67
1992	355	195.00	364.50	1.03
Total	1,363	1,585.00	3,514.50	2.05

Source: MOFTEC data, quoted by Li (1992: 42) and Chai and Tang (1993: 8)

The attitude of the Chinese authorities towards the internationalization of Chinese enterprises has drastically changed over time. Before 1985 the Chinese government devoted little attention to the development potential and the implications for their economy of the internationalization of Chinese enterprises. Until then practically all overseas subsidiaries were established by state owned foreign trade companies which mainly set up commercial activities abroad. The rapid growth of a number of overseas investment projects, carried out by industrial enterprises, after 1985 convinced the Chinese government that it was necessary to integrate these foreign activities into its overall economic development strategy. On the one hand a set of regulations about the approbation process of overseas subsidiaries, foreign exchange control, accounting systems, etc., were set up. On the other hand a number of large state owned enterprises were granted more general decision making authority and more autonomy as to the management of their overseas investment activities. Consequently several large Chinese enterprises controlled by the central government attracted worldwide attention with the acquisition of some important foreign firms. China International Trust & Investment Corporation (CITIC) spent US$140 million to buy a 10 per cent share in the Portland Aluminium Smelter Company in Australia in 1986. Shougang Corporation (formerly known as the Capital Iron and Steel Corp.) paid about US$312 million (including the outstanding long-term company debt) to acquire 98 per cent of the stock of Hierroperu SA in Peru in 1992 (Bowen 1993: 7). The liberalization of Chinese regional economic policies and the more autonomous management structure set up by Chinese enterprises in 1992 also allowed local industrial enterprises to engage in international activities.

The main Chinese overseas investors can be classified into four different categories according to their current business scope (Li 1992: 41; Luo *et al.* 1993: 48). To the first category belong the Foreign Trade Corporations (FTCs) which are part of the Ministry of Foreign Trade and Economic Co-operation (MOFTEC) or the Department of Foreign Trade and Economic Co-operation of provincial (and municipal) governments. It includes companies such as e.g. China National Chemicals Import and Export Corporation (SINOCHEM), China National Foreign Trade Transportation Corporation (SINOTRANS), Shanghai Animal By-Products Import & Export Corporation, etc. Before 1980 these state owned enterprises monopolized Chinese foreign trade in at least one particular business line. However, these companies lost their monopoly position with the decentralization of the Chinese foreign trade system in 1984. To deal with this new situation, they adopted a new corporate strategy focusing on diversification, internationalization and globalization. The business activities of the FTCs were therefore extended from pure foreign trade to domestic and overseas manufacturing production and services (UIBE 1992: 20–21).

The second category of CHMNEs consists of a number of Foreign Business Oriented Companies or Conglomerates (FBOCs), which were set up by the central and local governments in the early 1980s to develop and extend their foreign business activities. These enterprises were granted relatively more autonomy than the other Chinese enterprises and were allowed to use a special management and decision making structure whereby they could directly establish branches or subsidiaries abroad, at the beginning, mainly in Hong Kong. Since the business activities of FBOCs are very diversified, and include direct investment, portfolio investment, technology transfer, manufacturing, real estate transactions, international leasing, etc., they are usually considered as foreign business oriented 'conglomerates'. CITIC, which depends on the central government, and Yue Xiu Enterprises, of the Guangdong province, can be considered as typical examples of this second category.

The third group in this classification is composed of some large industrial corporations and hi-tech enterprises (LICs) which were designed as 'showcases' with regard to the ownership and management reform in China (e.g. the so-called contracting and shareholding system). They were allowed to expand abroad without too many restrictions. Shougang Corporation, which was selected to test the Contract Responsibility System[3] in 1979 and has continued to apply it since then, belongs to this group.

Besides these three categories a large number of small and medium sized firms (SMEs), in particular those from the Guangdong and Fujian provinces, are also quite active in establishing foreign operations especially in neighbouring countries, although the size of their overseas subsidiaries is generally small. Recently a new type of industrial organization, the 'township enterprises', have become a new source of growth for the Chinese economy, especially in the coastal regions. While these enterprises have gradually upgraded their level of technology through co-operation agreements and joint ventures with state owned firms and foreign companies, and adopted a flexible and market driven strategy, they have also started to invest abroad (Liu and Campbell 1995).

EMPIRICAL FINDINGS

The lack of systematic data at the firm level about the overseas production activities of Chinese firms obliges the researcher to combine many different sources of information, such as articles in newspapers and business reviews, internal reports, interviews, etc.

For this particular research project, 40 of the most frequently quoted Chinese companies with manufacturing operations abroad were selected on the basis of information collected from the above mentioned unofficial sources. As a result of preliminary contacts, more than half of these companies had to be excluded from the study because they either did not want to co-operate or because they refused to confirm the information which had been gathered about their overseas manufacturing investments. Although this elimination process left a sample of only 16 companies, it can still be regarded as quite representative with respect to the size, forms and sectoral characteristics of CHMNEs.[4] A structured questionnaire was used for the interviews in order to obtain data both about the Chinese parent company and about three of its overseas manufacturing subsidiaries, i.e. the most recent one, the oldest or first plant which was established outside of China, as well as the largest of their production facilities abroad. The survey data deal with issues such as the technology, production and marketing characteristics of both the Chinese parent companies and their overseas subsidiaries.

The empirical data were collected in China between August and November 1993 by way of personal interviews on the basis of a questionnaire for which the year of reference was 1992. Also, two Chinese overseas subsidiaries were included, which were visited in Thailand in 1992. The sample therefore includes 16 parent companies and 31 of their overseas subsidiaries located in 17 different countries, i.e. seven in the United States, five in Australia and New Zealand, four in Thailand, four in Hong Kong and Macau, two in other Asian countries, two in the former Soviet Union and the rest in Africa and Latin America.

Although the sample of 16 CHMNEs is rather small as compared with China's total direct investment figure (see Table 8.1), it is not quite without representative value. First, the sample includes companies of all four categories of the main Chinese investors which have already been discussed. Second, the surveyed firms are among the most important Chinese multinationals with regard to the number and size of their overseas production plants. The sample is therefore skewed to the larger CHMNEs. The surveyed CHMNEs own more than 50 overseas manufacturing subsidiaries, i.e. 3.7 per cent of the total foreign non-trade initiatives of China. Also the Chinese investment in 12 of the overseas subsidiaries of the sampled CHMNEs amounted to nearly $410 million, or 21 per cent, of the total Chinese overseas investment in non-trade sectors between 1982 and 1992. However, since the number of surveyed companies is relatively small, it is evident that the use of mean scores in the following tables can only have an indicative meaning and should be interpreted with the necessary care. More detailed case studies may provide additional insights (Zhang and Van Den Bulcke 1994).

Parent company

Four of the 16 surveyed parent companies are FTCs which belong to MOFTEC or to its former branches in provincial (and municipal) governments. Two firms (13 per cent) can be considered FBOCs. Seven surveyed companies (44 per cent) are LICs, of which several have recently diversified into service activities such as trading and banking. There are also three (19 per cent) medium sized industrial firms. With regard to the ownership control, six of the sampled CHMNEs (38 per cent) belong to the central government (i.e. MOFTEC and industrial ministries), nine (56 per cent) are related to local governments (several provinces and cities) and one (6 per cent) is collectively owned. The main activities of the FTCs in the sample consist of import and export of chemical products, overseas transport, trade of animal by-products and construction projects abroad. The industrial enterprises (LICs) are mainly engaged in manufacturing activities, such as the production of computing equipment, spinning and knitting of wool, iron and steel, nonferrous metals, cotton textiles, machine tools, food flavours and fragrances, pesticides, bicycles, etc. General data about the CHMNEs in the sample are shown in Table 8.2.

Table 8.2 Average profile of Chinese parent companies with direct investments abroad (1992)

Average	FTCs	FBOCs	LICs	Others	Total sample
Age of parent company	33.5	12.0	35.6	28.0	30.7
Number of employees in parent company	14,675.0	28,300.0	186,129.0	7,333.0	93,778.7
Sales volume (US$ million)	3,210.6	751.0	1,632.2	18.3	1,674.4
% of sales realized in foreign business related activities	100.0	n.a.	36.8	10.0	49.1
% of products exported (in terms of value)	100.0	n.a.	36.7	12.7	28.7
Number of domestic subsidiaries	41.5	12.5	78.7	37.0	53.3
Number of manufacturing domestic subsidiaries	22.3	n.a.	52.3	5.3	31.4
Number of overseas subsidiaries	48.4	22.5	10.7	2.3	20.0
Number of manufacturing overseas subsidiaries	3.0	7.0	3.8	1.3	3.3
Number of surveyed parent firms	4	2	7	3	16

Source: CHMNE survey (1993)
Notes: FTCs=Foreign Trade Corporations, FBOCs=Foreign Business Oriented Corporations, LICs=Large Industrial Companies

Most of the surveyed parent companies in the three first categories of the above mentioned typology are among the largest firms in their specific sector in China. Their average turnover reached nearly US$1.7 billion in 1992, while the number of their employees averaged more than 93,000.[5] Not only the foreign trade and business companies (FTCs and FBOCs) but also the largest industrial and technological enterprises or groups in the sample have been granted the Import and Export Authority by MOFTEC. In comparison with other Chinese firms, they are highly oriented towards foreign markets, as nearly 30 per cent of their production was sold abroad. On average the CHMNEs in the sample own 53 domestic and 20 overseas subsidiaries (including joint ventures), of which respectively 31.4 and 3.3 are in manufacturing. The business activities of the domestic subsidiaries are often vertically integrated with the parent companies. The LICs usually established trading and service subsidiaries, while the FTCs try to extend their activities into related manufacturing activities. These two groups of CHMNEs to some extent follow converging paths and will probably become more similar over the years. However, horizontal diversification into unrelated sectors is also an important feature of the CHMNEs, especially when they invest abroad.

Of 16 Chinese surveyed enterprises, 13 reported that they established joint ventures with foreign and overseas Chinese investors within China. They also entered into other business arrangements with foreign or overseas Chinese enterprises, as 11 out of 16 of the responding firms reported licensing agreements with foreign firms, while eight of these firms had concluded technical agreements and engaged in subcontracting. They considered these arrangements as important channels for acquiring new production technologies and participating in foreign business networks. Four out of 16 of the surveyed CHMNEs can be considered as high-technological enterprises. Their products are not only import substituting in the domestic market, but also competitive in the international market. They have established their own research institute or department to adapt and absorb foreign technology and to develop new products. Their efforts in developing new production processes and new machines or equipment are relatively limited, however.

Parent companies were asked to rank a number of items in their marketing strategy on a five point scale (from 1 – very limited to 5 – very important) in an attempt to measure their respective importance and the influence on their competitiveness. Highly ranked factors were: good quality of the products (with a mean of 4.3), own sales capabilities (4.0), low selling price (3.5) and brand names (3.1). It is therefore not surprising to find that five of the surveyed CHMNEs consider themselves to have a very good reputation with regard to their trademarks in China. The state distribution channels were considered as less important (3.0) than their own sales capabilities, especially by the industrial enterprises.

Overseas subsidiaries

The available data about the Chinese overseas manufacturing activities cover 31 subsidiaries. More specifically, information is provided about 16 of them which were established as the first plant abroad, nine which were the most recent establishment of the group, and six which were considered as the largest plants abroad owned by the parent companies. These sample data reveal some interesting features about Chinese overseas subsidiaries.

As a matter of fact, because of the recent origin of CHMNEs in general, the number of years the foreign subsidiary has been active shows little difference among the three categories of oldest, most recent and largest subsidiary. While the average age for the subsidiaries of the CHMNEs in the sample was 4.4 years in 1992, the oldest plant existed on average for only 5.3 years, while the most recent subsidiary had been operational for about 3 years.

The Chinese manufacturing subsidiaries abroad are mostly medium and small sized, as seven have less than 20 employees and only two employ more than 450 persons. Yet the data which are available for about 11 firms show that the average size of these subsidiaries in terms of total investment is more important than the average for all Chinese overseas nontrade projects taken together (see Tables 8.1 and 8.3). The new investment projects tend to be much larger than the first time investments, as the recent projects employ on average about 175 people and investment reaches about $28.6 millions, while the first plants that were established abroad have on average 130 persons and $5.9 million of investments. (Table 8.3).

Nine (29 per cent) of the surveyed subsidiaries of the CHMNEs manufacture the same products as their parent company, while 11 (36 per cent)

Table 8.3 Profile of Chinese overseas manufacturing subsidiaries: mean scores (1992)

	Most recent subsidiaries	Oldest subsidiaries	Largest subsidiaries	Total sample
Age	3.0	5.3	4.1	4.4
Number of employees	175.2	130.4	784.0	277.2
Project cost (US$ millions)*	28.6	5.9	61.6	26.3
Ownership (%)	58.9	59.2	56.5	58.6
Local sourcing (%)	33.3	33.1	78.0	42.5
Export ratio (%)	79.2	66.4	66.7	69.8
Number of surveyed subsidiaries	16	9	6	31

Source: CHMNE survey (1993)
Note: *Twelve available cases, of which one was excluded because its size was disproportionately large

operate abroad in sectors which are not specifically related to the major product lines of their parent firms. The vertically integrated subsidiaries produce directly for their parent companies (e.g. raw materials, new products, etc.) and/or provide information to the Chinese parent about the production process, engineering service, market information, distribution channels, etc. A great number of smaller subsidiaries of the sampled CHMNEs engaged only in simple manufacturing activities (e.g. assembly) and trading activities. The overseas subsidiaries of CHMNEs were mainly situated in the chemical sector, metal-working and machinery, and textiles and clothing, as respectively eight, seven and four out of the 31 subsidiaries in the sample were active in these sectors. Three subsidiaries were involved in natural resources (forestry and mining products).

Chinese overseas subsidiaries sourced about 42 per cent of their inputs from the local market in 1992, while the export ratio of these affiliates averaged nearly 70 per cent. The oldest subsidiaries abroad tended to export less than the most recent subsidiaries. This is probably to some extent due to the fact that it was the earliest ventures abroad which were established in order to enhance the export of the parent company itself, i.e. they usually imported semi-finished products from the parent company and they assembled or used them to serve the local market, rather than to export from the host country.

Motives for overseas production

While it is generally believed that foreign multinationals invest in China for its low production costs and its large potential market, much less is known about the motives for Chinese enterprises to venture abroad. Apparently the motives of the Chinese enterprises to produce abroad are mainly related to market expansion and information factors (Table 8.4). To expand into new markets, to advance the parent company's exports, to locate close to export markets, to get access to information abroad, and to build up international business experience, are ranked highest in a list of factors which were submitted to the evaluation of the Chinese managers. This result is quite similar to the findings of Ye (1992:128) where 16 out of 17 responding Chinese multinationals mentioned the opening up of new markets together with the need to acquire first-hand information on foreign production and markets as the second most important motive to invest abroad.[6] Although the CHMNEs seem to be seeking markets rather more often than resources through their overseas expansion, foreign direct investment in resource projects by CHMNEs is nonetheless important, particularly in terms of its size. However, the Chinese resource seekers have been more influenced by the home government than the market seeking CHMNEs.

The specific nature of Chinese enterprises in terms of ownership and management characteristics and the internal and external changes which

Table 8.4 Motives for Chinese enterprises to produce abroad

Factors[a]	Most recent subsidiary	Oldest subsidiary	Largest subsidiary	Total sample[b]
Expansion into new markets	3.4	3.8	3.3	3.6
To advance exports of parent company	3.4	3.6	3.2	3.5
To be near export markets	3.3	3.6	3.2	3.4
Access to information abroad	2.9	3.8	2.8	3.3
Following home country's strategy	4.0	2.3	3.2	3.2
To build up international experience	3.1	3.3	2.8	3.1
Access to third country markets	2.8	3.5	2.8	3.1
Diversification of production	2.3	3.2	3.0	2.9
Higher rate of profits abroad	2.9	2.2	3.3	2.6
To use product innovation	3.1	2.2	2.7	2.6
Trade barriers in host country	2.3	2.4	2.7	2.4
Investment incentives in host country	1.8	2.5	3.0	2.4
Desire to be near source of supply	3.0	2.2	1.8	2.4
Defending existing markets	2.6	2.0	2.3	2.3
Lack of raw materials in home country	2.7	1.7	2.5	2.2
To follow competition	2.0	2.5	1.7	2.1
Home country's agreements with host country	1.3	2.5	1.5	1.9
Cultural and language proximity	1.3	2.1	2.2	1.9
Competitive pressures in home country	1.9	1.7	1.5	1.7
Lower labour cost in host country	2.0	1.5	1.7	1.7
Lower land cost in host country	1.9	1.7	1.3	1.7
To use labour-intensive technology	2.2	1.4	1.5	1.7
To exploit managerial skills	2.1	1.2	2.0	1.7
To follow customers	1.6	1.2	2.7	1.6
Lower capital cost in host country	1.0	1.6	1.3	1.4
Political instability in home country	1.0	1.2	1.5	1.2
Diversification of financial risks	1.2	1.0	1.3	1.1
Market limitation in home country	1.0	1.0	1.2	1.0

Source: CHMNE survey (1993)
Notes: [a] There were 28 responding firms, of which 9 were most recent subsidiaries, while 8 were among the oldest and 5 among the largest subsidiaries
   [b] The importance of each factor is ranked on a 5 point scale: 1= very limited, 2=limited, 3=moderate, 4=important, 5=very important

are due to the rapid transitions in the Chinese economy, are likely to have an impact on the behaviour of the Chinese enterprises which engage in overseas production activities.

First, since the CHMNEs in the sample are all state owned (except for one which is collectively owned), the foreign investments of these firms must be in accordance with the economic development policy of the government, i.e. they should increase Chinese exports, provide access to raw materials and acquire foreign technology and management skills (Chai and Tang 1993: 8–12). The overseas corporate strategies of CHMNEs are therefore greatly affected by the initiatives and preferences of the government, e.g. the foreign direct investments of some FBOCs in unrelated resource extraction.

Second, the rapid transition of the Chinese economy from a planned economy to a market system presented Chinese enterprises with certain threats and opportunities with regard to their investment abroad. When for instance the Responsibility Contract System was introduced in the state owned enterprises, the contracting enterprises which signed on for this management system were permitted to diversify their products and markets freely as long as they fulfilled the state's planning production quotas and their diversification complied with the state's guidelines (Dong *et al.* 1992: 34). As a result of this reform, several state owned enterprises expanded abroad in order to sell surplus products (i.e. produced in excess of the state's planning quota) at a higher rate of profit; to earn foreign exchange; to acquire foreign technology; to get access to overseas market information and managerial skills and to have more management autonomy and production flexibility. Certain CHMNEs use their foreign subsidiary to transfer abroad profits realized at home in order to have more financial autonomy or to build up their own business units abroad[7], and even to benefit from the Chinese incentives for foreign firms when re-investing these funds within China.

Third, it has been suggested that the decision of Chinese enterprises to invest abroad is sometimes linked to the personal interests of the managers, as the affiliates allow them to travel more easily to foreign countries, to send family members or friends to work or travel abroad or to build up the career of overseas family members, etc. (Salem 1988: 66).

Entry mode and ownership pattern

According to the literature concerning the entry strategy of firms into international markets (Johanson and Vahlne 1977), the internationalization process of firms can be split up in stages with different degrees not only of resource and market commitment, but also of control. Firms may gradually develop their overseas operations by consecutively using direct export, a local agent, a sales office or commercial subsidiary, licensing, a technology or management contract, subcontracting, joint equity investment in a production subsidiary and wholly-owned production subsidiary[8]. However, the gradual internationalization process could not be confirmed for Chinese enterprises as neither a clear time sequence nor distinct stages could be distinguished. One of the state owned FTCs in the sample appointed its first foreign commercial agent as early as 1951, opened its first overseas representative office in 1952 and only established its first overseas production subsidiary in 1989. The first overseas manufacturing subsidiary established by one of the surveyed LICs dated from 1983, while its parent company obtained the Import and Export Authority only two years later. Also, the responding FBOCs in the survey mostly started their foreign business activities by establishing overseas trade, manufacturing and service (e.g. bank and/or real estate) subsidiaries practically at the same time in the early 1980s.

In establishing foreign manufacturing subsidiaries, Chinese FTCs and FBOCs enterprises often convinced other domestic industrial enterprises (e.g. their suppliers) to become joint investors in their investment projects, so that they could rely on their technology or their production experience. From their side the industrial enterprises also involved FTCs and FBOCs (which often belonged to the same industrial or administrative ministerial department) in order to facilitate the approval procedure for their foreign investment activities and to use their overseas business connections. Eight out of 30 overseas subsidiaries (27 per cent) in the sample were established in such a way. However, the equity participation of the joint investing enterprises was almost always below 25 per cent. The practice of investing abroad with other partners from the home country was clearly intended to enhance the specific endowments of the investing companies, and may to some extent be specific for the Chinese internationalization process. While it has been typical that domestic suppliers have followed companies abroad in order to maintain preferential links with the investing company and to limit the development of potential competitors, the Chinese state owned firms seem to have taken a more active role in bringing other Chinese companies into ventures abroad, maybe because they are often subordinated to the same industrial or administrative department or bureau.

The entry strategy of Chinese multinationals into foreign markets varied with the size and the foreign business experience of the parent company. The FBOCs and FTCs tended to use mergers and acquisitions (M&A) to invest in advanced technological firms in industrial countries and resource extraction projects. Seven out of 31 subsidiaries (22 per cent) in the sample were the result of an acquisition strategy,[9] of which five were undertaken by FBOCs and FTCs (38 per cent). However, middle-sized industrial firms in the sample usually expanded abroad by establishing new plants, especially in developing countries.

In terms of the ownership pattern, five out of 30 (17 per cent) responding Chinese overseas subsidiaries are wholly-owned, nine (30 per cent) are joint ventures with Chinese majority ownership, 13 (43 per cent) are joint ventures with a Chinese minority ownership and three (10 per cent) are 50:50 joint ventures. It is noteworthy that joint ventures with minority ownership are more often situated in the chemical sector (63 per cent as compared to 43 per cent in the total number of projects) and basic metal manufacturing (67 per cent), while the majority and wholly-owned subsidiaries are more frequent in the sectors of mining extraction

(100 per cent) and manufacture of machinery and equipment (67 per cent). The ownership of CHMNEs' subsidiaries does not seem to be particularly affected by their geographic locations, except that all subsidiaries in Hong Kong and Macau are majority controlled and wholly-owned.

Among the 25 foreign partners which were involved in the establishment of Chinese overseas joint ventures, there were 14 overseas Chinese investors, i.e. entrepreneurs of Chinese origin who are living outside of China. It has been observed that small and medium-sized Chinese industrial enterprises preferred to engage overseas Chinese as local partners, especially when they emigrated to neighbouring countries, such as Thailand and the Philippines. This practice is considered to allow CHMNEs to acquire local market knowledge at lower transaction costs because of the cultural and language similarity with the overseas Chinese. Local market experience of the foreign partners and their previous business relationship with the CHMNEs are generally regarded as important determining factors for the selection of joint venture partners. Factors such as personal reputation, brand names, financial capacity and sometimes even the level of technology do not seem to have been important considerations in the choice of local partners.

Decision making authority and control of overseas subsidiaries

The organizational structure[10] of the surveyed Chinese multinational enterprises is quite different according to the size and business activities of the parent company. 'Mother-daughter' relationships have been observed as the main feature of the organizational structure of the Western medium-sized industrial enterprises, i.e. their overseas subsidiary's operation is under direct control of the president (and/or first secretary of the Communist Party) of the parent company. In the case of the LICs, there is often an export department or an international division which is responsible for the overseas subsidiaries. However, the function of these divisions is mostly limited, as the important initiatives and decisions are often made at a higher level of management. The FTCs are all organized in a product structure (i.e. business line) and the activities of each business department are determined by its past administrative functions, rather than by its present corporate purpose. Recently some large FTCs have transformed their business departments into independent domestic subsidiaries. Their overseas subsidiaries, which were previously related to these departments, have been linked to these new domestic subsidiaries, where they sometimes have been organized into regional groups. However, the function of the regional groups is still quite limited (i.e. co-ordination centres), as the business activities of their overseas subsidiaries are often directly linked to the different domestic subsidiaries. The FBOCs are generally organized in a geographical structure and their overseas subsidiaries are directly dependent on a regional 'headquarter', which may be a holding company, an enterprise group or simply a trading or management company. In short, the main forms of the organizational structure of Chinese multinationals are still at an early stage of overseas expansion, according to Stopford and Wells' original classification (Vernon and Wells 1989: 33).

The decision making autonomy of the overseas subsidiaries was ranked by the managers of the parent companies on a scale from one to five. The decisions with the lowest score are the most centralized while those with the highest figures are the most decentralized ones. Table 8.5 shows that the decisions which are centralized by the parent company usually deal with financial and strategic aspects, such as the choice of new investment projects (average score of 1.33), disinvestment (1.40), royalty payments to the parent company (1.73) and budget decisions (2.20). These results are very similar to the findings of other studies about MNEs in developed and developing countries (e.g. Van Den Bulcke 1986: 120–123).

The selection of the top managers of the subsidiaries is also a relatively centralized decision (2.33). Yet, this latter aspect might be due to the

Table 8.5 Decision making authority of Chinese overseas subsidiaries[a]

Decision making authority[b]	Factors
Choice of investment projects	1.33
Sale of fixed assets	1.40
Royalty payments to parent company	1.73
Budget decisions	2.20
Recruitment of top managers	2.33
Entering export markets of parent company	2.71
Selection of suppliers	2.83
Choice of technology	2.93
R&D planning	3.00
Establishment of new department	3.27
Introduction of new products	3.38
Determination of prices	3.80
Setting of product range	3.85
Selection of distribution networks	3.87
Quality control	3.93
Setting production standards	3.93
Output volume	4.29
Recruitment of employees	4.87

Source: CHMNE survey (1993)

Notes: [a] There are in total 15 valid responses from the parent companies
   [b] The meanings of the scores on the five point scale are: 1 = autonomous decision by parent company, 2 = decision by parent company after consultation with subsidiary, 3 = decision made jointly by parent company and subsidiary, 4 = decision by subsidiary after consultation with parent company, 5 = autonomous decision by subsidiary

complicated Chinese administrative process (combined with the personal interests of the managers) for sending people abroad, rather than to the status of these management positions themselves. The data from the survey show that there are 214 Chinese expatriates in 22 overseas subsidiaries. This represents 25 per cent of the total employment in the foreign subsidiaries (i.e. 34 per cent in the earliest subsidiaries, 14 per cent in the most recent plants and 24 per cent in the largest affiliates). Nearly half of the Chinese expatriates are technicians. This high proportion of Chinese expatriates in total overseas employment, especially when compared with non Chinese MNEs, can be partly explained by the fact that two Chinese overseas manufacturing subsidiaries employed a large number of Chinese workers in order to acquire knowledge about foreign production skills in the host country. In another case Chinese workers were being sent overseas in order to earn foreign exchange. Excluding these cases, the proportion of Chinese expatriates in the total employment of the sample firms comes down to 13.4 per cent, which is still quite high.

As a large number of Chinese overseas subsidiaries (15 out of the 25 respondents) use technologies and equipment from the Chinese parent companies or other Chinese firms, it is not too surprising that the decisions related to technology and R&D are relatively centralized. The decision to enter export markets and the choice of the suppliers of the inputs are also highly centralized, probably because the Chinese overseas subsidiaries were often set up to advance their parent companies' exports (by using parent companies' semi-finished products as inputs) and to expand into new markets.

Nearly half of the overseas subsidiaries in the survey were operating under the 'contracting management system', i.e. the Chinese managers of the subsidiaries have contracted with parent companies to reach specific financial – and sometimes also production – targets. These companies are therefore not only allowed to decide about the daily operations, but also about certain important production aspects, e.g. the diversification into other activities. This feature is typical of the small and medium sized Chinese overseas subsidiaries with both trade and manufacturing activities. In the five largest Chinese overseas subsidiaries, the daily management was completely in the hands of the local managers or especially established management companies which were jointly set up by the investing partner companies. Because of the low degree of integration of the foreign subsidiaries into the parent companies' production activities, Chinese overseas subsidiaries have a good deal of autonomy in decision making with regard to production and marketing policy. The mean scores show high decentralization for the following aspects: the determination of the output volume (4.29), quality control (3.93), the selection of the distribution channels (3.87), the development of the production range (3.85) and the setting of prices (3.80).

Competitive position and performance

Among the group of the earliest established overseas subsidiaries of the CHMNEs in the sample, two failed within a few years after operations had started, while another one replaced its foreign partner. The main reasons for these failures are related to the fact that in one case the products of the subsidiary were not sufficiently suitable to the host market (i.e. Chinese traditional medicine in a Western country), while in the other case – which concerned a quota hopping investment project – the foreign partner did not succeed in exporting the products and providing the necessary working capital as was stipulated in the joint venture contract. In the third case, the original Western partner withdrew from the joint venture arrangement, because it could not cope with the 'business goals' of the Chinese partner. However, Chinese parent companies were generally satisfied with the results of their overseas operations, especially in terms of the achievement of their initial objectives, i.e. the expansion into new markets, the enhancement of the exports of the parent company and the building up of international business experience.

The competition to which the Chinese overseas manufacturing subsidiaries are exposed in the host countries mainly comes from local firms (2.29 on a 5 point scale), products imported from industrial countries (2.14) and other foreign subsidiaries (2.05). Products imported from developing countries (1.65) scored somewhat less. These evaluations of the competitive position of the overseas subsidiaries in the host countries should be related to the competitive advantages of the most successful subsidiaries from the point of view of the parent companies.

According to the perceptions of the managers of 11 Chinese parent companies (Table 8.6), the main competitive strengths of their overseas subsidiaries are their distribution networks, the high level or adaptability of their technology and the quality of their products. More than one third of the FTCs and FBOCs have extensive business connections both in the domestic and international markets. To fully appreciate the capability of Chinese overseas subsidiaries to engage in export activities, one has to realize that more than half of the foreign sales of the Chinese overseas subsidiaries were realized via the parent companies. The strong position of Chinese overseas subsidiaries in terms of technology and product quality is related to the fact that, on the one hand, many Chinese industrial parent companies are relatively well advanced themselves in technology and production innovation, and on the other hand that the technology of some overseas subsidiaries was acquired by the takeover of companies with advanced technology or at least with a technological level which is comparable to international standards.

The comparison made by the responding CHMNEs with the competitive position of their overseas subsidiaries vis-à-vis local industrial firms and other foreign subsidiaries applied mainly to Western subsidiaries

Table 8.6 Competitive position of Chinese multinational enterprises in host countries[a]

Factors[b]	Compared with local firms	Compared with other foreign subsidiaries
Distribution network	4.25	4.00
Technology	4.20	4.17
Quality of products	4.09	3.83
Better business information	3.89	3.00
Home country's support	3.80	3.50
Economies of scale	3.60	2.83
Productivity	3.50	2.67
Brand names	3.20	3.00
Product adaptation to local market	3.10	3.67
Low selling price	3.00	3.17
Access to financial resources	2.80	3.17
Low cost of capital	2.80	3.17
Low administration cost	2.78	3.60

Source: CHMNE survey (1993)
Notes: [a] There are 11 available responses with respect to local firms and 6 concerning other foreign subsidiaries
[b] The importance of each factor is ranked on a 5 point scale: 1=very limited, 2=limited, 3=moderate, 4=important, 5=very important

located in other developing countries. Chinese firms mentioned that they had lower administration costs than their Western homologues and their technology was more adapted to the local conditions. The favourable competitive situation of Chinese subsidiaries vis-à-vis local firms is most pronounced in terms of productivity and economies of scale.

DISCUSSION AND CONCLUSION

Previous studies on the multinationalization of state-owned enterprises (e.g. Kumar 1981; Anastassopoulos *et al.* 1985) revealed two key factors which largely determined the ownership (O), location (L) and internalization (I) patterns. The first factor is related to the public characteristics of the firms, i.e. the strengths and weaknesses that enterprises inherited from the bureaucratic system under which they operate. The second factor is derived from the so-called entrepreneurial logic of state owned firms, which refers to their specific behaviour and reactions in the marketplace. Building on this analytical framework an attempt was made to examine certain features of Chinese state owned multinational enterprises with regard to their investment strategies and management practices abroad (Table 8.7).

The firm-specific or ownership advantages of Chinese multinational enterprises can be mainly attributed, on the one hand, to the monopoly status and/or privileged positions from which they benefited in their

Table 8.7 Tentative summary of the characteristics of Chinese state owned enterprises with regard to their internationalization process

Aspects of internationalization	Main characteristics
FDI motivations	To expand into new markets and to advance exports of parent companies
	To earn foreign exchange
	To seek foreign market information and experience
	Home country policy
Entry mode and location	Tendency to invest in 'upstream' countries
	No clear sequence in the internationalization process
	Involving other domestic enterprises as joint investors in establishing foreign subsidiaries
	Acquisition of existing firms in the industrial countries to acquire advanced technology and small sized 'green field' investments in Third World countries
	Preference for overseas Chinese as local partners
Overseas production structure	Low production integration between parent company and subsidiaries
	Very diversified overseas business activities

specific and related sectors, and on the other hand to the product and process technologies that they have acquired to a large extent with governmental assistance. Although these characteristics also apply to other public multinationals both from Third World countries and industrial countries (Kostecki 1981: 171–173; Kumar 1981: 194–196), they are more pronounced in the case of China, due to the nature of its central planning economic system.

The product and process technology of Third World multinationals are generally considered as appropriate to the specific factor costs, input characteristics and demand conditions of Third World host countries (Lecraw 1977; Wells 1983; Lall 1984). They usually involve small-scale, flexible, labour intensive plants with considerable use of local inputs (Wells 1983: 65). The competitiveness of their products is based more on lower price than on product differentiation (Lecraw 1977: 48). Although the technological and innovatory capabilities of Chinese multinationals are very similar, two characteristics are quite different. First, most of the Chinese multinationals in the sample had established joint ventures with Western multinationals within China. These arrangements allowed them to acquire not only large-scale production technology, but also certain management skills and experience with different organizational structures. Second, the relatively frequent use of takeovers by Chinese multinationals to penetrate industrial countries often gave them direct access to foreign advanced production technology and management know-how.[11] However, because of the operating environment in China and the general technological level of the whole group, these assets in many cases are not fully absorbed by the parent company and domestic subsidiaries.

The main weaknesses of state owned multinationals are that they often suffer from poor management because of a deficient bureaucratic system, unprofessional managerial personnel, low motivation, etc., and that they have not developed sufficient marketing expertise, because they are accustomed to operating in protected national markets (Kumar 1981: 196; Blanc and Anastassopoulos 1982: 177). Apart from these well-known features of public enterprises, Chinese enterprises have suffered specific weaknesses derived both from their external (e.g. the effects of the state planning system, which has gradually been removed since the 1980s) and internal organizational structure (the typical parallel decision making structure) (Schermerhorn and Nyaw 1992: 11–17). These characteristics may pose obstacles not only to the development of a firm's specific competitiveness vis-à-vis enterprises with different ownership structures (especially foreign owned subsidiaries) in the domestic market, but also to their overseas expansion (see further). Of course the strengths and weaknesses of Chinese multinationals are quite different from one firm to another, depending on their size, jurisdiction (i.e. subordinated to the central or local government sector), etc.

An analysis of the motives of state-owned enterprises to venture abroad must take into account that they are 'instruments of achieving national objectives', i.e. that their goals have to be integrated with the wider interests of the country, rather than be driven only by the profit maximization principle (Kumar 1981: 190). This feature of state owned multinationals also applies to Chinese multinationals, as their overseas expansion is greatly affected and controlled by the government at various levels (e.g. the approbation process, foreign exchange control, taxation, etc.), at least with regard to the establishment of their first overseas subsidiary. Apart from the relatively large role and specific preferences of the Chinese government, the motives of Chinese enterprises to locate abroad are not all that different from other Third World multinationals (Wells 1983; Lecraw 1977, 1993), i.e. they invested abroad to expand into new markets, to build up international experience, to have access to foreign market information, to acquire foreign production technology and management skills, etc. A typical characteristic of Chinese outward investment, however, is that the personal interests of the managers might play a more important role in the decision making process.

In contrast to other early Third World multinationals which invested generally in neighbouring, 'downstream' developing countries with lower levels of industrialization and technological capabilities (Lecraw 1977; Wells 1983),[12] Chinese multinationals tend to invest more in 'upstream', higher income or industrial countries. More than 70 per cent of Chinese overseas subsidiaries, at least when those located in Hong Kong and Macau are excluded, are established in industrial countries (Luo *et al.*

1993: 47). The geographical patterns of CHMNEs seem to be determined by their previous foreign business activities (e.g. import and export, transfer of technology, etc.), which are mostly concentrated in industrial countries, especially in the case of FTCs and FBOCs. With regard to the internationalization process, the surveyed Chinese multinationals did not necessarily go through different stages before establishing overseas producing subsidiaries. The internationalization sequence of Chinese enterprises seemed to be determined more by the changes in Chinese economic policy than by the gradual development of the corporate strategies and resource endowments of these enterprises themselves.

It has been argued that the overseas subsidiaries of state owned enterprises were not necessarily different from other private local enterprises or foreign subsidiaries in terms of business behaviour and management practices, because to be successful they had to break away from the 'public characteristics' they possessed in the domestic market (Anastassopoulos *et al.* 1985: 128–135). This argument might be too general to be applied to CHMNEs, however. There are large differences amongst firms according to size, activities, multinational spread and organizational structure. The foreign business-oriented Chinese multinationals (FBOCs) usually set up a geographical structure, i.e. their overseas subsidiaries were generally under the direct control of a regional headquarters which was often located abroad. It could be assumed that although the headquarters might be to a large extent influenced by the Chinese bureaucratic system, the subsidiaries abroad should be less exposed to this and should be more similar to other foreign companies, especially when they have foreign partners or managers. On the other hand, CHMNEs with only a few overseas subsidiaries tended to apply the parent company's management system to their foreign affiliates without much adaptation. The reforms of the Chinese management system also had an impact on the business behaviour and the management practices of Chinese overseas subsidiaries, for example, CHMNEs using the 'contracting management system' or 'shareholding system' are given more leeway by the Chinese bureaucratic system in the management control of their overseas subsidiaries.

The above mentioned results not only reveal some characteristics of Chinese state owned enterprises and the internationalization process but also raise an interesting conceptual issue. Like many other multinationals from Third World countries, most of the CHMNEs are still in their early stages of development with regard to the investment patterns and the application of modern management techniques and styles. However, some of them already operate in ways that are quite similar to their Western homologues in terms of the entry strategies, the industrial and geographical patterns and some management characteristics. It is likely that the differences amongst Chinese multinational firms are to a large extent determined by two key factors, i.e. the 'influence of the governmental bureaucratic system' and the 'development of a real entrepreneurial logic'. As this latter aspect especially is still very much evolving in the Chinese enterprises (e.g. the introduction of a new management system), one might put forward the hypothesis that those enterprises which developed an early link between these two factors are likely to be more successful and competitive than those which have based their international business strategy only on the privileged position which they received from the government. Thus, the internationalization of Chinese state-owned enterprises should remain an interesting subject for future research – especially when more information becomes available – as the reforms of corporate management are likely to continue and the influence of the governmental bureaucratic system will also change.

NOTES

1 A company is considered multinational when it owns production facilities in at least two countries. This broad definition of the Multinational Enterprise (MNE) is widely used in the literature, especially with regard to MNEs emanating from developing countries (e.g. Wells 1983: 9; Lecraw 1977, 1993).

2 MOFTEC (previously named MOFERT) classifies Chinese overseas investment projects into two main types: trade and non-trade projects. The first category includes investment in service sectors such as banking, commercial office, travel agency, etc., while the second category covers projects in industrial manufacturing and resource extraction. The bureaucratic administration of these two kinds of overseas investment projects is relatively different, in particular with regard to the investment regulations and approval procedure. In general the procedure for overseas trade enterprises is simpler.

3 The Contract Responsibility System was developed as a management control system. The main objective of this reform is to increase the performance and profits of state enterprises by transforming them into self-supporting business entities (Maschmeyer and Yang 1993: 253–254).

4 During 1988–1989, the Institute of World Economy of Fudan University in Shanghai carried out a survey on CHMNEs under the supervision of MOFTEC and two other Chinese governmental institutions. This study also started out with a selected number of 37 Chinese enterprises with foreign affiliates. Even after repeated contacts, only 18 agreed to respond to the detailed questionnaire, however (Ye 1992: 127).

5 One should be careful with the interpretation of the financial and employment figures of Chinese groups, mainly because of the unclear organizational structure and administrative dependence. An enterprise group which is subordinated to an industrial ministry can for instance formally 'incorporate' a large number of organizations belonging to this ministry, i.e. factories, research institutes, universities, technical schools, etc.

6 All surveyed firms in the Fudan study answered positively to the description: 'to create conditions for other business activities of the enterprises' which stresses the learning experience CHMNEs are striving for. To acquire raw materials was quoted by 10 out of 17 (59 per cent) of the surveyed companies. In the Fudan survey (1992: 128) the same response rate applied to the motive 'to circumvent trade barriers and maintain export markets'.

7 This practice has already raised objections from the Chinese authorities, who

have tried to stop this 'flight of state property' by strengthening control over these kinds of transactions.

8 However, recent empirical studies have indicated that this clear sequence in the internationalization process of firms does not necessarily apply in developing countries (e.g. Lecraw 1993: 593; Zhang and Van Den Bulcke 1993: 15).

9 Luo, Chen and Yang (1993: 47) also found that 22 per cent of Chinese overseas subsidiaries were acquired by using M&A, while the other 78 per cent were the result of traditional 'green field' investments.

10 It is not possible to bring into this discussion the characteristics of the organizational structure and management of Chinese industrial enterprises such as the 'simultaneous system' and 'parallel authority structures' (Schermerhorn and Nyaw 1992: 11–17). Yet, these features are quite likely to have an effect on the organization of the overseas production units.

11 It has been observed (Lecraw 1993; Van Hoesel 1992; Plasschaert and Van Den Bulcke 1992) that more and more multinationals from Taiwan, Hong Kong, Singapore and South Korea rely on this strategy to get access to foreign distribution networks and technologies in industrial countries.

12 Recent studies however showed that more and more firms from Third World countries started to invest in 'upstream', higher income or industrial countries (Lecraw 1993: 592). The changes in geographical and industrial patterns of Third World multinationals have been explained by the investment development path (Dunning 1986, 1988; Dunning and Narula 1993) and the technological competence theory (Cantwell 1991; Tolentino 1993).

REFERENCES

Anastassopoulos, J.-P., Blanc, G. and Dussauge, P. 1982 *Les multinationales publiques*, Geneva: IRM.

Blanc, G. and Anastassopoulos, J.-P. 1983 'Les multinationales publiques', in A. Cotta and M. Ghertman (eds) *Les Multinationales en Mutation*: 161–193, Geneva: IRM.

Bowen, S. 1993 'A mutually beneficial link with China', *Financial Times* 21 September: 7.

Cantwell, J.A. 1991 'The Technological Competence Theory of International Production and its Implications', in D. McFetridge (ed.) *Foreign Investment, Technology and Economic Growth*, Toronto: University of Toronto Press.

Chai, Lin and Tang, Na 1993 'Faced with the world: China develops actively its foreign direct investment', *International Economic Co-operation* 3: 9–12 (in Chinese).

Dong, Shizong, Zhang, Danian and Larson, M.R. 1992 *Trade and Investment Opportunities in China: the Current Commercial and Legal Framework*, London: Quorum Books.

Dunning, J.H. 1986 'The investment development cycle and Third World multinationals', in K.M. Khan (ed.) *Multinationals of the South*: 15–47, New York: St Martin's Press Inc.

Dunning, J.H. 1988 'The eclectic paradigm of international production: a restatement and some possible extensions', *Journal of International Business Studies* 19(1): 1–31.

Dunning, J.H. and Narula, R. 1993 'Transpacific foreign direct investment and the investment development path: the record assessed', *Essays in International Business* May, 10.

Johanson, J. and Vahlne, J.-E. 1977 'The internationalization process of the firm – a model of knowledge development and increasing foreign market commitments', *Journal of International Business Studies* 8(1) Spring/Summer: 23–32.

Kostecki, M.M. 1981 'State Trading', in R. Vernon and Y. Aharoni (eds) *State-Owned Enterprise in the Western Economies*: 170–183, London: Croom Helm.

Kumar, K. 1981 'Multinationalization of Third World public sector enterprises', in K. Kumar and M.G. Mcleod (eds) *Multinationals from Developing Countries*, Lexington, MA and Toronto: Lexington Books: 187–201.

Lall, S. 1984 *Les multinationales originaires du tiers monde*, Geneva: IRM.

Lecraw, D.J. 1977 'Direct investment by firms from less developed countries', *Oxford Economic Papers* 29 (3): 442–457.

Lecraw, D.J. 1993 'Outward direct investment by Indonesian firms: motivation and effects', *Journal of International Business Studies* Third Quarter: 589–600.

Li, Zhaoxi 1992 'How to manage Chinese enterprises towards internationalization', *World Economy* 12: 41–45 (in Chinese).

Liu, Hong and Campbell, N. 1995 'An international perspective on China's township enterprises', *Paper presented at the International Conference about Management Issues for China in the 1990s* 23–25 March, Cambridge.

Luo, Long, Chen, Yunghong and Yang, Rongzhen 1993 'Some considerations on the management of Chinese multinationals', *World Economy* 5: 46–50 (in Chinese).

Maschmeyer, R.A. and Yang, Ji-Liang 1993 'Results of the contract responsibility system in the People's Republic of China: an analysis of two state enterprises', *The International Executive* 35 (3): 253–272.

Plasschaert, S. and Van Den Bulcke, D. 1992 'Changing dynamics of international production: an analysis of globalization and collaborative developments of multinational enterprises', in J. van den Broeck and D. Van Den Bulcke (eds) *Changing Economic Order*: 93–116, Groningen: Wolters Noordhoff.

Salem, E. 1988 'The China syndrome: Peking pours money into Hong Kong – for its own benefit', *Far Eastern Economic Review* 23 June: 64–66.

Schermerhorn, Jr, J.R. and Mee-Kau Nyaw 1992 'Managerial leadership in Chinese industrial enterprises', in O. Shenkar (ed) *Organization and Management in China 1979–1990*: 9–22, M.E. Sharpe, Inc.

Tai, Ming Cheung 1993 'Middle of the kingdom', *Far Eastern Economic Review* 21 January: 48–52.

Tolentino, P.E.E. 1993 *Technological innovation and Third World multinationals*, London and New York: Routledge.

University of International Business Economy (UIBE) 1992 'Internationalization, globalization and diversification of large Chinese foreign trade companies: problems and policy implications', *International Trade Review* 1: 20–26 (in Chinese).

Van Den Bulcke, D. 1986 'Role and structure of Belgian multinationals', in K. Macharzina and W. Staehle (eds) *European Approaches to International Management*: 105–126, New York: W. De Gruyter.

Van Hoesel, R. 1992 'Multinational enterprises from developing countries with investment in developed economies: some theoretical considerations, *CIMDA Discussion Paper* No: E/6, Antwerp: RUCA.

Vernon, R. and Wells, Louis T. 1989 *Manager in the International Economy*, Englewood Cliffs, NJ: Prentice Hall.

Wells, Jr., L.T. 1983 *Third World Multinationals: the rise of foreign investment from developing countries*, Cambridge, MA.

Ye, Gang 1992 'Chinese transnational corporations', *Transnational Corporations* 1 (2): 125–133.

Zaleski, E. 1983 'Les multinationales des pays de l'Est', in A. Cotta and M. Ghertman (eds) *Les Multinationales en Mutation*: 198–213, Geneva: IRM.

Zhang, H. and Van Den Bulcke, D. 1993 'Internationalization of overseas Chinese family enterprises: the case of the Philippines', in Vitor Simoes (ed.)

International Business in the Far East, Proceedings of the 19th Annual EIBA Conference: 30–55, Lisbon: CEDE.

Zhang, H. and Van Den Bulcke, D. 1994 'Strategic management of international diversification: the case of three Chinese multinational enterprises', *Paper presented at the 20th Annual Conference of EIBA* 11–13 December, Warsaw, Poland.

9 Hong Kong's China-invested companies and their reverse investment in China

Danming Lin

ABSTRACT

This chapter studies Hong Kong's China-invested companies (the CICs) with special reference to their reverse investment in China. Following a brief review of the history of the CICs, the chapter examines their characteristics based on field survey results. We suggest that, by playing the role of intermediaries between mainland China and the international market, the CICs possess a double-counted advantage due to their close relationships with higher PRC authorities and their current identification as 'foreign investors', providing them with a relatively strong strategic position in conducting China business. However, some key organizational aspects, such as technology and marketing, remain underdeveloped for the CICs. Contextual remarks concerning the implications of the CICs' operations for China's 'reform and open door' process and the evolution of China-Hong Kong connections are also provided.

INTRODUCTION

With 15 years of experience in implementing the 'reform and open door' policy, China has become linked with the interdependent world economy more and more closely. Significant increases in the volume of foreign trade and foreign investment continue. The important role foreign direct investment (FDI) plays in the open door system is a striking development of the 1980s (UNCTC 1988). Since 1992, a new round of economic reform, inspired by Deng Xiaoping's journey to south China and further confirmed by the Fourteenth Congress of the Chinese Communist Party (CCP), has attracted FDI on a nationwide scale. The FDI absorbed in 1992 exceeded the total FDI realised during previous years. In 1993, China became the world's second largest FDI receiver by utilizing more than U.S.$20 billion FDI inflow (*Hong Kong Economic Journal* 1994).

On the other hand, as the opportunities for external economic activities expanded, China's outward investment increased. So far, according to official statistics, China has invested around U.S.$20 billion in some 121 countries and territories (*China Daily* 1994). Taking the vast mainland investment in Hong Kong into account, however, some writers suggest that the official figures very likely underestimate China's actual capital outflow (Wu 1993; Shen 1994). Compared with the size of inward FDI, we may conclude that outward investment has become an important strategic factor in China's open door economic system.

From the very beginning of the reform period, China established overseas firms for outward investment. Subsequently – and interestingly – the overseas firms, notably those firms located in Hong Kong, have returned to the China market to initiate more and more reverse investment, which is counted officially as FDI regardless of the domestic background of the investors. Furthermore, various sources indicate that such reverse investment may account for a considerable part of the total FDI inflow in China. For example, in the first nine months of 1993, reverse investment launched by only four China-invested companies operating in Hong Kong, i.e. the Bank of China Group, the China Resource Group, the China Travel Service Group, and the China Overseas Group, amounted to US$1.5 billion, which accounted for around 14 per cent of China's total utilized FDI inflow during the same period (Cao 1994). In another report, a Hong Kong research institution estimates that, by the end of 1991, a China-invested company – the Guangdong Enterprises Group – made a total of HK$4 billion direct investment in Guangdong province, which accounted for 13 per cent of the total FDI inflow in that province by that time (Brooke Hillier Parker 1992). Accordingly, China's overseas firms have formed a group of 'foreign' investors with growing importance.

This chapter studies Hong Kong's China-invested companies (Zhong Zi Gong Si, or CICs as we will call them here), which constitute the bulk of China's overseas firms, with emphasis on their reverse investment in China. Here, CICs refer to the companies wholly or mainly funded by mainland capital sources when they registered in Hong Kong. Although there are other related topics, it is believed that, for the purpose of an exploratory survey, the scope of study must be limited.

The remaining part of this chapter is organized as follows. The next section briefly traces the development of the CICs; the following section explains the research methodology used in a survey conducted in a small group of CICs. Then, based on the results of that survey, the subsequent section looks at the strategic and organizational characteristics of the CICs with special reference to their reverse investment in China. Some contextual remarks are included in the final section, as suggestions for the further development of the CICs.

THE DEVELOPMENT OF THE CICs

Ever since 1949, the government of the People's Republic of China has operated state owned businesses in Hong Kong. Although some of the state owned business entities, such as the Hong Kong branch of the Bank of China, the China Merchants Steam Navigation Company, began in the early Qing dynasty and were subsequently taken over by the government, the significant history of the CICs dates from the birth of the People's Republic. Before the 1980s, however, the CICs undertook only a limited number of businesses, such as agency operations, distribution and retailing, and the size and scope of their operations were not very significant. For example, as the representative financial institution of the Chinese government, the Hong Kong branch of the Bank of China mainly dealt with the acceptance of remittances by Hong Kong and overseas Chinese and the purchase of foreign exchange for the PRC government, and it was rarely involved in direct borrowing and syndicated loans (Shih 1989).

The Chinese government began to implement the 'reform and open door' policy at the end of the 1970s. While the special economic zones (SEZs) and the open coastal cities were designated as the windows for developing foreign economic activities, the leadership recognized the fact that, to some extent, Hong Kong could be treated as an existing window with much more potential, and hence stressed the need to promote China's economic involvement in the territory. This strategic consideration was further facilitated by the expectation of smoothing the process of resuming Hong Kong's sovereignty and maintaining her prosperity after 1997.

Consequently, the centrally-administered units increased their investment in Hong Kong sharply. At the same time, through the process of domestic decentralization, local governments at various levels and domestic enterprises have obtained greater autonomy in their economic operations. With the hope of speeding up the economic development by pursuing the strategy of 'three points linked by a line' (the domestic market, the Hong Kong market, and the international market), those non-centrally-governed organizations have also released large amounts of capital into Hong Kong to set up their own firms. While some writers (Young *et al.* 1993) estimate that there are 37 Chinese local governmental organs represented in Hong Kong, further investigation conducted by this author indicates that the actual number is at least twice that.

There are inconsistent reports on the current number of CICs. Reflecting the viewpoint of the Hong Kong Association of Chinese Enterprises, Cao (1993) roughly estimates the number as more than a thousand, and the *China Economic News* (1993) reports more specifically that there are 1,701 CICs operating in Hong Kong. Young *et al.* (1993), however, conclude that the number of CICs should be around 5,000. This figure seems to be more realistic because a large number of the CICs are not members of the Association of Chinese Enterprises, and many CICs registered in Hong Kong without getting the formal approval of the domestic authorities. Concerning the size of investment, it is widely reported that China has invested a total of US$20 billion in Hong Kong and already become the largest foreign investor in the territory (*Heng Seng Economic Monthly*

1993; Cao 1994). Sung (1991) also points out that China's investment in Hong Kong exceeds Hong Kong's investment in the mainland. This fact reflects the important role mainland capital plays in Hong Kong's economic development.

There is an informal hierarchy of CICs. On the top level there are some well-known enterprise groups, such as the China Resources Company, the China Overseas Company, the Guangdong Enterprises Company, etc. Normally, such groups are representative organs of state ministries, huge state owned enterprises or provincial or large municipal governments, and the scope of operation of these groups is quite diverse. Under the umbrella of each group there are many companies, and such companies can roughly be classified into four categories:

1 Wholly owned subsidiaries of the enterprise groups.
2 Joint ventures established by the group and other mainland administrative authorities/enterprises.
3 Nominal subsidiaries which represent other mainland administrative authorities/enterprises which in turn entrust the group as the parent of these representative companies.
4 Joint ventures established by the group and other foreign companies, including Hong Kong companies.

It should be noted that there are other, unidentified Chinese investors' CICs registered through various channels, and those CICs are difficult to account for in the above hierarchy because their operations are rather independent.

The CICs have experienced rapid development since the 1980s and revealed some differences, as compared to the pre-reform era. First, the investing institutions are diversified. In addition to the centrally-administered units, which were previously the dominant investors of the CICs, various local governments and enterprises have also initiated their own CICs, and mainland private investors have started their operations in Hong Kong. Second, the scope of operation of the CICs extends to almost all of the industrial sectors in Hong Kong. In order to match international practice, large CICs have organized enterprise groups to facilitate integrated operations. Third, almost all CICs are involved in significant China business activities. For example, as the representative organ of the Ministry of Foreign Trade and Economic Co-operation (MOFTEC), the China Resources Group receives 30 per cent of its business revenue from the China market. For many smaller CICs the proportion is much higher still (Fu 1993).

METHOD OF FIELD SURVEY

Despite their growing importance, the CICs attract relatively little research attention due to their low profile and the difficulties faced by researchers in gaining access to these companies. In order to bridge this gap, we survey the CICs' strategic and organizational characteristics with special reference to reverse investment in China.

A field survey, administered by questionnaires and follow up interviews, was conducted during April 1993. Thirty CICs were identified through personal connections. Such a sampling method may prove to be acceptable for the purpose of an exploratory study, although the extent to which the survey results can be generalized remains to be discussed. For each sample company, the manager received a copy of the questionnaire from a person who had some connections with him. The manager was then asked to fill in the questionnaire and return it within two weeks to the writer or the person from whom he received it. Further face-to-face interviews were conducted with eight managers who were among the 22 respondents who answered and returned the questionnaires in time.

The questionnaire is divided into five parts. The first part is designed to obtain some general information on the company. Parts 2, 3, and 4 address issues related to investment strategy, organization, and performance, respectively. The final part includes five open-ended questions to elicit additional insights. Concerning data analysis, only simple statistics, namely, frequency counting and mean rating were performed, due to the descriptive nature of the study. The major results of the survey are summarized and analysed below.

THE CHARACTERISTICS OF THE CICs

General information

Of the 22 CICs surveyed, two of them were among the top level enterprise groups, and the others were subsidiaries of some top CIC enterprise groups in categories 1–3. Concerning the type of administration, these 22 companies could be further classified as three centrally-administered companies, 14 provincial government-administered companies, two local government-administered companies, and one CIC jointly established by a centrally-administered CIC and a provincial government-administered CIC. Furthermore, 21 CICs were established before 1990, with 10 of them established before 1985.

Twelve CICs focused on manufacturing and trading certain product(s), while the other 10 CICs were involved in both manufacturing and service industries. Concerning the sizes of the companies, 18 CICs reported less than US $100 million asset value, among which eight companies claimed the figure as less than US $10 million. Furthermore, 17 CICs hired fewer than 50 employees in their Hong Kong operation. Thus, by Hong Kong standards, most of these CICs would be considered as small or, at most, medium size companies as regards the value of assets and number of employees. Compared to China's domestic companies, however, these

CICs are relatively large in terms of value of assets. The limited number of employees hired by the CICs in their Hong Kong operations also suggests that the majority of the manufacturing activities of the CICs are probably undertaken outside Hong Kong.

All sample CICs have undertaken some manufacturing investment in China. The products these CICs manufactured in China include textiles, garments, packaging materials, agricultural products, construction materials, metal and non-metal products, video products, foodstuffs, beverages, electronics, electrical appliances, and shoes. The non-manufacturing activities of these CICs include real estate development, financial services, transportation, travelling, and hotels. In sum, we can see considerable breadth in China business. The CICs, however, tend to invest in small or medium size projects. While 11 CICs invested less than US $10 million in China, only one CIC had more than US $100 million reverse investment. Similar behaviour was observed from other Hong Kong companies by previous studies (e.g. Thoburn *et al.* 1990).

Like many other foreign investors, most CICs mentioned Shenzhen and the Pearl River Delta as the investment location. The CICs also preferred to invest in other SEZs and coastal regions. Furthermore, a number of CIC managers indicated that they were studying the potentials of the inner provinces, such as Liaoning, Guangxi, Jiangxi and Sichuan.

Strategic issues

Operational objective

Some studies, reflecting the PRC leadership's view, suggest that 'the foremost strategic purpose of the CICs is to open a window in Hong Kong to serve the needs of the China economy. Profit is only a secondary consideration' (Li and Rui 1992). In this survey, however, major concerns were expressed about the economic performance of the CICs themselves. As a CIC manager said: 'Without profit the company would not be able to survive.' Another manager added: 'In order to achieve and sustain better performance, we must invest back to China.'

Firm-specific and locational advantages

To date, no specific theoretical framework has been developed for the study of reverse investment. In this study a tentative strategy was adopted: first, if we accept the official definition and therefore classify the reverse investment of the CICs as a sort of FDI in China, then some FDI-related theories, especially the OLI eclectic paradigm (Dunning 1988), seem to be of relevance. Second, because the CICs were generated within a developing country – China – it is arguable that they could be further categorized, in the so-called Third World Multinational Enterprises (TWMNEs).

Consequently, in studying the strategic determinants of the reverse investment of the CICs, we placed emphases on the firm-specific advantages
and locational advantages of the China market because the investment
pattern of the TWMNEs is more nearly explainable by a factor endow-
ment than a market failure model (Dunning 1986).

Bearing the above considerations in mind, a number of relevant
variables were categorized through a literature survey and then included
in the questionnaire. In view of their special background, the CIC
managers were asked to rate the importance of the variables explaining
their firm-specific advantages against both the domestic and other foreign
firms (see Tables 9.1 and 9.2).

Some interesting findings can be concluded from Tables 9.1 and 9.2.
First, comparing their firm-specific advantages to those of the domestic
firms, the CICs gave greater importance to such factors as favourable
policy treatment (as foreign investors), better access to information, better
connections to export markets, and better managerial skills. Thus the CICs
seem to own some advantages, presumed to be enjoyed by foreign

Table 9.1 Importance of firm-specific advantages over domestic firms

Advantages	Mean rating
Favourable policy treatment*	3.182
Better access to information	2.909
Better connection to export markets	2.864
Better connection to administration	2.681
Greater flexibility and adaptability	2.545
Better managerial skill	2.409
Superior production technology	2.136

Notes: 1 = unimportant, 2 = less important, 3 = rather important, 4 = most important
 * This item, originally categorized as one of the locational advantages by the
 eclectic paradigm, was included in comparing the firm-specific advantages of the
 CICs with those of domestic firms because it seems to fit this context more
 appropriately, albeit at the risk of double-counting

Table 9.2 Importance of firm-specific advantages over foreign firms

Advantages	Mean rating
Better environmental knowledge	3.636
Better connection to administration	3.182
More PRC business experience	2.909
Better access to domestic market	2.818
Lower costs	2.545
Greater flexibility and adaptability	2.409
More appropriate technology	1.500

Note: 1 = unimportant, 2 = less important, 3 = rather important, 4 = most important investors, which give them a competitive edge over the domestic firms. However, it is worth noting that the above mentioned advantages are highly dependent on the CICs' specific operational site – Hong Kong – and their consequent identification as foreign investors. According to the strategic management interpretation (Porter 1986, 1990), the firm-specific advantages of the CICs over the domestic firms are mainly location-based, rather than system-based. Second, when asked to compare their firm-specific advantages with those of the foreign firms, the CICs paid more attention to the factors of better China environment knowledge, better connection to administrative sections, more China business experience, and better access to the domestic market. The emphasis on these China factors indicates that, given the same identification as foreign investors, the firm-specific advantages of the CICs over other foreign firms are domestically location-based: the major assets the CICs used to compete with other foreign firms stemmed from their mainland origins.

Third, many CICs claimed better connections to administration as an important firm-specific advantage over both domestic and foreign firms. This is not surprising because the CICs are closely related to high-level authorities, but it also implies the possibility of using such an advantage to decrease or even to exclude competition from both domestic and foreign firms, which is contrary to the original purposes of the CICs and, in a broader sense, to the development of the socialist market economy. Fourth, the CICs gave less importance to technology when comparing their firm-specific advantages with both domestic and foreign firms, reflecting their weaker technological base. Technology is, however, centred around any corporate operation and is considered by the Chinese government to be the highest priority. Future development of the technologies of the CICs, then, may prove to be important.

To further explain how the CICs secure their firm-specific advantages vis-à-vis both domestic and foreign competitors, we adopted and extended an institutional perspective developed by a study on the organizational dynamics in China's transitional economy (Nee 1992). Nee described the Chinese marketized firms, transformed from the traditional collective firms and with an incremental market-orientation, as an intermediate property form operating between and linking the market and planning ends of China's transitional economy. It was found that those marketized firms were operating under the conditions of stronger local administrative support, a higher degree of operational autonomy and looser state budget constraints than the state owned enterprises, as well as having better access to production factor inputs and markets than the privately owned enterprises. Because these conditions were well matched with the nature of a transitional economy, the marketized firms could enjoy their specific advantages over alternative governance structures.

The CICs could also be viewed as intermediaries linking domestic and international markets: they are firms locating in Hong Kong – arguably a foreign market – and they are also rooted in China. This two-site locational characteristic allows the CICs to enjoy the advantages of institution and information asymmetry over both domestic and foreign firms, given the significant impact of both factors on saving transaction costs when doing business in China's transitional economy. Both the CICs and Chinese domestic firms are subject to the institutional control and various administrative arrangements of the state government, but the CICs' operational base is in the environment of a market economy, rather than a transitional one in which the domestic firms operate. By operating in Hong Kong the CICs are subject to lower administrative constraints and even receive favourable policy treatment only given to foreign firms, as well as enjoying better access to international market information than their domestic counterparts. Although both the CICs and other foreign firms are exposed to market competition in the international marketplaces, the governance structure of the originally state owned CICs is fundamentally different from that of the other foreign firms. Accordingly, the direct relationship with the PRC administrative bodies becomes an indispensable competitive asset for the CICs over other foreign firms, as long as China's national economy undergoes the transitional stage in which state intervention in corporate operations remains significant.

Moreover, while entering the China market at the same time, the CICs have already mastered the necessary business networks and knowledge which will cost other foreign firms substantially to develop. In conclusion, the advantageous strategic position of the CICs in doing business in the China market stems from their intermediate role and the transitional nature of the Chinese economy, which allow the CICs to play different cards with different competitors: they play a 'foreign' card with the domestic firms and a 'domestic' card with other foreign investors. Whether the CICs can compete effectively in a market economy like Hong Kong, however, remains a big question.

Table 9.3 shows the CICs' perceptions of the advantages of the China market. The CICs emphasized such factors as huge market size, cheaper

Table 9.3 Importance of advantages of the China market

Advantages	Mean rating
Huge market size	3.636
Cheaper labour	3.545
Cheaper land	3.455
Familiar business environment	3.455
Favourable policy	2.955
Loan availability	2.091
Cheaper materials and components	2.049
Availability of advanced technology	1.455

Note: 1 = unimportant, 2 = less important, 3 = rather important, 4 = most important land, cheaper labour, and familiar business environment. Previous studies show that, in doing business in China, Western investors are more market-oriented and Hong Kong and Taiwan investors more resource-oriented (Daniels *et al.* 1985; Thoburn *et al.* 1990; Sung 1992). Results obtained from Table 9.3 suggest that the CICs tend to focus on both China's market and resources, further supported by a China background. According to the opinions of the CIC managers, China's favourable policies in treating FDI are also an important locational advantage. However, this statement must be interpreted cautiously because it largely depends on the way such policies are adopted, that is, on taking advantage of the policies subtly and fully.

It is also noted that the factor of cheaper materials and components only receives moderate attention. As further interviews suggested, this can be explained largely by two reasons. The first is that for many manufacturing processes imported materials and components are much cheaper than the local ones, and even after the recent devaluation of the RMB, this remains unchanged. Another reason is that, although it is cheaper to purchase some materials locally, the processing costs of such materials may prove to be too high, compared to the imported materials, thus increasing the total production costs considerably. As a result, in certain situations it is more appropriate to use imported materials. Combining the findings of Tables 9.1, 9.2 and 9.3, the CICs seem to invest in labour intensive projects because, on the one hand, their technological base is weaker and, on the other, they pay less attention to the advanced technology available in China.

Investment mode and partner selection

If reverse investment is to be conducted, then which mode(s) of entry would be selected? On a scale of 1 (least used) to 4 (most used), the CIC managers termed equity joint venture with a higher mean rating of 3.227 and wholly owned subsidiary and contractual joint venture equally with a moderate mean rating of 2.636. Interestingly, our respondents paid less attention – a mean rating of 2 – to the mode of San Lai Yi Bu (three processing/assembling and one compensation), which includes compensation trade and a number of processing/assembling arrangements. To be sure, Shan Lai Yi Bu represented an important source of Hong Kong investment in the early 1980s.

In the cases of joint venture (JV) operations, local partners are involved. The beginning of such a co-operative journey is the process of partner selection and negotiation, which has proved to be time-consuming for the foreign investors. As investors with excellent China business knowledge, the CIC managers were therefore asked to respond to a number of negotiation-related questions. Table 9.4 summarizes the major findings. It should be noted that the items were ordered according to the frequencies claimed by the respondents.

Table 9.4 Rank order of partner selection and issues related to negotiation

Type of China partner (in order of preference)	Criteria for selecting China partner (in order of importance)	Major issues in negotiation (in order of difficulty)
State owned enterprises Town and village enterprises Collective enterprises Private enterprises	Better connections with local administration Domestic market channels Mutual co-operative experience Similar scope of operation Sufficient capital Advanced technology	Management style Equity structure Amount of investment Pricing of technology and equipment Balance of foreign exchange Proportion of export

The table shows that state owned enterprises (STEs) are the most preferred JV partners of the CICs. As the respondents indicated, the preference for STEs is due to the fact that, in addition to enjoying more administrative support by working with the STEs, the CICs can also promote mutual trust with the STEs more easily because of shared 'roots', that is, the governmental authorities at various levels. Consequently, the JVs are likely to achieve better performance. The CICs are unlikely to choose private enterprises as their partners because, in spite of their astonishing development over the last decade, private enterprises are still less connected with the administration and get less support from other departments, such as banks, customs, etc., and thus encounter more difficulties in their operations, especially in their foreign economic activities.

The major criteria used by the CICs in selecting local partners also reflect concerns about administrative connections, or *guanxi*, and mutual trust. While access to domestic market channels stands as another important criterion, it is of interest to observe that the CICs gave less attention to the aspects of capital and technology.

Management style, i.e. the distribution of the functional delegation between the partners, is considered to be the major negotiating difficulty by most CICs. In fact, in some face-to-face interviews the managers emphasized the importance of keeping managerial control on their China investment projects because it is important to avoid the opportunistic behaviour of their local partners. 'We have to ensure control, blind trust is too risky,' one manager said. The greater attention paid to equity structure also reflects this concern. Rather unexpectedly, balance of foreign exchange and the proportion of export are considered important by fewer responding CICs. A tentative explanation is that, except for some CICs which heavily rely on export and encounter fewer problems of balance of foreign exchange, most can keep a balance by means of the swap markets and/or the underground markets. Some CICs even use most of their RMB revenue to re-invest in China, thus circumventing the problem of balance of foreign exchange. Concerning the proportion of exports, a frequently claimed solution is to persuade the administrative sections to qualify a project as import-substitution. Certainly, in addition to the characteristics of the project, the qualification process also depends on the *guanxi* with related administrative sections.

The managers of the CICs also measured the time frame required from signing the initial co-operation document to getting administrative approval for a selected project, in a normal situation. The general rule is more than a month but less than a year: no CICs spent less than a month or more than a year on this process. While some CICs indicated that the 'shared roots' among the partners and the administrations seem to facilitate the negotiation and approval processes, other respondents stressed that the CICs do not necessarily enjoy advantages over the Western and Hong Kong and Taiwan investors. Possibly the size and structure of the project and the proposed investment location are the most important determinants. The impression is that, currently, the negotiation picture in China is rather brighter than the descriptions of some previous studies (e.g. Davidson 1986; Campbell and Adlington 1988,).

Organizational issues

In the third part of the questionnaire the interviewees were asked to describe the organizational characteristics of the CICs from a number of aspects, including the basis for division of work, human resource structure, technological development, marketing, and other factors. Among the 22 sample CICs, 18 companies divided their work on a functional basis. Accordingly, the lines of products/services and the degree of internationalization of these companies are limited. This is understandable, taking the relatively new history of the CICs into account.

Table 9.5 summarizes some information concerning the human resource structure of the CICs. It is of interest to note that, while the CICs hire permanent Hong Kong residents as their employees in various proportions, they only hire a small number of local people as managers. This is

Table 9.5 Percentage of permanent Hong Kong employees and managers

Percentage	Nos. given by responding CICs in hiring employees	Nos. given by responding CICs in hiring managers
25 or less	7	17
26 to 50	5	3
51 to 75	6	1
More than 75	4	1
Total	22	22

similar to what happened in some Hong Kong-invested enterprises oper-ating in China, where relatives of the Hong Kong investors are often in charge of most of the managerial tasks. It is said that there are some undocumented directions concerning the priority of appointing mainland cadres in managerial positions, and it can be explained by the interaction of three factors, namely, the explicit or implicit arrangement of adminis-trative sections and *guanxi*, the requirement of keeping managerial control under the rather unique CIC structure and practice, and the sub-cultural gap between mainland China and Hong Kong. Recently, however, some CICs have issued documents emphasising the equality of mainlanders and permanent Hong Kong employees in the personnel promotion process. This development reflects the efforts of the CICs in attracting more qual-ified and knowledgeable local employees.

Among the 22 CICs surveyed, 13 of them are involved in some sorts of R&D activities. Further investigation, however, suggested that the emphasis is on product and market development, not technology. For most of the CICs, the channels for acquiring technology are from foreign firms. In fact, R&D only plays a marginal role in the operations of the CICs because, on the one hand, they still lack necessary R&D human resources and, on the other, R&D activities tend to be undermined by the managers of the CICs due to the retrospective effects of their past working experi-ence in mainland China, where R&D activities are mainly supported by the government, rather than by the enterprises.

Table 9.6 suggests that the China subsidiaries of the CICs purchase more materials but less equipment and machinery locally. It is, to some extent, consistent with the findings and discussions on the technological aspects of CICs. The fact that the CICs' subsidiaries purchase more materials locally may also be due to the fact that many of them focus on light manu-facturing and textile industries, and the local supply of the materials for such industries is relatively easily available.

Concerning the marketing activities of the CICs, this survey indicates that CICs tend to rely more on direct marketing channels, such as their own marketing teams, subsidiaries and regular clients, reflecting the tradi-tional Chinese business practices stemming from established trust and *guanxi*. The CICs conduct market research with varying frequency.

Table 9.6 Percentage of materials, machinery and equipment purchased in China

Percentage	Materials Nos. given by responding CICs	Machinery and equipment Nos. given by responding CICs
25 or less	4	14
26 to 50	1	5
51 to 75	10	2
More than 75	7	1
Total	22	22

Table 9.7 Percentage of export products of the China subsidiaries

Percentage	Nos. given by responding CICs
25 or less	8
26 to 50	3
51 to 75	5
More than 75	6
Total	22

Table 9.8 Major export markets of the China subsidiaries

Market	Nos. given by responding CICs
Hong Kong	11
Southeast Asia	8
United States	6
Western Europe	4
The former USSR and Eastern Bloc	3
Japan	3

However, market research may remain an underdeveloped area because 17 CICs, accounting for around 80 per cent of the sample, claimed that the research was conducted by their non-professional staff.

From Table 9.7, we note that eight of the 22 sample CICs exported less than 25 per cent of their China products. In fact, three CICs have no exports. Whether exploiting the domestic market in this way is in accordance with the original purpose of establishing these CICs is worth studying. Not surprisingly, Table 9.8 shows that the export market most quoted by the CICs is Hong Kong. However, many China subsidiaries of the CICs export their products to some other Hong Kong companies, and the destinations of these products are difficult to identify.

Performance

This survey studies the issue of performance step by step. At the first step, the analytical level is defined on the organization *per se*, with a longer time horizon. Thus the managers of the CICs were asked to evaluate satisfaction on the overall performance of their China projects. The time horizon employed here is from the establishment of the CIC to date. It must be noted that, at this stage, the purpose is descriptive rather than comparative. The managers were then asked to rank the importance of various criteria, which are supposed to be closely related to conventional corporate objectives by the current literature, in their performance evaluation.

On a scale of 1 (unsatisfactory) to 4 (very satisfactory), a mean rating

Table 9.9 Importance of factors explaining the performance

Factor	Mean rating
Return on investment	3.50
Sales growth rate	2.80
Total profit	2.75
Technology progress	2.00
Social welfare	1.50

Note: 1 = unimportant, 2 = less important, 3 = rather important, and 4 = most important

of 2.6 on the performance evaluation was obtained. Table 9.9 further indicates that, in assessing performance, the CICs focus on the financial and marketing indicators, and the technological and social welfare aspects are largely ignored.

The open-ended questions

Five open-ended questions concerning other aspects of the CICs' operations were asked in the final part of the questionnaire. Major responses of the CIC managers were summarized in Table 9.10. The key points seem to be:

1 Bureaucracy currently stands as the major barrier to conducting China business.
2 After a period of Hong Kong operation, some CICs still have not adjusted to business in a market economy.
3 In order to do successful business in China, much more attention must be given to the environmental issues.

DISCUSSION AND CONCLUSION

In the course of their China business operations, the CICs serve as promoters for China's foreign trade and foreign investment. In addition to trade with and investment in the mainland directly, the CICs are very active in introducing and co-ordinating foreign trades/investors. In line with the Chinese government's call to extend the scope of utilizing foreign investment, the CICs have also started to issue stocks (Red Chips) on the Hong Kong stock market, with around 40 CICs already listed. As such, the CICs seem to further strengthen their position as capital accumulators for the development of China's economy. Recently, however, the mainland capital influx directed towards the Red Chips indicates the paradoxical phenomenon of accumulating capital from China, rather than from the potential foreign investors.

Some roles the CICs have been expected to play, such as technology

Table 9.10 Typical responses to the open-ended questions

Questions	Responses
What surprised you in your China operation?	The policy is changing.
	There is too much administrative interference, the efficiency of the administration is too low.
	We are bothered by the frequent collection of various arbitrary fees.
	The domestic partners always breach their commitments and the contract; they don't act according to the normal business practice.
What surprised you in your Hong Kong operation?	The Hong Kong businessmen are too sensitive to political issues.
	The poor understanding Hong Kong people have about the mainland makes it very difficult to develop business here.
	It is so risky to operate in Hong Kong: competition is too intense, rate of personnel turnover is too high.
What is the prospect of your China operation?	We are very confident because China is one of the fastest developing nations.
	We are very confident because we have seen the great potentials associated with the opening of the inner provinces and the tertiary industry to foreign investors.
What is the prospect of your Hong Kong Operation?	We are confident because of the 'China' factor.
	We are less confident because competition among the CICs is too intense and not rational.
What would you advise people about doing business in China?	Develop smooth relationships with the administration, adapt to the policies flexibly, choose a trustworthy regular partner/client.
	Be careful about the devaluation of the RMB.
	Strengthen managerial control of the project.

innovators and information distributors, are less obvious at this stage. In other words, the CICs' performance is not completely in accordance with the strategic intentions of the PRC leadership. Rather, in order to enhance their own economic interests, the CICs tended to ignore administrative directions. Trade-offs between the planning mechanism and those market-oriented CICs have become more difficult to make.

The CICs started as socialist companies operating in a capitalist economy. Over time the state ownership structure changed, as the CICs began to accept the business values, norms and practices of a market economy. Consequently, the corporate behaviour of the CICs changed substantially. We can speculate, then, that the experiences of the CICs in such a 'transplant' experiment should have some institutional implications for the development of China's 'socialist' market economy, especially for the development of China's modern enterprise system.

Being heavily involved in the economies of mainland China and Hong Kong, the CICs constitute an interface in linking China and Hong Kong. As 1997 approaches, the CICs are also required by the Chinese government to take the responsibility of stabilizing Hong Kong's post-transitional period. To realise this end, the CICs are most likely to expand their operations in Hong Kong. Bearing the political, social and sub-cultural gaps between the CICs and local Hong Kong firms in mind, it will be of interest to see whether the future operations of the CICs will develop synergy with, and hence stabilize, or cause conflict with, and hence de-stabilize, the Hong Kong economy.

Taking a wider view and based on observation of the CICs, it seems to be valid to ask the following question: does a model of economic penetration in advance of reunification, which has already been applied to Hong Kong by the Chinese government, have any implications for the development of the relationship between mainland China and Taiwan?

ACKNOWLEDGEMENTS

The author wishes to acknowledge Dr John Frankenstein for his continuous encouragement and advice throughout the whole research process. Thanks are also due to the editors of this volume for their helpful comments.

REFERENCES

Brooke Hillier Parker Research 1992 *Chinese investment in Hong Kong*, Hong Kong: Brooke Hillier Parker.

Campbell, N. and Adlington, P. 1988 *China Business Strategies*, Oxford: Pergamon.

Cai, Ling and Na Tang 1993 'Toward the world: China develops overseas investment actively' (*Mian Xiang Shi Jie: Zhong Guo Ji Ji Fa Zhan Hai Wai Tou Zhi*), *International Economic Co-operation* (in Chinese) 3: 9–12.

Cao, H. 1993 'The characteristics and prospects of Hong Kong's China-invested companies' (*Xiang Gang Zhong Zi Qi Ye Di Te Dian Ji Qi Qian Jing*), *Economic Reporter* (in Chinese) 2301–2302: 35–36.

Cao, H. 1994 'China capital plays important role in the development of China-Hong Kong economic co-operation and trade' (*Zhong Zi Zai Zhong Gang Jin Mao Fa Zhan Zhong Fa Hui Zhong Yao Zhuo Yong*), *Economic Reporter* (in Chinese) 2351–2352: 49.

Chen, E. 1983 'Multinationals from Hong Kong', in S. Lall (ed.) *The new multinationals*: 88–136, Chichester: Wiley.

China Daily 1994 July 24–30 Business Weekly.

China Economic News 1993 No. 10.

Daniels, J.D., Krug, J. and Nigh, D. 1985 'US joint ventures in China: motivation and management of political risk', *California Management Review* 27(4): 46–58.

Davidson, W.H. 1986 'Creating and managing joint ventures in China', *California Management Review* 29(4): 77–94.

Dunning, J.H. 1986 'The investment development cycle revisited', *Weltwirtschaftliches* 122(4): 667–76.

Dunning, J.H. 1988 'The eclectic paradigm of international production: a restatement and some possible extensions', *Journal of International Business Studies* Spring: 1–31.

Fu, S. 1993 'On the operational strategy of Hong Kong's China-invested companies in Hong Kong's post-transitional period', unpublished Master of Economics Dissertation, Guangzhou: Zhongshan (Sun Yat-Sen) University.

Heng Seng Bank Limited 1993 *Heng Seng Economic Monthly* October.

Hong Kong Economic News 1994 10 January (in Chinese): 11.

Li, D. and Rui, M. 1992 'A study on the operational adaptability of Hong Kong's Shanghai-invested manufacturing enterprises' (*Shanghai Zai Gang Zhi Zhao Ye Qi Ye Jin Ying She Yin Xin Yan Jiu*), *Journal of Shanghai Social Sciences Academy* (in Chinese) 3: 31–39.

Nee, V. 1992 'Organizational dynamics of market transition: hybrid forms, property rights, and mixed economy in China', *Administrative Science Quarterly* 37: 1–27.

Porter, M.E. (ed.) 1986 *Competition in Global Industries*, Boston: Harvard Business School Press.

Porter, M.E. 1990 *The Competitive Advantage of Nations*, New York: The Free Press.

Shen, G. 1993 'China's investment in Hong Kong', in P.K. Choi and L.S. Ho (eds) *The other Hong Kong report 1993*: 425–454, Hong Kong: The Chinese University of Hong Kong.

Shih, Ta-Lang 1989 'The PRC's Hong Kong-based conglomerates: their role in national development', in E. Kaynak and K.H. Lee (eds) *Global business: Asia-Pacific dimensions*: 368–387, London: Routledge.

Standard Chartered Bank 1993 'Hong Kong's growing role as China's equity market', *Hong Kong Economic Indicators* 8.

Sung, Yun-Wing 1991 *The China-Hong Kong Connection*, Cambridge: Cambridge University Press.

Sung, Yun-Wing 1992 'The economic integration of Hong Kong with China in the 1990s: the impact on Hong Kong', *Asia Pacific Studies Research Papers* 1, University of Toronto and York University: Joint Centre for Research Papers.

Thoburn, J.T., Leung, H.M., Chau, E. and Tang, S.H. 1990 *Foreign investment in China under the open policy: the experience of Hong Kong companies*, Aldershot: Avebury.

Tian, Z. 1993 'Extending overseas investments and strengthening transnational operations actively' (*Ji Ji Kuo Da Wo Guo Qi Ye Di Dui Wai Tou Zi He Kua Guo Jin Yin*), *International Economic Co-operation* (in Chinese) 2: 27–29.

United Nations Center on Transnational Corporations (UNCTC) 1988 *Transnational corporations in world development*, New York: UNCTC.

Wu, F. 1993 'Stepping out the door: Chinese companies are upping their investments abroad', *The China Business Review* November-December: 14–19.

Young, K.Y., Chan, Chi-fai and Dan Lin Hsu 1993 'China's overseas investments in Hong Kong: theory versus practice', Proceedings of the 1993 Academy of International Business, Western and Southeast Asian Regional Meeting.

10 China's foreign trade corporations

Their role in economic reform and export success

Alasdair MacBean

ABSTRACT

The study explores foreign trade corporations (FTCs) in the reform process; the changes made, and responses of officials to change. It is based on discussions with officials, managers of FTCs and their clients, and comparisons with trading organizations of Japan, South Korea, Taiwan and Hong Kong.

Pre-reform, 12 specialized FTCs handled all China's foreign trade according to the National Plan. Now at least 3,600 FTCs exist, and 538 enterprises have direct trading rights. FTCs are now financially responsible; no longer subsidized, but permitted to retain profits and more foreign exchange. Many, nevertheless, are in debt.

FTCs are no longer the obstacle to commerce they were. But complaints against FTCs are many; bureaucracy, overcharging, monopsony, technical incompetence, poor feedback from clients. In our survey no enterprise preferred trading through a FTC. Direct traders had no wish to return to FTCs. Foreigners generally preferred to deal directly with enterprises.

The FTCs' unpopularity bodes ill for their future. In response, many propose to imitate Japan's *sogo shosha* by enterprising (vertical integration), grouping (mergers with other FTCs), and internationalization (becoming diversified multinationals with overseas affiliates). While this might help FTCs to survive through captive suppliers, the policies could increase monopsony and encourage risky investments. A better strategy might be to equalize export incentives for all, extend trading rights to more firms, and open all trade to all enterprises. Given fair competition the most efficient institutions for trade should prevail.

INTRODUCTION

Throughout its post-war history China relied on national foreign trade corporations (FTCs), at first to control international trade, and latterly to promote exports, and facilitate efficient importing. Pre-reform, their role was simply to carry out the directives of the central planning authorities.

The national plans laid down import requirements which were assigned in quota form to the relevant FTCs who had to fill them as best they could. To pay for imports the FTCs bought goods through contracts with Chinese state owned enterprises at controlled domestic prices and sold them at international prices. Profits were remitted to, and losses met by the central authorities. The responsibility of the FTCs was to meet the quantitative targets for exports and imports. Financial considerations were a minor concern.

China's economic reform, which has produced such dramatic material progress, involved two major features:

1 a shift from central command planning towards more market directed allocation of products and resources;
2 graduation and experimentation in the adoption of reforms (World Bank 1993; Singh 1993). Both these characteristics are exemplified in China's 'opening' to the rest of the world through progressively liberalizing foreign trade and investment. Most reforms were introduced one step at a time and many were tried out in special economic zones before being widely adopted. Imports of consumer goods remain highly controlled while export policy contains a mix of contracts between central or provincial and municipal authorities and FTCs, but with increasing emphasis on incentives to export.

(Lardy 1992; Panagariya 1993)

Since 1979, as China's international trade has been progressively liberalized the number of FTCs has been expanded, from the original 12 national FTCs to several thousand at provincial and even township levels. Instead of simply meeting national plans, FTCs, like other state owned enterprises (SOEs), have become increasingly responsible for their own commercial performance, with the threat of merger or bankruptcy as the ultimate penalty. Few SOEs, however, have actually met that fate so far.

China, with GATT ambitions, has continued its trade liberalization. General policy levers such as the exchange rate, tariffs and subsidies are being substituted for the direct controls of mandatory plans implemented through national FTCs. This progress certainly makes the old style FTCs obsolete and raises several questions for the 1990s: what is the FTCs' role in China's trade liberalization? Can they evolve into successful trading agencies, offering efficient services at competitive prices to China's manufacturing and service industries? What can such agencies offer which could not be achieved by direct dealing between Chinese firms and foreign firms? How should FTCs change in order to be most useful to China into the next century? Are there lessons for China from the experiences of Japan and South Korea's large general trading companies, or from the different models of smaller and more agile FTCs adopted by Taiwan and Hong Kong?

Suggesting answers to these questions forms the main objective of this chapter.

TRADE POLICY REFORM IN CHINA

China's pre-reform trade policy has been likened to an airlock which sealed the domestic economy from the rest of the world. Motives for this policy of self-reliance were partly strategic. After the withdrawal of Russian assistance China felt isolated in a hostile world. Political isolation fostered the desire for economic independence, but this was reinforced by the prevailing wisdom of dependency theorists and the export pessimism which permeated contemporary development literature. Import substituting industrialization policies were pushed to the limit in China. A major purpose of imports was to 'lay the foundations of China's industrial independence' (Lardy 1992: 16). Exports were purely determined by the need to pay for essential imports, with little if any attention paid to comparative advantage. China has a long history of trying to avoid contamination by foreign ideas through limiting contact between its citizens and foreigners. Under Chairman Mao this was taken to an extreme. Pre-1978 all trade was conducted through about a dozen state owned FTCs each of which had a monopoly over particular products. Most trade was conducted at biennial trade fairs held in Canton. With a few exceptions suppliers and end-users seldom met. This has been a source of errors, inefficiencies and complaint on both sides. It hindered the transfer of technology and managerial know-how from foreign to Chinese firms.

Export success

The return of Deng Xiaoping to power in 1977 signalled the start of China's 'Open Door' Policy. By 1979 the process was underway. Although reform was gradual the developments in China's international economic relations were dramatic. Between 1979 and 1992 exports grew at an annual rate of 17 per cent and imports at 15 per cent, the share of manufactures in exports rose from 47 per cent in 1980 to 80 per cent in 1990, while traditional exports of food, raw materials and mineral fuels fell from 46 per cent to 19 per cent. Labour intensive manufactures rose at a rate of 23.6 per cent. China's share of total world exports approximately tripled over the last decade. In 1978 there was no foreign direct investment in China but in 1992 there was over $58 billion in contracted value (World Bank 1993). Over 20,000 Sino-foreign joint ventures are in operation (World Bank 1992: xvi). There can be little doubt that these changes in China's trade and foreign investment have made a significant contribution to the record rates of growth of the Chinese economy: 10 per cent per year over the last ten years, of which 3 to 4 per cent can be attributed to improved productivity, unlike pre-reform growth which was due almost entirely to increased inputs of labour and capital (World Bank 1992: xvi).

The opening of the economy of China to the rest of the world has brought inflows of capital, technology, managerial and marketing know-how, some shift of resources towards China's comparative advantage, and improvements of efficiency within firms. A good deal of the latter can be attributed to the substantial growth in the share of township and village enterprises and of foreign owned and joint ventures in manufacturing in China. A highly significant contribution has come from the close relationships which have developed between Hong Kong and Guangdong businesses and between Taiwan (China) and Xiamen. Guangdong province accounts for 15 per cent of China's exports and about 50 per cent of foreign direct investment (World Bank 1992: 26).

The policies

The policies which have brought about these successes involved removing obstacles to international trade and investment, creating incentives, and decentralizing decisions. China moved from a centrally planned command economy to one in which market forces played a substantial role in resource allocation. First in time, if not in importance, was the passage, in July 1979, of a law which permitted joint ventures and set up special economic zones (SEZs) in the southeast coastal areas of China. In 1984, 14 coastal cities and Hainan island were also opened to foreign investors. These policies were designed to attract foreign investment and collaboration in trade from expatriate Chinese and others, and they allowed China to experiment with economic policies which, if successful, could be transferred to other areas. The law on joint ventures removed obstacles to foreign direct investment in China, and gave such ventures legal status and certain privileges. The SEZs provided tax incentives both to foreign funded firms and to Chinese corporations, including state owned enterprises. Imports used to produce exports, and imports which stayed within the zones were freed of duties and indirect taxes. Firms were allowed to keep 100 per cent of foreign exchange earnings and the first foreign exchange adjustment centre (FEAC) was set up in the Shenzhen SEZ in 1985. This enabled enterprises to swap foreign exchange for local renmenbi currency at a market determined rate which was much more attractive than the official exchange rate.

The local authorities in the zones were given delegated powers. Their investments are largely outside the national plan provided they are financed from their own resources. Enterprises within the zones, whether foreign or Chinese owned, can make their own decisions on investment, production and marketing. Experiments were conducted in freeing markets for commodities and factors of production. Apart from a few rationed goods commodity prices within SEZs are market determined. The first capital market was established in Shenzhen and joint stock companies were encouraged. Special 'B' shares were created to attract foreign portfolio investment. Experiments with banking have been allowed. In the labour market lifetime tenure has been largely replaced by short-term contracts. Hiring and firing have been made easier and government run social security systems have been developed to replace the services commonly provided throughout China by the work unit. The sale of land use rights, the development of secondary markets for land and property built on it, and rights for foreigners to develop land were all experiments first started in SEZs. The SEZs gave tax incentives to investors, freed firms from many bureaucratic controls and generally gave free rein within the zones to market forces.

Most of the experiments tried in the SEZs have now been extended throughout China. As a test bed for ideas the zones do seem to have been a great success. But any rigorous evaluation of their contribution to China's rapid economic development is fraught with difficulty (for two attempts at evaluation see World Bank 1993: Appendix 6.2 and Chen 1991). Clearly Chinese resources have been poured into the SEZs and their opportunity cost was high. The rapid growth of exports from the SEZs has been remarkable, but the local value added has been much less because much has been simple processing of imported materials and components. Also many of the exports were produced in other parts of China and simply passed through the zones. Much depends on a political judgment on whether, given the political situation in China, any other way could have been found to tap into the enormous advantage of collaboration with the business community of Hong Kong and the overseas Chinese communities of South East Asia, and whether any other way could have been found to introduce to China the various market driven reforms which were first tried in the SEZs.

Much of the decentralization which took place was in the break up of the large state FTCs and the setting up of new FTCs in provinces and townships. Along with the decentralization of authority to engage in international trade went a large reduction of the range of products controlled by the central plan. Before the 1980s all trade was supposed to be under the control of the foreign trade plan which covered about 3,000 individual commodities exported, and some 90 per cent of imports. It was the responsibility of the 12 national and sector specific FTCs to export and import the physical quantities laid down in the plan. By 1988 planned imports had dropped to 40 per cent and only 112 exports remained in the plan, but as some were large this was still 45 per cent of exports (Lardy 1992: 39–41; World Bank 1990: 87–88 and 1993: x–xi).

A system of export and import licensing, and tariffs, enabled the state to continue to exert some control over foreign trade as the system of command control was relaxed. This system served several objectives. At the macroeconomic level it gave the government one means of balancing the use of foreign exchange with the amounts of foreign exchange received, but it also enabled protection of selected domestic industries and some means of correcting for domestic price distortions. For example, where the domestic prices of goods were controlled at levels below world prices, export licences could prevent excessive exports which could create domestic shortages. There are also a few goods such as tungsten, antimony, tin and some rare earths where China's large market share gives some market power. For these, and for agricultural exports to Hong Kong, the Chinese authorities believe export restrictions can improve China's terms of trade and be welfare improving for China (World Bank 1993: xiv–xv). A final use of export licences is in allocating sub-quotas for goods restricted under the Multi-Fibres Arrangement or by voluntary export quotas (Lardy 1992: Chapter 3).

The overvalued exchange rate, a major disincentive to exporting, was successively devalued. Together with the introduction of FEACs these measures helped to make some exporting profitable and relaxed to some extent the constraints on enterprises of foreign exchange licensing. In addition, a system of foreign exchange retentions, started in 1979, gave extra incentives to exporters. Previously all foreign exchange had to be handed over to the Bank of China, but from 1979 exporters were allowed to retain claims over the use of foreign exchange in ways designed to give incentives to additional exporting. Finally, a system for obtaining rebates of tariffs and indirect taxes levied on inputs used to produce exports was introduced. For many products and firms these foreign exchange retentions and tax rebates did little more than offset a bias against exports created by an exchange rate which was still overvalued, and by high levels of protection (World Bank 1993: Chapter 2). The tariff on imported cars, for example, was 220 per cent, recently cut to 150 per cent (*Financial Times*, 20 January 1994).

In short, by the mid-1980s, in trade, just as in agriculture and industry, China had made significant moves away from central planning towards a more market directed economic system. Most of the devices to be used in the transition were in place, but much remained to be done.

THE FTCs AND THE PROGRESS OF FOREIGN TRADE REFORM

Further decentralization of the foreign trade system took place after 1984. A key element was the shift of FTC branches to provincial and township control and the creation of many new FTCs. Some were set up by large manufacturing enterprises such as Panda Electronics to handle their own exports and imports. Others, like Hubei Provincial Chemical Import–Export Corporation, were branches of national FTCs, in this case Sinochem, China's largest trading company. Yet others like Jiashan General Trading Company were new township export–import enterprises (World Bank 1993: Chapter 11; Appendix: Survey 1992). By 1986 there were 1,299 FTCs; by 1988 the numbers peaked at over 5,000. This rapid expansion was not free of problems. Some new FTCs had few staff experienced in foreign trade. They had inadequate financing, lacked familiarity with international product standards and business conventions. As a result there were complaints from foreign companies of contracts not delivered, of sub-standard products, delays and uncertainty. In addition there was a particular problem over silk.

Exports of silk and silk products are one of China's great successes. Competing FTCs scrambled for export contracts and then bid furiously for the limited supplies. As a result prices of silk cocoons were driven high and China's National Silk Export Corporation lost business and profits. The export prices received for some silk exports were also probably reduced by the competition. Some FTCs also transgressed various regulations.

The central authorities reacted by investigating abuses, withdrawing licences to export and import from many of the new FTCs, and by merging others. By the end of 1988 the authorities had shut down about 1,400 FTCs. The remaining 3,600, all publicly owned, continued to be supervised by the Ministry of Foreign Economic Relations and Trade and its local offices at national, provincial or municipal level. The authorities were clearly right to act firmly to defend China's international reputation from the effects of lowered quality, failures to meet delivery dates and so on. But whether restricting competition among FTCs was the appropriate remedy is debatable. Restoring the National Silk Exporting Corporation's monopoly was unlikely to maximize China's gains from silk production and trade.

Despite extending direct trading rights to larger SOEs, over 90 per cent of imports and 80 per cent of exports were still handled by the FTCs in 1992. Although the government has encouraged a shift towards the 'agency system' (trade on a commission basis) most FTCs continue to buy exportables at local prices and sell them abroad at international prices. The foreign exchange retention system gives them a powerful incentive to do this. If they act as the exporter they retain 60 per cent of the foreign exchange left after the central government has received its 20 per cent. If they act as agent this share goes to the manufacturer. Only 10 per cent of exports were on an agency basis in 1990 (World Bank 1993: 113).

Even firms, such as wholly owned foreign companies, which have direct exporting rights sometimes choose to sell some products through FTCs because of bureaucratic problems in claiming back import duties and indirect taxes on inputs (Survey 1992).

Efficiency through competition

Competition and efficiency in exporting and importing have increased greatly since the early 1980s when only 12 companies had monopolies over non-overlapping commodities. Knowledge of foreign languages and overseas trading experience have increased. Formal business training is widespread, indeed most FTC managers use the language of the market-place and the business school to describe their tasks and constraints.

Those interviewed in our survey described their environment as much more competitive than hitherto and were clearly worried at the threat from further extensions of direct trading privileges. Some, in provincial FTCs, felt that they were losing business to township FTCs, sometimes because local governments put pressure on local companies to channel exports and imports through the municipal FTCs. Other evidence of increased competition shows in estimates that almost a third of the foreign trade of Hubei and Shandong is handled by FTCs from other provinces, which suggests that local enterprises have more choice as to which FTC to use and this should increase their bargaining power (World Bank 1993: 124). A Taiwanese textiles buyer in Nanjing described how he arranged deals with Chinese enterprises directly and then left it to them to find the FTC which would give the best deal. The sales manager for a woollen cloth and garments manufacturer said that he could use any of 10 FTCs and obtained good prices by bargaining with them. Nevertheless he would have preferred to trade directly (Survey 1992).

The surge in China's exports of manufactures in the latter half of the 1980s seems *prima facie* evidence of the success attending China's decentralization of the authority to trade, but it should not be accepted without question. Substantial elements of monopoly and monopsony remain and efficiency varies a lot among China's FTCs (Survey 1992; World Bank 1993: 113–114).

The fact that over 50 per cent of China's exports are to Hong Kong, from which most are then re-exported suggests that a great deal of the initiatives to export have come from Hong Kong traders and manufacturers. Most of Hong Kong's labour intensive industries have migrated to Guangdong Province, attracted by China's lower labour costs. China's FTCs have been mere facilitators in most of this trade. Evidence from foreign buyers suggests that they often deal directly with manufacturers (and generally prefer to). But regulations and sometimes the need for export licences mean that the deal then has to be ratified and exporting carried out by an appropriate FTC (Survey 1992). Many orders for garments, toys and consumer electronics are repeat orders from foreign buyers to Chinese firms with whom they are quite familiar. Links between Chinese businessmen from Taiwan and Singapore and their mainland Chinese business counterparts are often strong, sometimes even family based. They perform a similar role for the Hong Kong business community for another large slice of China's exports and imports. The role of the FTC as intermediary in these cases seems superfluous.

In a country as large and diverse as China it is natural that FTCs should also vary a great deal. Both we, in our survey, and the World Bank in its 1992 mission on trade policy (World Bank: 1993) found FTCs which were striving hard to expand markets for their clients, were eagerly contacting foreign buyers and putting them in touch with Chinese suppliers. Often they were also providing medium-term finance to local firms to help them produce to meet new orders. Some were investing or intending to invest in manufacturing in order to ensure future supplies. The World Bank reports cases of the FTCs financing overseas trips for clients, and assisting in training workers of local enterprises. Where firms are involved in processing imported raw materials (more than half of China's exports are based on this form) the FTC helps to procure the materials and machinery. These more dynamic FTCs have also helped to transfer technology and more general know-how to local manufacturers. In the past they relied heavily on their contacts in Hong Kong, but more recently have been seeking out new markets and developing their own information networks (World Bank 1993: 113–114).

Despite evidence of successes among the FTCs there is also evidence of FTCs which are doing little to improve China's foreign trade. Foreigners complain of excessively protracted negotiations with staff who refer all decisions to superiors. Local firms complain of FTCs which fail to give adequate information on markets and feedback from foreigners. Some accuse FTCs of withholding information – to the extent that in a few cases local firms did not know the international prices for their products (Survey 1992; World Bank 1993). Others point to the advantages of direct trading: contacts between foreign buyers and exporters often lead to much informal technical assistance, advice on standards, suggestions on methods of production and new machinery. A World Bank study of South Korean exporters strongly supports the gains from such contacts (World Bank 1984: 61–62). But how can FTCs which cause dissatisfaction among their clients stay in business, and even, in some cases, stay profitable?

Evidence of continued monopsony

Despite much decentralization and some scope for enterprises to shop around for a better FTC many, if not most, FTCs still exert considerable monopsony powers. One local FTC in our survey in 1992 still had total control of exports of the largest selling item in local paper manufacturers' range of products (though it did expect to lose this privilege). But, more generally, foreign trade policy still confines most trade to FTCs. Only 538 manufacturers could trade directly by mid-1992 (World Bank 1993: 14). Some local enterprises were still getting prices for their exports which were well below the international prices. This tends to confirm the survival of monopsony powers in the FTCs. Enterprises, particularly in inland areas, lack information, and find it difficult to get access to FTCs from other provinces (World Bank 1993). This weakens their bargaining power *vis à vis* local FTCs. As noted earlier, local authorities who benefit directly from local FTCs' profits and foreign earnings may put pressure on local enterprises to use local trading companies.

In addition, some products can be handled only by designated national or provincial FTCs. They are thus given monopoly powers which in some cases allow them to extract monopoly rents. Sinochem, for example, has gained enormously from its exclusive right to sell petroleum (World Bank 1993: Box 56.1). Products which are sold on the domestic market at controlled prices: steel, fertiliser, coal and oil, could be sold abroad at much higher prices. To prevent a flood of exports only designated FTCs are allowed to export them so as to limit exports and conserve supplies for domestic use, but they make vast profits from this. FTCs are given monopolies over still other products in which China may have market power: tin, tungsten and some others, so as to prevent excessive supplies from depressing China's terms of trade – recently China's tin exports do seem to have depressed world tin prices (*Financial Times* 3 September 1993). Trade in agricultural products to Hong Kong is also exclusively through designated FTCs to ensure stability of prices in seasonal products.

Multiple objectives and soft budget constraints

Many FTCs complain of the multiple objectives given them by their controlling authorities: foreign exchange targets and job creation as well as profit. When, in the past, FTCs were forced to sell exports below costs or import goods at prices above domestic ones they were normally compensated by subventions from the national budget or by grants of profitable business such as licences to import goods which could be sold very profitably in China. Now they are supposed to be responsible for their own profits and losses, but they have been allowed to borrow from state banks at low rates of interest and indefinite repayment terms. In this way soft budget constraints have continued, at least till very recently. These confusions over targets, confusions over responsible authorities (provincial government or continuing relationship with their national trading company), and soft budget constraints have provided an environment in which inefficiency can continue without check.

More competition from direct trading and from other FTCs is forcing further change upon existing FTCs. Many are running at a loss. New regulations raising their share of retained foreign exchange from 12.5 to 60 per cent were probably partly intended to ease their financial difficulties (World Bank 1993). But more freedom for enterprises to choose among FTCs is increasing the pressure of competition (*Beijing Review* 1992: 13–14). The question has to be posed – are FTCs necessary? Is trade better handled directly by producers and users? Of the industrially developed market economies probably only Japan makes much use of such organizations. But Japan's success with the *sogo shosha*, South Korea's use of similar large general trading companies and the successes of Taiwan (China) and Hong Kong with their forms of trading companies argues that at least in East Asia they have been a major ingredient of exporting success. There seem to be circumstances where FTCs have advantages over direct trading.

FTCs' advantages over direct trading

Specialization and economies of scale FTCs provide economies of specialization and scale. By concentrating on foreign markets and suppliers they can build up far more information and trading contacts than would be possible for medium and small companies in manufacturing. Even large companies, if their main market is the domestic economy, could find the costs of acquiring necessary marketing information and contacts more expensive relative to overseas sales than making use of agencies which specialize in foreign trade, and handle many similar products. The high costs of mounting one's own foreign exhibitions should also tell in favour of the FTC which can do this on behalf of many products and companies simultaneously.

Economizing on scarce resources Resources such as staff trained in foreign languages, experienced in doing business in foreign environments with different laws, customs and cultures, and well-versed in the practical details of trade and finance in target markets are scarce in most economies, even more so in developing countries. The use of specialized trading agencies economizes on such scarce resources, making them available when they are needed to firms which could not afford to hire them on a permanent basis. This was a major motive in the case of Japan's early development of FTCs (Kunio 1982). A similar, though less convincing case can be made on buying machinery and technical know-how from abroad (manufacturers' own staff are likely to have a better grasp of their own technical requirements than would the employees of a FTC).

A single, convenient point of contact Provincial FTCs often handle many products from one sales outlet whereas many manufacturers are more specialized. But often a foreign buyer would find it excessively time consuming and difficult to deal with many scattered suppliers for the variety of products that they wish to buy. Dealing through a FTC gives the foreign buyer access to the local knowledge of the FTC, and avoids the language, transport and communication problems of dealing at a local level in an economy like China's.

Market power Another argument made for FTCs in China concerns market power and risks of spoiling the market. There are those few products, mainly minerals and some foods, where China has a dominant market share. For these, independent producers competing for a larger share of the market may drive down the international price. If national FTCs have the sole rights to sell these products abroad the government can exercise control over the supply so as to maximize profits. (There are other ways of doing this, such as export taxes and, of course, any policy designed to raise prices above the cost of production will tempt new entry, substitution or the expansion of existing foreign supplies. Such policies may make short-term gains at the risk of long-term losses as Ghana found out with cocoa in the 1960s and 1970s.)

Curbing seasonal export surpluses Sales of fresh foods to Hong Kong are a special case where seasonal variations in supplies need to be monitored and controlled to avoid excessive swings in prices, but whether FTCs are the appropriate method is again questionable.

Quota control and allocation under the MFA The necessity to control exports to avoid exceeding Multi-Fibre Arrangement quotas is another special case. In China this is handled by giving FTCs sole trading rights. This is not the only way of rationing out quotas, but clearly some supervisory organization is needed to ensure quotas are not exceeded, even if the quota rights are auctioned off to manufacturers.

Curbing excessive competition for domestic inputs (raw materials or intermediates) An argument has been made that too much competition between suppliers can drive up the price of a domestic raw material such as silk, thus squeezing the profits of the manufacturers and trading companies. But although in the past that could have affected government tax revenues the government is increasingly diversifying its revenue sources and it is not obvious why a redistribution of income towards silk farmers should be bad.

Finance, and risk assessment control It is likely to be the case that FTCs will have a better knowledge of suppliers, customers and markets than ordinary banks. This enables them to assess risks better. Their close involvement with their clients and the latters' dependency on them for many other services gives them some hold over the clients which should help to reduce risks. This enables them to borrow at lower rates than their clients and to pass some or all of this benefit to the clients. Where the FTCs are large and able to spread their risk over a diverse range of products and customers their credit should be even better. For the *sogo shosha* their role as financial intermediaries has been crucial to the services they offer (Kunio 1982; Kojima and Ozawa 1984).

Further reforms

Given that there is a general case for foreign trade intermediaries such as the FTCs how should China's FTCs respond to the challenges of the mid-1990s? In interviews, most FTCs said that they proposed to follow reform strategies suggested by the central authorities. These seemed loosely based on the ways in which the Japanese *sogo shosha* evolved. They were described as enterprising (vertical integration), grouping (mergers with other FTCs) and internationalization (creating overseas affiliates). In a sense these represent survival strategies for FTCs, but they may not be in the best interests of China.

Vertical integration is a way in which a FTC could ensure at least some supplies of products for export from affiliated manufacturers, but unless they can start new, efficient factories or improve the efficiency of existing ones there is no gain to the economy, and there would be risks to their own finances. It should only be done if there are clear gains, due to the complementarity of the organizations, that cannot be achieved through arms-length trading, or informal methods of co-operation.

Grouping or merging of FTCs is put forward partly on the basis that there are too many of them and that too much competition between them is not in the national interest because of raising domestic supply prices, possibly lowering export prices, and perhaps damaging foreign confidence if smaller, less experienced FTCs fail to deliver on time or meet quality standards. But grouping FTCs which deal in similar products in a particular region runs the risk of increasing their monopsony power over local suppliers. This would damage incentives to export. Other means, such as public or private sector standards organizations with approved testing laboratories, exist for dealing with risks to quality standards and delivery times.

Internationalization may be premature for most of China's FTCs and is liable to take place for the wrong motives. There is some evidence that foreign subsidiaries have been used to evade China's laws, engage in risky speculation in real estate and to re-invest in China to take advantage of incentives created to attract genuine overseas investors (World Bank 1993).

The lessons from a brief review of the trading companies of Japan, South Korea, Taiwan (China) and Hong Kong are that there is no single model for a successful FTC (MacBean 1993: 14–21). Nor has the Japanese model of the *sogo shosha* proved easy to transplant. Despite strenuous efforts it did not take root in Taiwan, and Hong Kong's model is quite different. Given China's size and diversity no single model is likely to be appropriate everywhere and for all time. The most successful FTCs in China in terms of volume of exports and profits are probably those in Guangdong which have generally been small and rather similar to their counterparts in Hong Kong. But their success could be due largely to proximity to Hong Kong and the activities of the Hong Kong FTCs in re-exporting their products to world markets.

China already has some giant FTCs such as Sinochem or the main China International Trade and Investment Company (CITIC) trading company.

They may well be able to evolve into multinational conglomerates, but there does not seem to be any reason for China to provide special help or inducements for them to do so. In the presence of high uncertainty it probably makes more sense to try to construct a level playing field in which large and small enterprises with freedom to trade directly can compete so that the more efficient routes for exporting and importing can emerge. This requires the central authorities to remove special privileges from the FTCs and to ensure that any incentives to exporting are available to all enterprises. This would fit well with the thrust of China's general economic reforms which aim to grant greater autonomy to business enterprises. It would also make sense to permit the FTCs to trade within China to allow them to spread their overheads over a larger volume of business, to make use of their marketing skills in wider markets and to provide more competition in China's retailing and distribution system. In 1992 only one FTC could trade within China. That was the main trading company in the large conglomerate, CITIC (Survey 1992).

Greater competition, leading to better services to clients, would be promoted by allowing private companies and joint ventures to become FTCs. As this is already common in manufacturing the precedent already exists. Control over foreign trade can be maintained by tariffs and licensing so long as these remain compatible with membership of GATT and the new World Trade Organization. In so far as non-tariff measures of control over trade have to be relaxed to meet GATT standards the use of FTCs to exert control over imports and exports would similarly offend. The central and provincial authorities would still have a substantial role in providing support to exporters through information services for foreign buyers and organising trade exhibitions at home and overseas.

ACKNOWLEDGEMENTS

I am grateful to the Economic and Social Committee on Research of the Overseas Development Administration for a research grant in support of this work. They bear no responsibility for any of the analysis or views expressed in this study. I am also grateful to Liu Zhenya of Renda University for assistance and interpreting in several discussions in Beijing, to David Brown of Lancaster University for introducing me to his Chinese friends and to former students for aid in arranging interviews in China. Without their help and the courtesy and frankness of Chinese officials and managers this research would have been impossible. I have also to thank Rajiv Lall of the World Bank for discussions on China's trade policy reforms. But none of the foregoing bears any responsibility for errors or views expressed. That is mine alone.

APPENDIX: THE SURVEY 1992

The bulk of the survey was carried out during February to June 1992, while I was a visiting professor at The People's University (Renda), Beijing. It involved meetings with officials of the Ministry of Foreign Economic Relations and Trade (MOFERT), other state institutions, and companies in Beijing. During that period I visited Hangzhou, Nanjing, Taiyuan and Xiamen. In each place I had meetings with trading companies, a few manufacturing enterprises, and provincial officials concerned with international relations and commerce. It was supplemented by further interviews in Shanghai, Xiaoshing, and Jiashan (a township near Shanghai) while I was in Shanghai for a seminar on China's coastal development zones in September 1992. Where interpreting was needed I was fortunate to have the help of Liu Zhenya (Assistant Professor at Renda) in Beijing, Associate Professor Zhang Ru of Fudan University in Shanghai and Jiashan, and several former students of Lancaster University in other cities. Back in Britain I had meetings with relevant managers in ICI, Rolls-Royce and Snapdragon Pottery Export–Import Company, who were interviewed on their experiences of dealing with China's FTCs over the years.

It was not possible to construct a random sample of FTCs to be formally interviewed. In Beijing I had a list of officials who had taken part in a UN project at Lancaster. Introductions from my management school colleague, David Brown, opened doors magically. Visits in other cities were arranged by former students of Lancaster University, now in responsible positions in government offices and FTCs. I explained my research objectives and then accepted what they were able to organise through their contacts. Time for visits was short as I usually gave lectures in the places visited, but all lasted over an hour and several much longer. A list of organizations visited is appended.

On my return journey I visited Osaka in Japan and Seoul in South Korea to meet with relevant officials and FTC managers. I had hoped to meet with the retired president of one of Japan's *sogo shosha* (C. Itoh), but this proved impossible. I did, however, meet with a senior official of Japan's international chamber of commerce who was able to describe trade relations with China, and experience of dealing with China's FTCs. In Seoul I met with the chief of the international trade section of the Korean Planning Board, managers in Korea's Trade Promotion Corporation (KOTRA) and in two major trading companies: Daewoo and Samsung.

I cannot claim that my sample of officials and businessmen has statistical validity. On the other hand the answers I got were very consistent and they accord with the findings of the World Bank missions in 1990 and 1992 whose reports deal incidentally with China's FTCs. I also sent, in August 1992, an early draft of my findings to Rajiv Lall (desk officer for China and Mongolia in the World Bank, and the principal author of the

1993 Report) for his comments. I met him in Washington in June 1993 and had a general discussion with him on China's trade reforms and the FTCs. We had no areas of disagreement. I do therefore have some confidence in the findings.

Organizations visited

Beijing (April and May 1992)

    Ministry of Foreign Economic Relations and Trade (MOFERT)
    Divisions: North American and Australian
                Personnel
                Research
    Commission for Restructuring the Economic System
    Academy of Social Science
    CITIC Trading Company (FTC)
    China National Textiles Export–Import Corporation (FTC)
    London Export–Import Corporation
    Satake (UK) Ltd (Flour Milling Engineering Co.)
    Midland Bank Beijing

Nanjing (May 1992)

    Jiangsu Province Commission for Foreign Economic Relations and Trade
    China Jiangsu Machinery and Equipment Import–Export Corporation (SUMEC) (FTC)
    Jiangsu Provincial Foreign Trading Co. (FTC)
    Panda Electronics Group and Nanjing Panda Import–Export Corporation (manufacturer and FTC subsidiary)

Hangzhou (April 1992)

    Provincial, Commission for Foreign Economic Relations and Trade
    City, Foreign Economic and Trade Bureau
    Department of Foreign Affairs Zhejiang Province
    China National Export–Import Co. (Provincial Branch, FTC)
    Zhejiang Knitwear and Home Textiles Import–Export Co. (FTC)

Jiashan (September 1992)

    Zhejiang Jiashan General Electric – Acoustic Factory (provincial enterprise)
    Jiashan Woollenmill (township and village enterprise)
    Jiashan Tractor Factory (state enterprise)

Zhejiang Xing Xing Silk Industrial Trade Company (manufacturer with direct trading rights through joint venture)
Zhejiang Province Trading Company, Export–Import, Jiashan Branch (FTC)

Shanghai (September 1992)

Shanghai Kaolite Bedding and Clothing Co. Limited, Pudong
China-Britain Trade Group (Shanghai office)
Fudan University

Taiyuan, Shanxi Province (May 1992)

China National Light Industry Products (Import–Export Corporation, Shanxi branch, FTC)
Zhao Jia Bu Heater Grill Industry Co. of Qingxu, Shangxi (manufacturer of central heating radiators, a township enterprise)
High Tech. Development Corporation, Shanxi University
Department of World Economics, Shanxi University

Xiamen (April 1992)

Jutai (Taiwanese company in real estate, textile manufacture and wooden products, able to trade directly but also used Chinese FTCs)
Nam Wah International Trading Co. (FTC)
Business School, University of Xiamen

Xiaoshing (September 1992)

Zhejiang Provincial Trade Commission (Xiaoshing)

Osaka (June 1992)

Japan-China Association on Economy and Trade
Staff in Economics Department, St Andrew's University

Seoul, South Korea (June 1992)

Trade Policy Division, Ministry of Trade and Industry
Korea's Trade Promotion Corporation (KOTRA)
Daewoo Corporation
Samsung Corporation

United Kingdom (February/March 1993)

> ICI (East Asia Division)
> Snapdragon (Export–Import Company, Ceramics)
> Rolls-Royce (Corporate Services Division)

REFERENCES

Beijing Review 1992 'State-owned enterprises no longer state run', November: 16–22.

Chen, J. 1991 'Foreign direct investment in China – policies and performance', PhD Thesis, Lancaster University.

The Financial Times 1992 and 1993 various issues, London.

Kojima, K. and Ozawa, T. 1984 *Japan's General Trading Companies: Merchants of Economic Development*, OECD Development Centre Study, Geneva.

Kunio, Y. 1982 *Sogo Shosha: the Vanguard of the Japanese Economy*, Oxford: Oxford University Press.

Lardy, N. R. 1992 *Foreign Trade and Economic Reform in China, 1978–1990*, Cambridge: Cambridge University Press.

Lee, R. *et al.* 1984 *Korea's Competitive Edge: Managing the Entry into World Markets*, World Bank/Johns Hopkins University Press.

MacBean, A. I. 1993 'China's foreign trade corporations (export–import companies): their role in economic reform and export success', *Discussion Paper EC19/93*, Lancaster University: The Management School.

Panagariya, A. 1993 'Unravelling the mysteries of China's foreign trade regime', *The World Economy* 16(1).

Perkins, D. H. 1992 'China's "Gradual" Approach to Market Reforms', *UNCTAD Discussion Paper* December, 52.

Rosario, L. do 1993 'Big is still beautiful', *Far Eastern Economic Review* 11 February: 51.

Singh, Ajit 1993 'The plan, the market and evolutionary economic reform in China' UKCTAD Discussion Paper No. 76, December, Geneva.

Song, Byung-Nak 1990 *The Rise of the Korean Economy*, Oxford: Oxford University Press.

World Bank 1990 *China Between Plan and Market*, Washington, DC.

World Bank 1992 *China: Reform and the Role of the Plan in the 1990s*, Washington, DC.

World Bank 1993 *China, Foreign Trade Reform: Meeting the Challenge of the 1990s*, Washington, DC.

Young, A.K. 1982 *Sogo Shosha, Japan's multinational trading companies*, Charles E. Tuttle.

Name Index

Subject Index

absorptive capability, definition of 55
Accountancy Law 1985 14
ad hoc middle men *see* middle men
age, respect for 4
authority, respect for 4

Bangkok Declaration 1993 15, 16, 19
bargaining *see* negotiations
bilateral treaties 19–21; *see also* China–US memorandum of understanding
bureaucracy: intervention by 4–5; 'mothers-in-law' of government and 13

central government *see* government
China Market Access Agreement *see* China–US memorandum of understanding
China–US memorandum of understanding 19–21; telecommunications industry and 20–1; transparency and 20; *see also* US–Chinese joint ventures
Chinese Multinational Enterprises (CHMNES): advantages of 157–8; competitive position and performance 156–7; Contract Responsibility System 144, 151; contracting management system 155, 160; control of overseas subsidiaries 153–5; decision making authority 153–5; decisions on technology and R&D 155; distribution networks 156; entry mode 151–3; firm-specific advantages 157–8; geographical patterns 160; insufficient marketing expertise 159; international

management strategies of 141–61; local partners 153; location in higher income/industrial countries 159–60; motives for overseas production 149–51, 159; organizational structure 153–5; overseas subsidiaries 148–9; ownership advantages 157–8; ownership pattern 151–3; parent company 145–7; performance 156–7; personal interests of managers 151; poor management of 159; product and process technology 158; Responsibility Contract System 144, 151; sale of surplus products 151; selection of top managers 154–5; shareholding system 160; state owned 150, 157, 159; township enterprises *see* township enterprises; unprofessional managerial personnel 159; weaknesses of 159; *see also* Foreign Business Oriented Companies or Conglomerates; foreign trade corporations; large industrial corporations; small and medium-sized firms
Christianity, Western legal tradition and 18
CICs *see* Hong Kong's China-invested companies
civil society 11, 16–17, 18; privateness and 16; regulation of 16–17; rule of law 14, 17, 19, 26; *see also* law; legal system
Co-ordinating Committee for Export Controls (COCOM) 20
collective enterprises 61; expansion of 61; ownership of 61; transfer of skills/technology and 61